GROWING TOGETHER
PARENT AND CHILD
DEVELOPMENT

GROWING TOGETHER

PARENT AND CHILD DEVELOPMENT

Robert D. Strom

Arizona State University

BROOKS/COLE PUBLISHING COMPANY
Monterey, California
A Division of Wadsworth Publishing Company, Inc.

To Shirley,
Our Parents, Our Grandparents,
and Our Children

Printed in the United States of America

10 9 8 7 6 5 4 3 2 1

Library of Congress Cataloging in Publication Data

Strom, Robert D
   Growing together.

   Includes index.
   1. Child development.   2. Parent and child.
I. Title.
HQ767.9.S77   649'.1   77-22752
ISBN 0-8185-0244-4

Production Editor: *John Bergez*
Interior Design: *Jamie S. Brooks*
Cover Design: *Katherine Minerva*
Photographs: *Shirley Strom*

PREFACE

Parent education is becoming a national priority. The increasing demand of mothers and fathers for access to training in parenting reflects their awareness of the favorable results that usually take place. According to recent follow-up studies of early-childhood intervention programs, those educational efforts that focus on both parent and child rather than on one party or the other register the greatest long-term gains. The purpose of this book is to show how parent and child development can proceed together from birth through adolescence.

This book is written for people learning about child development, family relations, and parent education. The content is divided into six aspects of growth that are common to the parent and child goals of each generation: achieving acceptance from peers, learning to enjoy life, coping with fears and anxieties, finding a model for success, achieving a favorable view of self, and choosing a worthwhile set of values. Throughout the book, my emphasis is on improving the expectations that parents, children, and teachers have of one another.

If we want to attain a better partnership between the home and school, some books should be written with both parents and teachers in mind, but this has seldom been the case. Parents expect that material for them will be written in a simple, straightforward manner, with an emphasis on pat answers to problems in family relationships. By contrast, college students preparing to teach are often assigned books on child development that have a broader focus than the family but that are written in jargon and that contain more references to research than practical suggestions. In this book I try to blend the strengths of both approaches, combining research knowledge and practical advice in a presentation that I hope both parents and teachers will find worthwhile.

For those persons who wish to become more understanding of the ways in which parents and children can grow together, I have edited a companion volume to accompany this book. *Parent and Child in Fiction* is composed of 23 short stories that have been selected to illustrate the concerns discussed in *Growing Together*. Although either book can be helpful if read independently, they offer greater benefit when considered in combination.

A number of people have helped in the preparation of this book. The following people reviewed the manuscript and offered valuable suggestions: Carol Copple, Institute for Research and Human Development, Educational Testing Service (New Jersey); Cheryl Goeree, Carmel High School; Freda Rebelsky, Boston University; and Elaine Smith, North Seattle Community College. John Bergez of the Brooks/Cole staff has improved the manuscript by his insightful editing, while Todd Lueders and Jamie Brooks carefully planned the design and format. I am also grateful to my wife, Shirley, for her ideas and photographs.

Robert D. Strom

CONTENTS

1

PEERS
AND
BELONGING

ONE

GETTING READY FOR SCHOOL

What should children learn before they begin school? Should they recognize the letters of the alphabet? Should they be able to count to ten, write their names, identify shapes? Should they know the parts of the body? Should they be familiar with certain stories and children's books? These questions come from parents who wish to prepare their sons and daughters for formal education. Many parents are disappointed that the school does not specify its initial expectations beyond such advice as "Talk to your child a lot" or "Be sure that he likes himself." This reluctance to identify expectations seems unreasonable in view of research about the potential of early childhood education. According to Benjamin Bloom at the University of Chicago, 50% of mature intelligence is developed between birth and age 4. Another 30% is developed between ages 4 and 8. Finally, from age 8 to age 17, youngsters develop the remaining 20% of their intelligence. Stated another way, it appears that as much intellectual development occurs before children start school as during the many years they spend in a classroom. These estimates do not depreciate the importance of elementary and secondary education, but they do urge us to improve the conditions for learning in the years before kindergarten.

DIFFERENCES AMONG FAMILIES

Parents can disadvantage children by not knowing what schooling they should provide at home. Although the relationship between family influence and a child's readiness for school is complex, it is possible to identify certain features of the environment and make some assessment of their collective impact. For example, a number of differences separate what have been termed *deprived* and *abundant* homes, the two environmental extremes in our culture. When these terms first became popular in the mid-1960s, they were used primarily to distinguish between low-income and middle-income families. Today we take a more balanced view of what is required to be a successful parent. It now seems that teaching parenting skills, which can be learned by people of every income group, is the best way to eliminate deprivation in childhood.

We no longer suppose that every low-income child is necessarily deprived or that all boys and girls from middle-class and affluent homes are necessarily advantaged. What matters more than parents' income is parents' behavior. Given this redefinition, an abundant home is one in which parents are aware of their responsibility to help children get ready for school. They attempt to make available the materials, guidance, and types of situations that will increase the chances for academic success. Boys and girls growing up in these homes experience frequent conversations with their parents; they are often read to; they are encouraged to use symbols correctly, to identify objects, to ask questions, and to think about the environment in terms of relationships. They are provided with many toys to stimulate their imaginations, to develop their perception, and to help them find pleasure in learning. Their parents regularly arrange time to play with them and act as interpreters of television shows. These children also learn to value solitude.

By contrast, the parents in deprived homes do not recognize how they can help their children prepare for school. Although these mothers and fathers may offer as much love as those in abundant homes, they do not give the children as much knowledge. There are thus fewer opportunities for parent-child conversation and corrective feedback to improve speech. No one reads to the children or encourages them to ask any questions. The parents seldom play with the children or buy the toys the children need to develop their skills and exercise their imaginations. Children are not taken to the park or other places in the community where they could see new and different relationships. Televiewing usually takes place without any grown-up interpreter, and there is rarely a chance for solitary play.

What are the consequences of growing up in these two contrasting kinds of environment? After an extensive review of studies on the development of intelligence, Benjamin Bloom tried to answer this question. He concluded that the distinction between deprived and abundant homes can be translated into measurable differences. Let's suppose that two infants who have the same genetic equipment, the same intelligence, are placed in different homes. According to Bloom, between birth and age 4 the child from the deprived home may be expected to fall 5 IQ points below the norm, while the child from the abundant home rises 5 IQ points above the norm. Thus, at the end of only four years of life, the environment alone has already made a difference of 10 points between the children's IQs. Later, between the ages of 4 and 8 the child from the deprived setting may be expected to fall 3 more IQ points below the norm, while at the same time the child from the abundant setting gains 3. Now they are 6 more IQ points apart. Finally, between ages 8 and 17, the deprived child loses 2 points, while the other child gains 2 points. When we add this all together, it appears that the difference between living in an abundant environment and living in a deprived environment from birth to age 17 may be around 20 IQ points.

If as much intellectual growth occurs between birth and age 4 (50%) as during the next 13 years (50%), and if general intelligence is a developmental characteristic related to the time it takes one to learn skills and concepts, it would seem reasonable that lack of learning in the early years might be difficult or even impossible to remedy fully at a later time. On the other hand, excellent learning during early childhood is unlikely to be lost. From this view of intellectual development has come the persuasion that we must find ways to improve the environment of children, especially during the preschool years, so that as adults they will have greater intellectual ability than they would otherwise. It was precisely this goal—to provide a better preschool experience for children from deprived homes—that led to the establishment of the nationwide Head Start project in 1965. Of course, there is more to child development than just the growth of intelligence. A child's personality is also being formed during the early years. Indeed, the preschool environment can influence the development of personality even more than it does the development of intelligence. For both kinds of development, the question asked by parents is usually the same: "How important is the influence of our environment?" Actually, environment can influence people of any age, but the younger the person, the greater the impact of the environment. Therefore, the younger the children, the more influential those who teach them can be.

Some further implications of Bloom's research deserve elaboration. For one thing, it implies that parents have an important teaching function from the time a child is born. Consequently, parent education ought to be available nationwide so that parents can learn how to fulfill their function as teachers. The school can help define part of the curriculum for parent education by making known the kinds of learning it expects of kindergartners. A second implication is the need for mutual curriculum planning by teachers who work in day care, nursery school, preschool, kindergarten, and first grade. In the absence of such planning, some children are destined to repeat nearly the same program for several years.

Obviously the evaluation and recording of children's progress before kindergarten demands more attention. At present, children who have regularly attended one or another form of preschool program seldom have a record of their progress to present to the next teacher. Yet experimentation for the 1975 revision of the Metropolitan Readiness Test confirms that young children are learning a great deal through the combined influence of *Sesame Street* and their other school experience before first grade. When a representative sample of today's first-graders were compared on the 1964 Metropolitan Readiness Test with the norming group for that version, their average performance was significantly better than that of their peers of a decade ago. For example, the average score of contemporary first-graders corresponds to a percentile rank of 73 in the 1964 distribution of scores. An analysis of the subtests shows that the greatest gains made by low-income pupils over those of a decade earlier is in letter names. Perhaps a number of factors are responsible for the improvement, including *Sesame Street*, which is brought to us by the letters J, K, L, and so on.

THE FIRST DAY

Regardless of how much a child has learned, parents cannot be completely sure what children's responses to starting school will be. Some boys and girls who say they want to come suddenly become afraid on arrival. Others seem to belong immediately. A few appear uncertain and withdraw. When we consider the range of adjustment, we should realize that some children have experience with nursery and preschool groups, while others do not. Some have brothers and sisters at school; others do not. Some have always had playmates; others have not. Some have been taught to be suspicious of strangers and now are expected to quickly place their complete confidence in the teacher.

Since a wide range of adjustment is typical, parents and teachers should consider some of their alternatives beforehand. To begin with, all parents should try to safeguard their children against the possible stress of sudden separation and the fear of an alien environment. This shock can be partially reduced if parents are honest with a child about school. An honest interpreter will tell the child that most boys and girls are nervous and unsure when they start. "Mom and Dad were scared too, at your age. It's natural to be a bit lonely at first, but part of the teacher's job is to help the children become friends. Even so, you might meet a few kids you don't like." The child needs to realize that there will be more rules and more directions to follow in school but that there will also be a lot of time for playing, taking trips, having parties, listening to music, making things, and learning from the teacher, who wants to be a friend. This kind of honest introduction to the school experience can help children far more than leading them to believe that any dissatisfaction they encounter is unnatural.

It is also worthwhile for teachers to schedule a few short play periods at school during the spring previous to kindergarten. This experience helps children confirm that school is going to be an enjoyable place. In addition, youngsters get to meet peers they'll look forward to seeing again in the fall. Furthermore, the chance to perceive the kindergarten teacher as a play observer invites a child's confidence and respect. This type of direct contact with the school should be more common, because it encourages adjustment and begins the relationship by honoring a child's strength—imagination.

The first day of school finally arrives and invariably some children feel deserted, frightened, out of place. When this happens, certain parents are embarrassed and resort to bribery.

Others blame themselves aloud for not preparing the child to fend for himself or herself. A small number of parents consciously appreciate the fact that their child seems helpless without them. No one profits by the decision that any of these parents should leave. The contention that desertion strengthens a child's character is unwarranted. We don't promote children's trust in the new teacher by encouraging parents to abandon them. Parents should stay, if not in the classroom, then in a room nearby. The important thing is that the child realizes that Mom or Dad is close by if needed. Kindergarten teachers who have training in parent education don't resent the presence of mothers or fathers. Instead these teachers quickly recruit them for instructional tasks in such a way that parental embarrassment dissipates and they cease to be seen as hangers-on. The length of time a parent will need to attend school with his or her child may vary from one day to several weeks. In every case a child's feelings ought to be respected.

Helping a child get ready for school includes starting the child's school experience at the proper time. This may be somewhat later than the earliest date allowed for entrance to kindergarten. Typically, the legal requirement for admission states that children can enter kindergarten if their fifth birthday occurs before December 31 of the school year. The result is that some kindergartners with autumn birthdays are as young as 4 years, 8 months. According to their parents, the fact that they are a few months younger than their classmates won't really matter in the long run. But are they right? Kindergartners in California who were about 4 years, 9 months of age when enrolled were compared with those who were enrolled at 5 years, 7 months. After six grades of schooling, children in the younger group achieved less well than those in the older group in all subjects at each grade level, except for one subject in which achievement was equal. A similar study was conducted in Tennessee, where it was found that Stanford Achievement scores taken in sixth grade strongly favored the older children. Other investigations of age and grade placement present an equally grim forecast for the child who enters elementary school too soon. These studies predict that the child will likely stumble insecurely through kindergarten and the primary grades. Friends who were delayed a year or so will quickly catch up and pass them—and usually become more stable and interested in school.

Perhaps the most compelling evidence is the research of Frances Ilg and Louise Ames. They discovered that the children referred to their guidance clinic at Yale University often had two things in common: a record of poor adjustment and test scores indicating they started school too early. But this was a population of disturbed children. In order to determine the magnitude of grade misplacement in the general population, Ilg and Ames obtained a grant from the Ford Foundation to pursue an intensive seven-year study of 1000 children in kindergarten through second-grade. When their work was finished, the Yale investigators concluded that as many as half of all students are a grade or more ahead of where they should be to do their best work. Moreover, in terms of mental health, most of the emotional consequences are detrimental and tend to remain with children throughout their school careers.

Parents are naturally puzzled by what appears to be a contradiction in the logic of researchers. Families have been told that intellectual development proceeds more rapidly during the preschool years than at any other time in life; yet the surprising recommendation of experts is that some children should enter kindergarten as late as possible. How can these two seemingly incompatible conclusions be reconciled? There is no dispute about whether early learning ought to be encouraged. The issue centers on what kind of education is most desirable for young children. One view is that recent changes in the kindergarten and first-grade curricula tend to eliminate certain kinds of potential in children while supposedly developing others. For example, everyone agrees that at some point boys and girls should learn to read and write, but, when we insist that these skills be acquired right away, the necessary formal instruction supplants the play and social interaction that children at this age may need more. In short, we pay a price for the trade, for choosing to emphasize reading rather than imaginative or social play. Although most people agree that creativity is becoming more necessary, unlike literacy its development is often taken for granted. Some youngsters even discover upon entering school that expressing their imaginations no longer brings adult approval. These boys and girls thus learn to depreciate fantasy, and their ability to pretend is left behind.

Our society's inclination to push children, to introduce them ever earlier to academic expectations, is best illustrated by a story involving Swiss psychologist Jean Piaget. After completing a lecture term at Harvard University, the renowned authority on child development consented to reflect on his experiences in America. One of the newspaper reporters began "Is it true, as Harvard's Jerome Bruner asserts, that if we try hard enough we can teach almost any child at any age to do almost any task in some reasonable way?" Piaget's short reply was "Only an American would ask." Indeed, in his later writings, he called this inquiry "The American Question." Let's assume Piaget is justified in doubting the appropriateness of our academic expectations for young children. In that case the guiding question changes from "What can children learn?" to "What kinds of learning are best during childhood?" This shift in concern is overdue, according to many former kindergarten teachers whose disappointing experience with forcing academic goals led them to seek assignments at a higher grade level. For parents the answer to our question can be given in the form of a recommendation. To enroll your child in kindergarten at the earliest legal age may be a good idea, *if* the experience there includes a generous portion of time for play, conversation, and curiosity. If these kinds of experiences are unavailable, a child is better off at home with the family, in a socially oriented preschool, or with some other caretaker who respects imagination and will accept the child's preference for learning through play.

SHARING YOUR IMPRESSIONS

1. Try to remember your first days in school, and tell something about your experiences.
2. How do you suppose being in the first grade is different now from the way it was when you were there?
3. What do you think the success or failure of a child's beginning days at school should be based upon?
4. Identify the conditions that would enable most children to enjoy life at school.

5. What advice can you offer parents and teachers for improving the experience of beginning students?
6. Comment on the importance of the nonacademic aspects of primary school.
7. What are your thoughts about the influence of *Sesame Street, The Electric Company, Mister Rogers,* and *Captain Kangaroo*?
8. Speculate about the self-concept of parents in their role as teachers of preschool children.

REFERENCES AND SUGGESTED READING

Ames, Louise. "Don't Push Your Preschooler." *Readings in Human Development.* edited by Phillip Rosenthal. Guilford, Conn.: Dushkin Publishing Group, 1974. Pp. 80–82.

Bloom, Benjamin. *Stability and Change in Human Characteristics.* New York: Wiley, 1964. Pp. 72–89.

Bloom, Benjamin, Davis, Allison, and Hess, Robert. *Compensatory Education for Cultural Deprivation.* New York: Holt, Rinehart & Winston, 1965.

Havighurst, Robert. *Developmental Tasks and Education.* New York: David McKay, 1972.

Ilg, Frances. "The Child from Three to Eight with Implications for Reading." In *Understanding the Young Child and His Curriculum,* edited by Bellin Mills. New York: Macmillan, 1972. Pp. 315–322.

Ilg, Frances, and Ames, Louise. "Your Child May Be in the Wrong Grade." *Teachers and the Learning Process,* edited by Robert Strom. Englewood Cliffs, N.J.: Prentice-Hall, 1971. Pp. 76–81.

Maier, John. "Children: USA." *Rockefeller Foundation Illustrated,* December 1976, pp. 4–5.

Mitchell, Blythe. "Changes Over an Eight and a Nine-Year Period in the Readiness Level of Entering First-Grade Pupils." Paper presented at National Council on Measurement in Education Annual Meeting, April 16, 1974.

Moore, Raymond, and Moore, Dennis. "The Dangers of Early Schooling." *Harpers Magazine,* July 1972, pp. 58–62.

Steinfels, Margaret. *Who's Minding the Children?* New York: Simon and Schuster, 1974.

Todd, Virginia, and Heffernan, Helen. *The Years Before School.* New York: Macmillan, 1977. Pp. 587–628.

Zigler, Ed, and Hunsinger, Susan. "Bringing up Day Care." *APA Monitor,* March 1977, pp. 1, 8–9.

BOOKS TO SHARE WITH YOUNG CHILDREN

Adelson, Leone. *All Ready for School.* New York: David McKay, 1957. It is natural for children entering school for the first time to have mixed feelings. In this story a little girl's animal friends observe her kindergarten class and find the activities quite different from what they think she should learn.

Binzen, Bill. *First Day in School.* New York: Doubleday, 1972. Boys and girls need reassurance that school is a place where people care about them. By looking together at these photographs of an actual opening day at school, parent and child can see ahead of time some fun things to anticipate and how certain adjustment problems are overcome.

Blue, Rose. *I Am Here: Yo Estoy Aqui.* New York: Franklin Watts, 1971. Teacher aides are seldom given the credit they deserve for helping boys and girls. On her first day in kindergarten, Luz, a Puerto Rican girl, feels overwhelmed by the unfamiliar language and expectations until Mrs. Rios comes along.

Cohen, Miriam. *Will I Have a Friend?* New York: Macmillan, 1967. Peers usually have more influence than adults when it comes to providing children a sense of belonging at school. This explains why some beginners like Jim worry that, if every friend is already taken, he will be left out.

Cole, William. *What's Good for a Five-Year-Old?* New York: Holt, Rinehart and Winston, 1969. The introduction of children to school should include some time for things they like to do. Mrs. Revere wants her class to learn the rules, but she also intends for them to share their goals and have fun playing together.

TWO
LEARNING FROM BIG KIDS

Whenever I talk with boys and girls about how age prejudice can deny someone a sense of belonging, I begin with a couple of questions: "Have you ever wanted to be older than you are? How old would you like to be?" Usually they answer 12, 16, 18, or 21. Most children want to be older because to them it means getting bigger, growing stronger, and having more privileges, such as staying up late or driving a car. Sometimes they also tell me what it is like to be left out because others consider them too young. Maybe a group of 9-year-olds has said "You can't play with us because you're only 7." Youngsters can attach great importance to only a few months' difference in age. I can't imagine a group of 35-year-olds suggesting "That couple shouldn't be invited to our bridge party because they're only 33." In any event, little children do look to older kids for an example of what comes next and of how to live. These are important reasons for examining how the influence of older children can be improved.

Perhaps we should begin by helping parents answer a related question: "Why should my children spend time with persons their own age?" Since they share the same interests, age-mates are willing to repeat things many times and still remain enthusiastic. This tolerance for repetition is essential for certain kinds of early learning, even though the practice may seem boring to bigger and more competent children. It follows that, to find out how well they're doing, young children need someone their own age for self-comparison rather than the example of persons with whom they can't realistically compete. In the company of larger boys and girls there is also less chance for little ones to assert themselves or to assume a leadership role. Whereas age-mates encourage one another to protest family decisions and to strive for independence, older peers often demand dependence from younger ones. Ordinarily the cost of associating with bigger kids is that the strengths a child hasn't yet developed are the only ones that count. By contrast, small children readily accept one another's imaginations, spontaneity, and fears. Thus, peers of the same age are less likely to ridicule one another about competence or to overstimulate and strain their companions as often as older children would. While big kids frequently lead small ones to feel unwanted, age-mates share secrets and private jokes, offer a feeling of being special, and help give that sense of belonging to a group that everyone needs.

Sometimes parents who favor interaction among age-mates worry when children of different ages spend much time together. The fear is that the younger party may be abused, exploited, or taught some undesirable lessons. Although these disappointing results can happen, it is also possible that older children will provide a beneficial influence that is unique. Certainly they are looked up to and imitated. One reason for their hero status is that their behavior can be readily observed and is easier to approximate than is a long-range occupational aspiration. Our own adult experience underscores this need for having proximate models when it comes to keeping motivation alive. For example, a golfer who finds out that a new acquaintance also plays immediately inquires about the person's typical score. The usual purpose of this checking is to learn how good the other player is before deciding whether it would be self-deflating to play that person. In a similar way the behavior of older kids presents a goal that is easier for little children to approximate than is adult performance. Moreover, the recency of older children's own experiences as little kids can cause them to be less demanding and more sensitive helpers. Finally, young boys and girls need acceptance from older companions in order to feel the sense of belonging that goes with being a member of a community.

THE HELPING RELATIONSHIP

The United States is considered by some social scientists to be the most peer-oriented culture of any in history. Despite the educational possibilities of peer influence, undesirable outcomes more often receive attention. As a result we hear reports about adolescents who lead their companions to drugs and about elementary school cliques that reject minority children. Even preschoolers are not spared from blame, because they teach age-mates the dirty language they have learned at home. It is sometimes easy to resent children's reliance on one another, but the worthwhile potential of that reliance should not be overlooked.

Some societies do not recognize children as capable of teaching anything. In certain primitive cultures no one becomes influential until the age of puberty. The opposite extreme describes countries in which peer teaching is excessive. For example, compulsory school attendance ends at age 11 in Portugal and at age 14 in Spain. These same ages represent the minimal qualification for someone who wishes to become a primary teacher. The result is that many immature children are being taught exclusively by somewhat older but still immature peers. In the Soviet Union, it is understood that age-mates are responsible for maintaining school discipline. If a student misbehaves during class, peers are expected to punish the offender outside of the school. Most Americans are not favorably impressed with these kinds of peer teaching.

In the United States, the one-room schoolhouse and peer teaching probably began at the same time. The practice was not always successful, but it did recognize children as being capable of teaching peers. For a long time we assumed that the children being taught deserved all of our attention. Only in recent years have we begun to look seriously at what happens to the children who teach. Consider the Mobilization for Youth Project, a massive program intended to help elementary school students in New York City who have trouble with reading. Typically, the MFY volunteer tutors were high school or college students. One of the project consultants observed that, even though some children receiving instruction did not improve in reading, their untrained tutors experienced significant gains in self-concept. It seemed that, independently of how well they were doing as teachers, the tutors felt good about themselves simply because they were trying to help someone else learn. This kind of special satisfaction can be appreciated by adult teachers.

Similar findings in other peer-teaching studies made it clear to Ronald and Peggy Lippitt at the University of Michigan that tutor preparation must be carefully designed in order for both parties to succeed. If they are properly trained, tutors gain a sense of accomplishment, because they have feedback about the worthwhileness of their teaching. This is a better arrangement than having to resort to self-approval just for holding noble intentions. The Lippitts have conducted a number of successful experiments with what they call cross-age helpers. By this procedure, upper-grade students are helped to understand what young children are like and what causes some of them to have difficulty in school. The participants learn ways of cooperating with the younger child's classroom teacher as well as techniques for helping the child directly. Cross-age teaching is scheduled several times a week during school hours. There are many less sophisticated programs than the Lippitt design, but, whatever the format, almost all of them appear to be successful. Herb Thelen, a leader in the peer-teaching movement from the University of Chicago, has observed that the benefits do not seem to depend on the subject matter or on the nature of the lesson plan. What does appear important is whether the helping relationship is formally recognized by the school.

In some ways children may be better candidates for teaching than we suppose. At the University of Wisconsin, Vernon Allen has studied the ability of young tutors to infer whether lessons are being understood. In one experiment a tape-recorded arithmetic lesson was heard by ten children, all of whom were alone at the time. Since the lessons were either simple or extremely difficult, every child clearly understood or did not understand. A video recording was made of the children while they listened to the lesson. After a 30-second excerpt had been taken from each of the ten segments, these were made into a single videotape that was shown to observers. It was found that third- and fourth-graders were able to discriminate significantly between the easy and difficult lessons by judging nonverbal facial cues. But when a sample of primary school teachers who were attending graduate classes observed the tape, they could not significantly identify which children had or had not understood a lesson. Everyone could benefit if the perceptions of children were properly recognized. Certainly the insights of peer teachers when added to our own would be more diagnostic than the traditional practice of assigning grades based on how hard the teacher supposes a child is trying.

MOTIVATION AND GAMES

Since play is the preferred way of learning for most boys and girls, it deserves a place in peer teaching. Most grown-ups would intuitively agree with this recommendation. For example, parents are convinced that their children need to play with peers outside of school. This belief implies that youngsters can learn through play and from people who are about their own age. Similarly, teachers daily witness the powerful influence older children exert on younger ones during recess. For primary students, playing with bigger kids is the next best thing to being bigger themselves. Given this common circumstance, one might expect teachers to ask "What kinds of games ought to be used for peer teaching? Which social values can games help us reinforce?" However, these sorts of questions are uncommon. Instead, an opposite concern is more likely to be expressed: "How can the amount of play in school be reduced so that children can get down to the business of learning?" The time scheduled for play during kindergarten and first grade has recently declined in favor of early reading activities. This transition has occurred in part because teachers do not have sufficient understanding of the merits of play to defend its presence in the curriculum. As a result educators find themselves emphasizing a set of child-development priorities with which they may disagree but for which they are held accountable.

At the same time that play is decreasing to make way for other activities in elementary school, play is increasing at the college level. This shift in the age groups who are expected to benefit from games warrants an explanation. A decade ago some professors reluctantly concluded that their traditional methods of teaching about social problems were no longer working. Often the students appeared content merely to verbalize knowledge without acting on it. While searching for approaches that would bring more student involvement, a number of scholars independently decided on games. It seems that, while playing games, people become participants in a different type of process from the usual "learning" experience, one that includes feelings as well as thought. Naturally this revelation was disturbing, because university teachers, like the rest of us, have been educated to believe that play and learning don't go together; to link them would mean a lowering of standards. Most of us can recall being told by a teacher to "quit playing around and get to work." Professors were also aware that certain claims about traditional games, such as "Football develops character," are unsubstantiated.

Thus the university attempt to connect games and learning was understandably cautious. It began by conceding that game-like conditions promote learning. However, given the frivolous design of commercial games, players in the past have been denied a chance to practice important values. Therefore, what students needed was a variety of new games, original at least in terms of their social purpose. Many new games based on this rationale began to appear about 1970. Now there are games for improving police-community relations, games for understanding elderly people and the aging process, even games for learning to cope as a foreigner abroad. Most of these playthings come with elaborate directions, lengthy time requirements, and debriefing procedures. Nevertheless, gaming is now accepted as a teaching device by many policymakers, professional planners, municipal administrators, management officials, and professors. Indeed so popular has the adult play movement become that in 1973 the University of Michigan School of Education established an extension service to help interested parties better understand the use and application of games, to assist in selecting appropriate games, and to design games for special organizational needs.

In view of the mounting support for play as a way to learn in college, business, and industry, perhaps we should reconsider whether gaming also has merit for peer teaching in elementary and high school. Certainly there is no question about motivation. That games are more appealing to the young than to adults is apparent not only by observation but in retail sales. In addition, a special benefit that games can offer children is the opportunity to practice decision making. What we know about the future suggests that people will need the ability to accept increasing complexity, cope with more uncertainty, see alternatives, and make independent judgments. As we enter what is being called the era of over-choice, children must have experience with decision making in order to adopt a set of coherent values. Although most parents and teachers would agree that growing up and decision making go together, it doesn't always turn out that way. Instead adults often justify making themselves the only decision maker because wrong choices by their children could bring serious consequences. So we are faced with the dilemma that, while boys and girls need preparation in making decisions, for their own protection the chance to make choices is often denied them. Since children are expected to remain students for longer periods of time than were their parents, it follows that for some youngsters the initial chance to decide for themselves may not come until the stakes are high.

Rather than assume that the only way children today can safely learn is by being taught, the gaming approach supposes that they can learn by experiencing the consequences of their own actions. Within a context of emotional and intellectual involvement, games permit players to try out situations and solutions that are either irreversible or too risky and expensive to test in the real world. Games offer the chance for virtually risk-free, active exploration of yet-to-be-experienced social and intellectual problems. Unlike blunders in life, however, mistakes can be made in games at no expense to the society and at a relatively low cost of ego deflation to the learner.

If certain conditions are met, games can be an effective means of peer teaching. What matters most is the attitude of the tutor. It is essential that the tutor respect the existing play style of beginners when introducing them to games. Otherwise the teaching task will be seen only in terms of helping a young child understand how to play. The larger problem with games from a beginner's view involves the devaluation of imagination. Previously the child relied upon imagination as a guide for play behavior and as a source for sensing power and control. This means that some beginners at games may be expected to become frustrated easily, especially when involuntary setbacks are imposed, such as "lose one turn and go back three spaces." A natural response to the new sense of powerlessness that children feel is reflected in their request to occasionally suspend or at least alter the rules of the game. If we honor this request and before a game invite beginners to make up alternative rules, we can help them keep alive their respect for pretending while gradually raising the priority they assign to rules.

A second obstacle for beginners is learning when they should participate. From their dramatic play children have grown used to moving around, reacting spontaneously, and participating full-time. Most board games, however, require players to sit still and respond only when it's their turn. So, during a group game it isn't surprising to find that some beginners easily become bored, others don't recognize when it's their turn, and a few assign themselves too many turns. Rather than complain that these children can't follow directions, let's acknowledge that the roles of spectator or part-time participant may be unnatural and therefore unappealing to them. A better way to start is with games that have few rules and involve only two players. These conditions minimize yet teach turn taking while respecting spontaneity.

It is worth noting that, more than other age groups, the very young take pleasure in the play itself. Since their sense of reward is continual during play, they need not rely upon the completion of an activity to achieve satisfaction. By contrast, adults who play games may find some pleasure in the action but usually look forward to the primary reward, which does not come until the game ends and the winner and loser are determined. Given these differences in the timing and source of satisfaction, it follows that to stop a game before completion will be unacceptable to some experienced players. They may resort to coercing the beginner who makes such a request. Similarly, some experienced players hurry the beginner so that the game can reach its conclusion, urging them to "go ahead and move" without so much information, gesture, and conversation unrelated to the goal of determining a winner. Teachers and tutors of every age should recognize that, when a beginner's chance for victory is more of a concern to the teacher than to the child, having fun should replace winning as the primary reason for playing the game. To ensure that both parties enjoy themselves, it's a good idea to alternate between playing games and playing at pretend. In this way the rules and competitive orientation of tutors and the pretending ability of their younger peers can both be respected.

The results of peer teaching and play research together suggest that the student role should be modified. If students are expected to teach as well as to learn, their definition of accomplishment can enlarge to include helping other people achieve. If children learn to share themselves, it seems likely that as adults they will be more willing to share affluence. We may be unwise to complain that the modern marketplace does not offer boys and girls an arena in which they can learn responsibility as some of us learned it through youthful employment. In fact, having to work may have trained us to see responsibility in the most narrow sense; surely it did not teach most of us to share with people outside our family. Instead we were taught to feel proud that no one needed to share with us. Unlike past generations, many children who are growing up now must learn to be responsible in school, or they may not learn it at all. Peer teaching represents one possibility for improving the ways children see themselves and one another.

SHARING YOUR IMPRESSIONS

1. Children of the same age often give each other a sense of belonging, while older children sometimes do not accept them. Describe several memories of age prejudice among children.
2. Give some reasons why young children need playmates their own age. Then give some reasons for having them spend time with older kids.
3. Make some guesses about how age prejudice begins for most of us.
4. Think of some advantages that being a peer teacher has over being a classroom teacher.
5. What kind of student would you expect to benefit the most from teaching others? Which students would you anticipate to be the most effective peer teachers?
6. How do you think parents and teachers feel about peer teaching at school? Outside of school?
7. Recall some of the games you played as a child. Then identify

the kinds of games you recommend for big and little kids who play together.

REFERENCES AND SUGGESTED READING

Abt, Clark. *Serious Games*. New York: Viking, 1970.

Allen, Vernon. *Children as Teachers: Theory and Research on Tutoring*. New York: Academic Press, 1976.

Bronfenbrenner, Urie. *Two Worlds of Childhood: U.S. and U.S.S.R.* New York: Pocket Books, 1973. Pp. 15–73.

Coleman, James. "Learning through Games." In *The Study of Games*, edited by Elliot Avedon and Brian Sutton-Smith. New York: Wiley, 1971. Pp. 322–325.

Gartner, Alan, Kohler, Mary, and Riessman, Frank. *Children Teach Children*. New York: Harper and Row, 1971.

Goldschmid, Barbara, and Goldschmid, Marcel. "Peer Teaching in Higher Education: A Review." *Higher Education*, 5 (1976), 9–33.

Goodman, Frederick. "Gaming and Simulation." In *Second Handbook on Teaching*, edited by Robert Travers. Chicago: Rand McNally, 1973. Pp. 926–939.

Johnson, Roger T., and Johnson, David W. "Cooperation and Competition in the Classroom." In *Readings in Educational Psychology: Contemporary Perspectives*, edited by Robert Dentler and Bernard Shapiro. New York: Harper & Row, 1976. Pp. 287–291.

Horn, Robert D. *The Guide to Simulations/Games for Education and Training*, Volume I. Cranford, N.J.: Didactic Systems, 1977. Pp. 1–16.

Lippitt, Ronald, and Lippitt, Peggy. "Cross-Age Helpers." In *Education for Affective Achievement*, edited by Robert Strom and Paul Torrance. Chicago: Rand McNally, 1973. Pp. 166–170.

Robison, Helen. "The Decline of Play in Urban Kindergartens." *Young Children*, August 1971, pp. 333–341.

Shears, Loyda, and Bower, Eli. *Games in Education and Development*. Springfield, Ill.: Charles C Thomas, 1974.

Strom, Robert, and Engelbrecht, Guillermina. "Creative Peer Teaching." *Journal of Creative Behavior*, Summer 1974, pp. 93–100.

Thelen, Herbert. "Tutoring by Students: What Makes It So Exciting." *The School Review*, September 1969, pp. 229–244.

BOOKS TO SHARE WITH YOUNG CHILDREN

Alexander, Martha. *Nobody Asked Me If I Wanted a Baby Sister*. New York: Dial Press, 1971. Children are disappointed when their brothers or sisters receive more attention than themselves. Oliver decides he can solve this problem by giving his baby sister away to whomever will take good care of her.

Guilfoile, Elizabeth. *Have You Seen My Brother?* Chicago: Follett, 1962. Parents hope their children will know what to do if they ever get lost. Andrew loses his older brother and searches without success until someone gives him a good suggestion.

Mallett, Anne. *Here Comes Tagalong.* New York: Parents Magazine Press, 1971. Sometimes children move into a neighborhood where no one else is their size. Seven-year-old Steve finds that tagging along with an older brother presents certain difficulties that cannot be entirely overcome.

Zolotow, Charlotte. *Big Sister and Little Sister.* New York: Harper & Row, 1966. Older children don't mind babysitting their younger siblings if parents don't require it too often. In this story the little sister tires of being constantly supervised and wants a chance to make her own decisions for a change.

Zolotow, Charlotte. *If It Weren't for You.* New York: Harper & Row, 1966. In a family with several youngsters, there are times when each of them may wish that he or she had been an only child. The older boy in this story tells his younger brother all the reasons why it would be fun to be alone—and then he reconsiders.

THREE
FAMILIES ON THE MOVE

Some people need to move. In the United States, we depend upon 300,000 migrant workers to harvest our fruits and vegetables. Business and government require the continual traveling of salesmen, military personnel, and construction workers. Even our entertainment calls for large numbers of actors and athletes to be on the road much of the time. In addition, there are many adolescents who now lead lives of perpetual movement. And nearly two million retired persons migrate south for the winter. All these groups rely on thousands of bus and truck drivers as well as pilots, stewards, and stewardesses to move with them. The rest of us may envy such people or feel sorry for them; yet we may be more like them than we suppose. During a single year, 40 million persons in the U. S. change their home address. Often they move to get ahead or to get away, to find somewhere better, somewhere new. Whatever the reason, all this mobility seems to underscore the contention that we are becoming a nation of strangers.

THE NEWCOMERS' EXPERIENCE

According to Vance Packard, the social cost of uprooting a society is enormous. In his nationwide study of mobility, Packard found that an increasing number of transient men and women are indifferent to community problems. When talented people behave in this way, the towns they move in and out of must settle for lesser leadership. Newcomers assess the matter differently; they suggest it is the community response that is in question. No one bothers to welcome them or invite their participation in the life of the community. As a result, some people undergo an identity crisis and suffer a feeling of powerlessness, the insignificance that goes with being unknown. Others who move report that the most serious loss is one of continuity. Without friends and familiar environment, the security of belonging is replaced by loneliness. All these losses contribute to a deteriorating sense of well-being for the individual and society.

The adjustment of children is the major worry of parents. They often wonder whether there is a best time for moving— when the kids are younger or older, while they are in school or during the summer. The first concern is justified by studies indicating that age is related to adjustment. Louise Ames of the Gesell Institute for Child Development identifies the period from ages 2 through 4 as an undesirable time to move. It is hard to overrate 2- to 4-year-olds' need for continuity. During this interval children want everything to remain the same; they don't appreciate even the family vacation if it involves a departure from the familiar. With this in mind, the Playskool Company, a Milton-Bradley subsidiary, offers a series of "familiar place" toys. One of the favorites is a miniature Holiday Inn that includes a swimming pool, playground, and people figures. This home-away-from-home is intended as a rewarding place for children to stop on the way to wherever their imaginations may take them. Many of the same play opportunities provided by the traditional doll house can be found at the Holiday Inn, plus the added modern elements of travel—staying in new places and meeting new friends. For some youngsters, the Holiday Inn may stir memories and give the chance to relive a family vacation, while for others this new type of playhouse can introduce some of the fun that goes with being on the road. Perhaps the big Holiday Inn will seem more familiar and appealing to little boys and girls who have experienced some of its attractions beforehand in their own homes. Similarly, whether a family is on vacation or moving, children's preference to eat in familiar places such as McDonald's should be considered by parents.

Returning to the issue of adjustment following a move, children between ages 5 and 9 seem to cope the best, for they no longer need a changeless environment and haven't yet become members of a clique. After age 9, and especially during the teenage years, moving can again be traumatic. The problem then is more than just leaving old friends. In the teens, loneliness is greater because it takes longer to make new friends. Even the adolescent college students, who now represent approximately half of their age group, report being lonely. Although the campus is usually referred to as a community, many people attending large institutions for the first time do not feel a sense of belonging. At the University of Wisconsin a special group center has been established primarily for students who are lonely and yearn for a chance to talk.

Most parents believe that it's better for a child to move in the summer than during the school year. This decision has always meant difficulty for the moving industry. To change the prevailing attitude, Allied Van Lines sought the support of experts for the notion that it may be better to move while school is in progress. When this effort failed to produce results in its favor, the moving industry turned its attention to campaigning for year-round schools with staggered vacations. School systems are being urged to adopt something like the Atlanta plan, in which a student can elect to stay out for any one of the four quarters or to keep studying throughout all four. An increasing number of school boards find the year-round school appealing because of its improved utilization of buildings and faculty. Meanwhile, parents still want to know what will happen if they move during the school year. Actually, the research is less than conclusive; but it seems that children of above-average ability tend to adjust well, while those of average or below-average ability can expect some difficulty.

If your family is among the 20% of the U. S. population who will move this year, remember that the process of child adjustment is sometimes undermined even before the family leaves town. Generally this mistake takes the form of a lawn or garage sale. Parents eager to reduce hauling costs frequently include children's toys as sale items. Perhaps the youngsters are told they can keep the profit to buy other toys in the new town. Although parents would not consider selling some items they are fond of, the favorite possessions of children are viewed differently. The point is that children do need continuity; they need some familiar things when they arrive in a new place. Consequently, they should be allowed to keep their toys or to sell only those they feel should be left behind.

The single factor that appears to matter the most when people move is family cohesion. For a while the members of a newcomer's family may be the only persons who listen and share concerns, who provide the help needed in unfamiliar situations, and who respect the abilities and competence that strangers don't yet recognize. Although these needs describe everyone in the family, the press to quickly get settled often results in parents being less accessible than they ought to be. Initially, it's better to delay some household tasks in order to spend more time as a family exploring the new community.

DIVORCE AND BELONGING

Moving can be especially difficult for boys and girls whose relocation is caused by marital separation or divorce. Almost 20% of American children have parents who decide to live apart—that's about 13 million kids. For many of these children, the usual problems of adjusting to a new environment are compounded by loneliness for the absent parent. More often than not, Dad is the person left behind, and Mom must return to work. Together these factors intensify a youngster's feelings of aloneness. Generally some attempt is made to compensate for the missing party. One promising example is the Nurtury, an early childhood center in Los Angeles, which was set up to serve families from fatherless homes. Most of the Nurtury staff are men so that children can be guaranteed access to a favorable influence that is otherwise lacking in their lives.

There are other, more widely available programs to assist single parents with child rearing. One of these is Big Brothers of America, a nationwide volunteer organization that provides counseling and companionship for boys from father-absent homes while giving mothers time off for themselves. If Dad is assigned custody of the children, then Big Sisters of America may be an appropriate resource. Despite their merit, these types of compensatory experiences aren't enough to ensure child adjustment. We must also acknowledge that the single parents themselves have a need for social contact. And, unless this need is fulfilled, the influence of parental discontent may overshadow whatever sacrifices are made by others on behalf of the children. It is unfortunate that few people seem willing to welcome the divorcee with children as she arrives in a new neighborhood or town. Usually she feels rejected, not merely ignored. To remedy this situation, there are now 800 local chapters of Parents With-

out Partners. Made up entirely of single parents, PWP arranges for adult companionship as well as family activities.

Our schools must join community groups in determining their own special role for helping people cope with divorce. That classwork is undermined by marital distress is illustrated in a study of Marin County, California. The Marin project, involving 131 children from 60 White, middle-class families, began five years ago as a free divorce-counseling service. Each of the participating families is studied for six weeks at the time of separation and followed up a year afterward. The researchers look for changes in psychological functioning and in intellectual and social adjustment. According to the project administrator, Judith Wallerstein, the most important single factor influencing a child's well-being is the amount and duration of anger between divorcing parents. To date the findings indicate that about one-third of the children function less effectively on the follow-up profiles. Preschoolers seem to comprise the most vulnerable age group. One year after the divorce, half of them look worse, compared to 30% of adolescents, who ranked second in being adversely affected.

Teachers often wonder what they can do for students undergoing domestic shifts—children who feel alone because they miss the absent parent and helpless because they can do nothing about it. A clue to our best response may be found in the advice given young adults who are divorcing while in college. Typically they are urged to take a semester off so that the preoccupation, strain, and depression will not jeopardize their academic success. Obviously a third-grader whose custodial parent decides to move to a new town will not be offered the option of dropping out for a term. Yet, because the temporary emotional disturbance of such a child is predictable, teachers can help most by modifying their own expectations. This change may take the form of shorter or less frequent assignments, longer time limits, greater individual attention, or a chance to receive an incomplete grade rather than a failure. What matters is that no child involved in a divorce situation be expected to perform at school as though conditions were normal. The first changes required are not on the part of the child but on the part of those who teach the child. Teachers govern their own expectations, and these expectations are crucial, since they determine whether anger, disappointment, tolerance, or support will be shown to the children of divorce.

RECOGNIZED AND WELCOME

In order to facilitate the adjustment of children whose seasonal moves in farming and fishing are predictable, the Migrant Student Record Transfer System was recently established. All 50 states, as well as Puerto Rico and other trust territories, are included in the system. The 450,000 student records maintained in the data bank are accessible from 130 computer terminals located throughout the United States. If a new migrant student arrives lacking records, a computer inquiry will yield critical information within six hours about family background and school placement. One day later a mail packet from the MSRTS headquarters in Little Rock, Arkansas, will be forwarded with achievement data. Of course, the anxiety of being a newcomer cannot be erased by having the faculty aware of one's background. A student will still feel more or less alone, depending on how the school system responds to people who transfer.

In Los Angeles, where over 100,000 transfers are reported annually, a project known as the Reception Room has been established. The inner-city schools involved have the highest turnover rate in the city, with 25 or more children entering each week. Many of these new arrivals come with no school records. In order to grade-place them properly and provide an orientation, a full-time teacher for remedial instruction, another for testing, and a part-time child-welfare worker are available to each of the Reception Room schools. Close contact is maintained with the health and welfare departments, as well as with church groups and charitable agencies, so that, if home visits indicate a need, prompt access to food, clothing, and medical services can be arranged. The Milwaukee Public Schools also operate a migrant program through which children and their parents are welcomed to the community and given assistance. The orientation features of these programs should be available to more affluent transfers as well—not only because they comprise three-fourths of the moving population but because adjustment is hard for all children, regardless of their family income.

Teachers appreciate continuity too, but they seldom find it. Out of 110 high school seniors interviewed at Montvale, New Jersey, only two were still living in the house where they were born. Almost half had spent part of high school somewhere else. This kind of mobility prohibits teachers from experiencing the pride they have traditionally received in watching former students grow. Certainly something is missing when a teacher perceives a new student as an extra burden, someone to resent but tolerate. Under these conditions the newcomer feels unwanted, and peers learn that strangers deserve to remain outsiders. Of course, most teachers welcome new students and try to hasten their sense of belonging by appointing a buddy, arranging a place on some team, or having a party. All these efforts could be improved if a child's new teacher understood more about the child than is provided by current school records. I favor having elementary teachers write letters of introduction when students transfer. Since the intent of these letters would be to facilitate adjustment, they would emphasize subjective information about the child's interests, sources of embarrassment, and peer preferences.

In the final analysis, classmates have the most significant effect on student adjustment. If they come from families that choose not to welcome new neighbors, from towns that discourage nonresidents from moving in, or from schoolrooms where teachers resent any increase in class size, the chances are that they will have missed an important example of how a newcomer should be treated. Fortunately, some children have been educated to surpass the example of most grown-ups; their initiative can serve as the model for the class. When teachers witness this initiative of students who try to ease the burden of newness for others, they should recognize such efforts as an important form of accomplishment. It may be that in some ways children have fewer responsibilities than we prefer, but the obligation to accept a newcomer in their midst is one that only they can fulfill.

SHARING YOUR IMPRESSIONS

1. Describe one of your own experiences with being a newcomer.
2. Speculate about the best and worst times for moving a family.

3. In what ways do the problems of belonging or adjusting in open classrooms differ from those in self-contained classrooms?
4. What suggestions do you have for teachers about how they can help students and faculty newcomers feel welcome?
5. Think of some techniques a school or classroom could develop to ease the burden of newness for transfer students.
6. In what ways can parents make the experience of moving less difficult for children?
7. When children are moved, is their most difficult adjustment to the other kids? The teacher? The curriculum? The neighborhood?
8. List some activities parents and teachers separately encourage that give children feelings of being left out instead of belonging.

REFERENCES AND SUGGESTED READING

Cavenagh, W. E. *Juvenile Courts, the Child and the Law.* Baltimore: Penguin Books, 1967.

Despert, J. Louise. *Children of Divorce.* Garden City, N. Y.: Doubleday, 1962.

Eddy, John, and Silverman, Manuel. "Children of Divorce: Implications for Counseling," *Kappa Delta Pi Record,* October 1974, pp. 7–8.

Goldburg, Martin. "The Runaway Americans—A Report on the Findings of a Study of the Mental Health of People in Flight," *Mental Hygiene,* January 1972, pp. 13–21.

Grollman, Earl. *Talking about Divorce: A Dialogue between Parent and Child.* Boston: Beacon Press, 1975. Pp. 1–18.

Hope, Karol, and Young, Nancy. *Momma, the Sourcebook for Single Mothers.* New York: New American Library, 1976.

Kantor, Mildred. *Mobility and Mental Health.* Springfield, Ill.: Charles C Thomas, 1965. Pp. 1–42.

Maddox, Brenda. *The Half-Parent.* New York: New American Library, 1975.

Packard, Vance. *A Nation of Strangers.* New York: David McKay, 1972. Pp. 160–178, 247–256.

Packard, Vance. "Nobody Knows My Name." *Today's Education,* September-October 1973, p. 24.

Parker, Seymour, et al. "Migration and Mental Illness—Some Reconsiderations and Suggestions for Further Analysis." In *Social Science and Medicine* (Volume 3). Oxford: Pergamon, 1969. Pp. 1–18.

Slater, Philip. *The Pursuit of Loneliness.* Boston: Beacon Press, 1970. Pp. 100–112.

Springam, Natalie. "Children on the Road." *The New Republic*, April 7, 1973, p. 13.

BOOKS TO SHARE WITH YOUNG CHILDREN

Goff, Beth. *Where Is Daddy? The Story of a Divorce.* Boston: Beacon Press, 1969. The personal distress of divorcing parents can cause them to underestimate how lonely and confusing the situation is for children. Janey's sudden change in surroundings, her fear of abandonment, and the adjustment to mother taking a full-time job are almost too much for the preschooler to face.

Lisker, Sonia, and Dean, Leigh. *Two Special Cards.* New York: Harcourt Brace Jovanovich, 1976. Parents who can no longer live together should still cooperate in making the life of their child secure. Eight-year-old Hazel is tormented by questions she cannot answer, but she learns to see that divorce can have some positive outcomes.

Martin, Patricia. *Be Brave Charlie.* New York: Putnam's Sons, 1972. The loneliness that accompanies moving can result in poor schoolwork. Charlie, a Navajo boy, misses his parents and has a difficult time adjusting to the boarding school until he is needed by someone else who is lonely.

Thompson, Vivian. *Sad Day, Glad Day.* New York: Holiday House, 1962. When children move, they should be allowed to bring their familiar toys with them. Kathy had to change from a country house to a high-rise apartment, but this transition bothered her less than leaving a beloved doll behind.

Zolotow, Charlotte. *Janey.* New York: Harper & Row, 1973. Being a newcomer is hard, but those who are left behind also feel lonely and helpless to change the circumstance. Janey's girlfriend recalls the good times they had together and hopes that someday, when they are adults, it will be possible for them to live near each other again.

FOUR
THE CHILDREN'S TERRITORY

So far we have considered opportunities for children to get to know one another at school, ways for them to feel a greater sense of belonging in the classroom. But what happens when boys and girls seek to be with one another outside of school? Where should encounters take place, and under what conditions? First let's recognize that the availability of play space depends on a child's residential circumstances. For example, when I was a boy in rural Wisconsin, playgrounds were a luxury, because we didn't need them. Few of us had much free time, and, when we did, there were plenty of places to get together. My impression then was that city children were the lucky ones, because they could have so many playmates. Maybe I was right, but several things have changed since then. Most of the vacant city lots have disappeared; there are more cars; high-rise apartments have become common. In combination these factors have brought about a contradiction of my childhood guess regarding peer play in the city. The fact is that, today, millions of urban children have fewer playmates than they need, because there is no safe place for them to meet.

NO PLACE TO PLAY

Parents respond in different ways to the problem of inadequate play space. One alternative is to reluctantly accept the situation and hope that children will learn to cope with it. In practice this means that a youngster has many chances to encounter other children, but only under the most dangerous conditions. Surely all children need to be warned about playing in the street, but grown-ups usually overestimate a child's ability to comprehend traffic danger. An average person does not attain the degree of traffic maturity necessary to be a pedestrian until some time between the ages of 9 and 12. Before then children are at risk whenever they are unescorted in the street. The size of that risk has been calculated by Swedish researchers who estimate that children's accident rate is six times greater in neighborhoods where pedestrian and car traffic are not completely separate.

Of course, street life can adversely affect child development in other ways, too. When they are not within their parents' reach, children are likely to form peer groups at an earlier age. As one mother has said, "It's hard to supervise play from the fifth floor." Studies of low-income families in Washington, D. C., indicate surprisingly early cutoff points in parent control. Children as young as 6 years old who live in high-rise apartments seem to seize control of family decisions involving themselves. One can hardly overlook the relevance of this pattern to the impression of many parents that boys and girls cannot reasonably be kept in the house for extended periods.

A nearly opposite view is expressed by parents who require their children to stay inside most of the time. A London survey revealed that 72% of the preschoolers living in high houses seldom play with others of their age because no safe opportunities have been provided for them. Their parents contend that, besides being unsafe, the busy street below is too far away to hear a child cry, that it is too long a distance for a child to reach the bathroom in time, and that the elevator button is often placed so that a small child cannot reach the right one. A similar study made in Stockholm found that young children seldom leave their homes alone or with playmates because traffic is too dangerous. Of 2000 Swedish mothers who were interviewed, 98% said they would rather have access to safe, supervised playgrounds than a car park or other amenity. Yet neither they nor the London mothers were ever consulted in the planning of their homes. Until this situation alters, many children must spend every day confined to their apartments. To be sure, they are safe from traffic, but they are also separated from peers.

The decision to reduce a child's environment to the confines of the home is costly. Not only must one stay with the same people all the time but this continuous contact can have frustrating effects. Under these conditions, family members are prone to become bored with each other. This boredom or lack of stimulation sometimes leads to destructive conflict—family members striking out at one another or else totally ignoring one another. Then too, with more time indoors and fewer social contacts, there is a low incidence of novel stimuli at the time in life when they are needed most. If children cannot explore or control their environment, it follows that they will have fewer new experiences that otherwise could add to their imaginations and intelligence.

When boys and girls lack outdoor play space, they try to compensate by being especially active inside. Unfortunately, parents know that, in order to avoid complaints from neighbors, they must minimize the sound and movements of indoor play. This unnatural restriction limits the kinds of play that are possible and thus the kinds of interaction, discovery, exercise, and learning that can take place. Typically, the parents decide to emphasize sedentary activities, such as board games. The less active mode is further reinforced by regarding television as the primary source of family stimulation. In effect, this priority urges everyone to perceive all other competing sounds as interruptions. Children who are scolded for attracting more attention than the television may conclude that active play is less important than being a spectator, or they may learn to dislike grownups for always discouraging pleasure. In either case, the parent preference for subdued play often results in children being denied the chances they need to talk. This consequence is serious, because 90% of a child's speech development is patterned by the age of 6.

In the high houses, a child's playthings must compete with other family needs for space. The low priority usually assigned to toys dictates that they be picked up and put away before bedtime. Children who express disappointment with this daily procedure are usually reminded that they are learning to be responsible, to achieve a sense of order. What some parents overlook is that their intended lesson may be less valuable than what could be gained if the playthings were sometimes allowed to remain in place overnight. For example, the persistence needed to solve complex problems is unlikely to develop unless a task begun today can be continued tomorrow without starting all over again. Instead of developing the habit of reaching premature conclusions, a child can learn to feel comfortable with incompleteness and ambiguity if his or her occupied play space is respected as being "work in progress."

Although boys and girls are seldom aware when they lose an opportunity to learn, they are acutely conscious of the loss of possible friendships that is imposed by isolation from peers. Consequently, among youngsters who are confined in the house all day because it is unsafe to play outside, extreme loneliness is a common experience. Given the ban on active indoor play and movement as well as the prohibition of normal speech and encounters with peers, perhaps we should not be surprised at the child's lack of exercise, bad posture, overreliance on television, poor imagination, and relative inability to relate successfully.

THE GOOD PLAYGROUND

Naturally, parents are dissatisfied when they must choose between allowing dangerous street play and keeping children at home. The usual recommendation to build a playground nearby makes sense if there is careful planning. Although many playgrounds are unsuccessful, people are remarkably unconcerned about the causes of their inadequacy and about what could be done to correct the situation. Actually, there are several ways to measure the success of a playground or the need for its redesign. The first consideration should always be safety. Nevertheless, the insistence that toys be safe has seldom carried over to playground equipment. According to the Consumer Product Safety Commission, park and school playground apparatus such as merry-go-rounds, jungle gyms, and swings account for the greatest number of play injuries to the preschool and primary school age group. In the United States in 1976, public and home playground equipment was associated with an estimated 100,000 injuries that required hospital-emergency-room treatment. Unlike toys, these unsafe playthings are usually not selected by parents; instead they are chosen for parents by people they trust—recreation directors, teachers, and school administrators.

The need for more judicious selection of play apparatus is linked to the less obvious need for a change in attitude toward outdoor education. It is well known that, except for field trips, elementary teachers place a low value on learning outside the classroom. If this were not the case, fewer schools would continue the practice of assigning only one teacher to 150 children during recess. This procedure conveys the impression that what takes place outdoors is unimportant for teachers to observe. That children at play believe otherwise is apparent from their nearly constant appeal for teachers to see their accomplishments: "Teacher, watch me go down the slide"; "Teacher, see how fast I can get to the fence"; "Teacher, look at how far I can throw the ball." During the early years, when the need for recognition is urgent, it is unfortunate that so few grown-ups make themselves available for the audience role.

Perhaps the most charitable explanation of why teachers are inclined to discount outdoor play is their preference for intellectual achievement. Such a position assumes, as we have for so long, that mental development and active play are mutually exclusive. But research during the past decade has determined that under certain conditions play can be a superior medium for intellectual and emotional learning. Consequently, it has become legitimate to ask "What kinds of learning can playgrounds provide that are unavailable elsewhere? What types of equipment and spatial arrangement are needed to support this learning?" These questions have initiated a new trend in playground design that unashamedly aims to produce both fun and learning.

In addition to safety, a second factor that identifies a good playground is its record for child appeal. We might call this a boredom index. It's true that children will play with almost anything, but a look at usage patterns indicates that conventional playgrounds don't hold the attention of boys and girls. G. R. Wade's study of playgrounds serving different socioeconomic areas in Philadelphia showed that children visited only once per day and then for only 15 minutes. Even the youngsters from low-income housing projects, the children with supposedly the least opportunity for play and perhaps the greatest need, demonstrated this same attention span. It was learned that, on the average, the nonmanipulatable play apparatus was vacant at least 89% of the time during the peak period of visitation. This typically low score for attraction suggests that play equipment is used only when nothing else is happening.

Although better toys have been developed because of consumer pressure, most playgrounds continue to look very much as they did 50 years ago. M. J. Ellis attributes this time lag for improvements to certain erroneous assumptions the public makes about play space. For one thing, we tend to assume that kids will sustain play whether we alter playgrounds or not. This notion contradicts our belief that in other learning centers, such as the school, it is important to manipulate and change the environment. The fact is that, if a playground doesn't modify, it soon becomes redundant and boring, no longer functional. A second mistake is to suppose that a playground can be designed and maintained for just the capital cost. According to this impression, a good playground is one requiring virtually no maintenance. However, since play is a process of consuming information, it follows that, when materials and human resources are consumed, a playground must be changed in order to retain its stimulation function. Perhaps this feature of being responsive to the growth needs of children is what makes the "adventure playgrounds" of Europe so popular.

Adventure playgrounds *are* appealing to children, including the 8- to 15-year-olds who are tireless explorers of discovery. What makes these playgrounds special is that they are constructed and operated by the youngsters themselves. A visitor is likely to see a group of older children hammering and sawing wood in order to build a hut while other participants are building a fire for cooking, watching, or warmth. Usually, as soon as children become fascinated by fire, grown-ups warn them not to play with matches. Have you ever observed a 6-year-old boy when candles are lit? He wants to blow them out again and again. Although we tire easily of a child's preoccupation with fire, the same fascination affects us—witness the fireplaces we build into our houses so that we can watch the flames and dream. In any event, the fires at adventure playgrounds are built in protective places, such as barrels, for roasting hot dogs or beans or just for watching. Meanwhile, some boys and girls might be seated on burlap bags, sliding down barren hills or mounds of dirt. A simple philosophy supports all this activity. It is that life demands courage, decision making, endurance, and strength but that grown-ups at school and at home underestimate the capacity of children for taking risks, enjoying the stimulation of danger, and finding things out for themselves. Even though an adventure playground serves more children for longer periods of time than does a conventional playground, accidents are less common. In fact, England's insurance rates are lower for adventure playgrounds than for any other type.

Only one rule guides adventure-playground children: their actions must not hurt, upset, or interfere with other people. To ensure that kids have access to help if they need it, a trained play leader is available each day for the 12-hour period the playground is open. This nondirective supervision represents a third criterion by which to judge a good playground. Generally the play leader is accompanied by volunteer assistants who are expected to respond when called upon by children but otherwise to refrain from interference, especially in terms of organizing play. Play leaders believe so much of life at school and home is adult determined that it would be a mistake to carry this condition onto the playground as well. Thus they reject the preference manifest in the United States for adult-organized activities, such as little-league sports, in which grown-ups feel they have a right and an obligation to direct children's play.

The popularity of adventure playgrounds in Europe has brought many visitors from the U. S. who want to see for themselves whether the favorable publicity is warranted. Usually these recreation directors and child-development experts return home with mixed feelings. On the one hand, they acknowledge the high level of participation and satisfaction. On the other hand, they doubt whether parents in the U. S. would be willing to accept the untidy appearance and child independence that go with adventure playgrounds. My own, contrary view is that parents will support whatever experiences children can safely enjoy. For this reason I believe that a recent study in Champaign, Illinois, may be more suggestive of what we can expect. By comparing the behaviors between two groups of youngsters whose play occurred in different settings—one a conventional playground and the other an adventure type—the researchers were able to identify certain socialization effects. The 5- to 16-year-olds who participated at the adventure site showed a greater increase in social skills; in fact, they tended to make more new friends at the playground than did the conventional-playground group. Perhaps this was because of the kinds of activities. It does seem that cooperation and group loyalty grow whenever children build things together. What about parent resistance? Of the parents whose children took part in the adventure program, 95% felt that it should be continued and enlarged.

Improving play supervision, choosing more stimulating types of equipment, and establishing better standards for playground safety are important objectives that imply a reevaluation of how we use urban space. There are psychological consequences when 70% of a nation lives on less than 1% of its land. If high-rise development is continued, it will be necessary to accept the implications. At the same time that crowding is increasing, there is more leisure time. Reason dictates that we establish the proper relation between these two factors or suffer the predictable consequences. We already are running out of play space where people can find peace and tranquility, places that historically have offered a welcome relief from the tense affairs of urban residents. Of even greater significance is the need to arrange protected and accessible spaces for children to play. What good is it to educate students for leisure if in their closest environment, the high-rise development or apartment complex, there is no room for play? All of us, especially the young, need leisure space. Unless we make adequate provision for play, the curiosity, imagination, and spontaneous gaiety of children will be lost.

SHARING YOUR IMPRESSIONS

1. What problems have you seen at public playgrounds?
2. How do you feel about the space available for your child's play?
3. What kind of a playground would you like for your child?
4. Make some guesses about how crowding can influence child development.
5. Think of some ways to make more room for play in crowded neighborhoods.
6. Suggest some things teachers can do for children who come from crowded homes and neighborhoods.
7. Although elementary teachers feel that peer play is valuable,

recess duty is an unpopular assignment. This is your chance to invent a better role for whoever must supervise recess.

REFERENCES AND SUGGESTED READING

Aaron, David, and Winawer, Bonnie. *Child's Play: A Creative Approach to Play Spaces for Today's Children.* New York: Harper & Row, 1965.

Abernethy, Drummond. *Playgrounds.* London: National Playing Fields Association, 1976.

Asbell, Bernard. "Can We Survive the Madding Crowd?" In *Values and Human Development*, edited by Robert D. Strom. Columbus, Ohio: Charles E. Merrill, 1973. Pp. 162–169.

Bengtsson, Arvid. *Adventure Playgrounds.* London: Crosby Lockwood and Sons, 1972.

Ellis, M. J. *Why People Play.* Englewood Cliffs, N. J.: Prentice-Hall, 1973.

Hall, Edward. *The Hidden Dimension.* Garden City, N. Y.: Doubleday, 1969.

Hurtwood, Lady Allen. *Planning for Play.* Cambridge, Mass.: M.I.T. Press, 1968.

Lambert, Jack, and Pearson, Jenny. *Adventure Playgrounds.* London: Penguin Books, 1974.

Newson, John, and Newson, Elizabeth. *Four Year Olds in an Urban Community.* Middlesex, England: Pelican Books, 1970. Pp. 142–171.

Sandels, Stina. "Children in Traffic: The Real Danger." *Where*, August 1971, pp. 229–231.

Shivers, Jay. "The Need for Children's Play Space in the Modern World." Paper presented to the International Playground Association in Vienna, Austria, September 1972.

Taylor, Anne, and Vlastos, George. *School Zone: Learning Environments for Children.* New York: Van Nostrand Reinhold, 1975.

Thompson, Frederick, and Rittenhouse, Ann. "Measuring the Impact." *Parks and Recreation*, May 1974, pp. 24–26, 62–63.

Wade, G. R. "A Study of Free Play Patterns of Elementary School-Age Children on Playground Equipment." Unpublished master's thesis, Pennsylvania State University, 1968.

BOOKS TO SHARE WITH YOUNG CHILDREN

Binzen, Bill. *Miguel's Mountain.* New York: Coward-McCann, 1968. City planners can please children by letting them have some control over play space. Miguel discovers a huge pile of dirt that has been temporarily placed in the park, but this mountain is scheduled to be removed unless the boy can figure out some way to keep it.

Hanlon, Emily. *What If a Lion Eats Me and I Fall into Hippopotamus' Mudhole?* New York: Delacorte Press, 1975. Some children lack confidence to explore the special places their city has planned for them. One boy offers many imaginative excuses for not going somewhere new; so his companion also uses imagination rather than teasing to introduce the zoo and make it appealing.

Keith, Eros. *A Small Lot.* Scarsdale, N. Y.: Bradbury Press, 1968. Urban space is expensive, but some of it should be reserved for children. The small lot where Bob and Jay have always played is being considered as a site for shopping until the boys propose a better idea.

Meeks, Esther. *The Hill That Grew.* Chicago: Follett, 1959. Children without a safe place to play will play in unsafe places. Dick and Tom have nowhere to ride their Christmas sleds downhill; so the townspeople work together and create a hill just for snow sports.

Schick, Eleanor. *City in the Summer.* New York: Macmillan, 1969. Urban children should get to leave the city once in a while. Like many kids, Jerry has no place to play except on the apartment roof. His outlook improves when an elderly friend introduces this city boy to the beach.

2

PLAY
AND
CREATIVE
BEHAVIOR

FIVE

THE VALUES OF PRIVACY

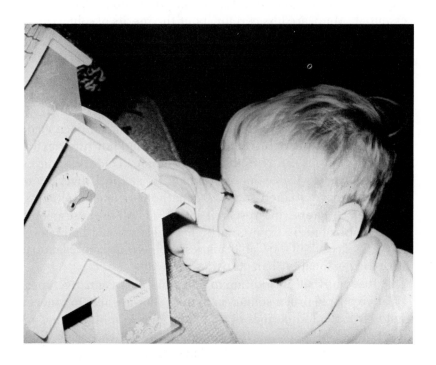

Most parents want their young children to have playmates. Play with peers is expected to foster the ability to get along with others and to share—social skills that will be required in school. In some families in which child rearing is left entirely to the mother, her own natural desire for periodic relief can also be a motivation for encouraging peer play. Whatever the reason, parents tend to agree that during early childhood peer play is essential. Many are less certain about the merits of solitary play and consequently less enthusiastic about arranging uninterrupted time for children to be alone. Recent research on creativity may call for a reconsideration of these attitudes.

CREATIVITY

Over the past 15 years, numerous attempts have been made to determine what creative people are like and how their extraordinary abilities can become more common. Under the direction of Donald MacKinnon, psychologists at the University of California have studied some 600 mathematicians, architects, engineers, writers, and research scientists. All of these people were nominated by experts in their fields as being highly creative. As a result of the California research, we are more familiar with the personality characteristics of creative adults.

It seems that, in addition to being highly imaginative, most creative people prefer solitary activities; they are able to concentrate for extended periods of time; and they exhibit an unusual level of task persistence. But how did they get this way? What growing-up experiences do they have in common? Some clues are provided by their autobiographical narratives. Generally, because they were either the eldest child in a family or were distantly spaced from brothers and sisters, they spent more time alone and with adults than did their peers, and they learned at an early age to enjoy the company provided by their own imaginations.

High and Low Daydreamers

Although the privacy most creative adults experienced during childhood is suggestive of an environment other people may need to become more creative, the value of solitary play has generally been overlooked. In the 1970s, however, Jerome Singer and his colleagues at Yale University made some important discoveries. One experiment involved a population of 9-year-olds who were similar in intelligence, level of education, and social background. After intensive interviews, the children were divided into two groups. The so-called "High Daydreamers" were boys and girls who created imaginary companions, enjoyed playing by themselves, and reported more daydreams. Children qualified as "Low Daydreamers" if they preferred more literal play, expressed disinterest in solitary activities, and reported infrequent daydreams. All the youngsters were told that they were being considered as potential astronauts. The "candidates" were told that, since astronauts must spend long periods of time in a space capsule without moving about much or speaking to others, the purpose of the experiment was to see how long they could sit quietly without talking to the experimenter.

The results were significant. The High Daydreamers were able to remain quiet for protracted periods of solitary activity and to persist without giving up—factors closely related to concentration ability. In addition, the High Daydreamers were less restless, less eager to end the test, and seemed serenely able to occupy themselves inwardly to make time pass. Later it was learned that they each had transformed the situation of forced compliance into a fantasy game that helped them increase their waiting ability. By contrast, the Low Daydreamers never seemed able to settle down. They would repeatedly leap up and inquire "Is the time up yet?" They continually tried to involve the experimenter in conversation. Further testing revealed that the High Daydreamers were also superior in creativity, storytelling, and need for achievement.

LEARNING TO BE ALONE

Teachers and parents can confirm Singer's findings for themselves. It is a common observation that slum children are usually crowded together and seldom have a chance for solitary play. As a result, many of them come to school restless, unable to sit still or persist at tasks, inclined to act out impulses rather than reflect on them. Because these children tend to lack the ability to concentrate, they often interrupt and distract each other. In one study of inner-city schools, Martin Deutsch found that teachers had to devote as much as 80% of their time trying to establish the discipline they felt was necessary for learning. Many of these teachers complained that their students had never developed the inner resources needed for sustained inquiry. The forecast is not much better in homes of higher-income levels where children are heard to complain "There's nothing to do" when playmates or television are unavailable. It is a sad commentary when the very young already bore themselves.

Fortunately, if solitary play is permitted a larger place in early childhood education of the future, boredom and inattention may become far less common. The transition will not be easy, because grown-ups have traditionally felt that children don't need privacy. On the contrary, children are often led to feel that being alone is more a form of punishment than an opportunity. When we say "Go to your room and stay there," the solitude is usually intended as a form of punishment, a type of solitary confinement. Although adults themselves resent child intrusion when they are trying to concentrate, their tendency to underestimate the seriousness of children at play is nearly universal. Moreover, researchers have found that the frustration effects of interrupted solitary play include reduction of a child's persistence for mental tasks and a lowering of the ability to concentrate. A further finding is that the younger the child the more vulnerable to play disturbance he or she will be. This comes as no surprise to the many day-care and preschool teachers who express disappointment about being unable to grant the request of some children for periodic privacy.

The conflicting privacy needs of some mothers and their children bear mention. More fathers should assume their proper share of child rearing in order to reduce the necessity of mothers having to be with children more than they can tolerate. A probable consequence would be a decline in the need to rely too much on early peer encounter for the sake of maternal relief.

Unlike learning to be with age-mates, which is a socialization skill that can be acquired after starting school, a child's learning to be alone will probably begin at home or not at all. Obviously the number of children in a class and the frequency of interruptions make solitary play a low-priority activity at school. Moreover, once the school years begin, such organized groups as Cub Scouts, Brownies, Little League, and YMCA are available, along with other peer pressures to spend less time alone. Some of these group experiences can offer a child much and should be encouraged. At the same time, however, parents should help children arrange a schedule that allows ample opportunity for solitude each day. This will be especially difficult for men and women who have been unsuccessful in finding uninterrupted time for even their own important business.

Many adults today appear unsure of their identity or sense loneliness even though they belong to social groups they can identify with and seek companionship in. Apparently, belonging is not enough. By setting aside a time for solitary play, parents avoid depriving youngsters of the early self-encounters every child needs.

FANTASY AND SOLITARY PLAY

When children engage in solitary play, they fantasize more than during peer play or parent-child play. Still, even though we recognize solitude as the best condition for fantasy practice, we sometimes look with concern upon the child who prefers to play alone. This apprehension relates to the high esteem our culture attaches to extroversion and sociability. Indeed, we generally tend to ignore the evidence suggesting that two-thirds of creative people are introverts and that 90% of them are intuitive. Some parents even express anxious reservations about whether their child's solitary play is healthy. One father suggests "Playing alone is fine, but our 4-year-old seems to be the victim of hallucinations. He often makes reference to Roy, a nonexistent companion." If such parents would listen more closely, they might realize that unlike the mentally ill person, who is dominated by hallucinations, during solitary play the child controls the imaginary friend. In fact, this total control of the companion may be what bothers some parents the most. Perhaps they suppose that being the boss isn't good for children because it invites them to develop uncooperative behavior in their relationships with real people. The fact is that cooperation implies sharing power. Children who feel powerless cannot cooperate; they can only acquiesce.

In any event, if imaginary companions appear at all, they are usually created by children between the ages of 3 and 6; seldom will they remain beyond the age of 10. Incidentally, these children cannot be classified as lonely, timid, or maladjusted. Instead, they are normal children who can be found in families of all sizes and social circumstances. Estimates ranging from 20% to 50% are given for the proportion of us who at some time experienced fictitious companions. That bright persons are more likely to have fantasy friends shows up in child studies and later in studies of creative college students, whose recall of imaginary companions is one of several retrospective variables that they have in common.

Society now tolerates the consequences of failing to provide uninterrupted time for solitary play. Hyperactivity, disruptive behavior, impulsiveness, inattentiveness—these are problems teachers and parents reluctantly feel they are obliged to cope with. But can we live with the long-term effects, the adult consequences? When people have no recourse to imagination, reflection, analytic thinking, and self-examination, then their mental health and the well-being of others they can influence are both in jeopardy.

Consider the elderly. During their employment years they may have been with groups most of the time; then, when they retire, they are suddenly all alone. Since they have never learned to be by themselves, many of them cannot accommodate solitude. These persons often die of loneliness. The key seems to lie at the other end of life, where our educational process may run counter to the goals we aim for. To illustrate, many children are placed all day in preschool and then told to play outside with friends when they get home. Later, after dinner, they are expected to be with their parents. For these boys and girls, there is no time for solitude, because parents haven't scheduled it. Similarly, for youngsters living in high-density housing, it is teachers who must provide solitary space at school, perhaps in a cubicle-style arrangement. All boys and girls should be given a chance to experience in some way the benefits of privacy.

A better future for all is likely if more parents and teachers come to see solitary imaginative play as a base for problem solving through its direct influence on the development of concentration, task persistence, self-control, and delay of closure. Then our emphasis on getting to know others will be joined by an enthusiasm for getting to know oneself. Surely children must learn to relate effectively with peers, but, unless they also learn the productive uses of privacy, they will have little to offer when in the company of others. Thus, to achieve either goal requires that we support both. In my view, these are sufficient reasons to recommend that every child's experience include a generous period of time for solitary play.

SHARING YOUR IMPRESSIONS

1. Give some reasons why you occasionally feel the need to be alone.
2. As a child, when were the times you played alone?
3. How do you feel when your child or student prefers to play alone instead of with others?
4. What do you suppose are the benefits of solitary play for children?
5. What are some materials that are appropriate for the solitary play of preschoolers? Elementary school children? Teenagers?
6. How can solitary play be arranged within the early-childhood facilities where some boys and girls spend most of their time?
7. "Some children classed as having learning disabilities or as 'problem children' are only normal children suffering from the need to spend some time alone." Give your reasons for agreeing or disagreeing with this assertion.
8. Think of some ways for children in crowded neighborhoods to experience privacy.

REFERENCES AND SUGGESTED READING

Buchsbaum, B. C. "The Effect of the Frustration of Interrupted Play on Cognitive Level as a Function of Age." Doctoral dissertation, Yeshiva University, Ann Arbor, Mich. (University Microfilms No. 66-2882)

Clepper, Irene. *Growing Up with Toys: A Guide for Parents.* Minneapolis: Augsburg Press, 1974.

Deutsch, Martin. *Minority Group and Class Status as Related to Social and Personality Factors in Scholastic Achievement.* Ithaca, N. Y.: Society for Applied Anthropology, Monograph No. 2, 1960. Pp. 3–23.

Farnham-Diggory, S., and Ramsey, B. "Play Persistence: Some Effects of Interruption, Social Reinforcement and Defective Toys." *Developmental Psychology* 4 (1971), pp. 297–298.

Freyberg, Joan. "Increasing Children's Fantasies: Hold High the Cardboard Sword." *Psychology Today*, February 1975, pp. 62–64.

MacKinnon, Donald. "Testing to Identify Creative People." Speech to the College of Education at The Ohio State University, Columbus, Ohio, February 19, 1965.

Singer, Jerome. "Exploring Man's Imaginative World." In *Teachers and the Learning Process*, edited by Robert Strom. Englewood Cliffs, N. J.: Prentice-Hall, 1971. Pp. 333–350.

Singer, Jerome. *The Child's World of Make Believe.* New York: Academic Press, 1973.

Strom, Robert. "Dangers and Advantages of Solitude." In *Psychology for the Classroom.* Englewood Cliffs, N. J.: Prentice-Hall, 1969. Pp. 233–236.

Strom, Robert. *Teaching in the Slum School.* Columbus, Ohio: Charles E. Merrill, 1965.

Strom, Robert. *The Inner City Classroom: Teacher Behaviors.* Columbus, Ohio: Charles E. Merrill, 1966.

Winnicott, D. W. *The Child, the Family, and the Outside World.* Baltimore: Penguin Books, 1971. Pp. 143–146.

BOOKS TO SHARE WITH YOUNG CHILDREN

Bennett, Rainey. *The Secret Hiding Place.* Cleveland: World, 1960. Many children in day care or preschool know the difficulty of trying to be alone. In a little hippo's case, he is overprotected to the point where his curiosity and desire to explore are nearly eliminated by the older animals, who insist that he never be out of their sight.

Browne, Anthony. *Through the Magic Mirror.* New York: William Morrow, 1976. Parents can help avoid boredom by arranging solitary play. Toby was fed up with television and toys but didn't know what to do with himself until one day he discovered that occasionally playing alone with a magic mirror is a good recipe for boredom.

DeRegniers, Beatrice. *A Little House of Your Own.* New York: Harcourt, 1955. Parents and teachers can together make sure that every child has some chance for privacy. In this story we are told where to find secret places for being alone and reminded not to interrupt other people when they are trying to spend time by themselves.

Schick, Eleanor. *Andy*. New York: Macmillan, 1971. When children rely upon peers too much, they have a difficult time if conditions force them to be alone. All of Andy's friends are busy one day; so he tries to discover some of the things that are more fun to do all by yourself.

Zolotow, Charlotte. *The Three Funny Friends*. New York: Harper & Row, 1961. The invention of make-believe companions is often a sign of creativity. Before she meets Tony from next door, the new girl in town eliminates her loneliness by relating to three imaginary friends.

SIX

THE DISARMAMENT OF CHILDREN

Most parents admit to being uncertain about which toys are best for their children. However, some parents are quite certain about the toys they find undesirable. For example, we can seldom discuss the selection of playthings without entering into a controversy over whether toy weapons are psychologically safe. In this chapter, I try to present both parent and child points of view on this issue and to suggest some new ways of effectively teaching values.

THE DILEMMA OF PARENTS

Barbara is 35 years old, a housewife, and a mother of three. She lives in suburban Columbus, Ohio. Even before their children were born, Barbara and her husband felt that violent toys breed lawlessness. In her words: "The position we have taken has not been easy to maintain. We knew that being unlike the group would be hard for our children to understand. The pressure and ridicule from other parents is tremendous, for we are the only ones in the neighborhood who have taken this stand. It would be easy to conform to the majority, but to us that would mean a lowering of our personal standards of integrity."

The willingness of Barbara and her husband to uphold their beliefs is commendable, but their assumptions about the adult consequences of weapon play during childhood are open to question. If those who oppose toy weapons are correct, professionals who deal with violence day after day might be expected to verify the claim that play with toy guns is a factor contributing to an individual's use or acceptance of violence in adult life. To find out, Frank Gavitt contacted chiefs of police in 200 cities and asked them. By a ratio of 12 to 1, the police chiefs said that in their experience children's play with toy weapons is not a contributing factor in the acceptance or use of violence by adults.

It is well known that children in other cultures also play with toy weapons. Indeed, some nations are less inclined than we are to control the content of children's fantasy play and to suppose that young players have pathological motives. To fault these countries for permissiveness would be unwise, because these same nations accept the difficulty and necessity of controlling adult access to firearms. Their remedy for adult violence is to disarm the grown-ups rather than the children. For example, England and France have strict gun-purchase laws, and they each report fewer than 100 gun murders each year. By contrast, in the U. S., where it is easier to obtain guns, the annual number of fatal victims exceeds 12,000. Taking into account the differences in population size among these countries, this means that approximately 30 times as many people are killed in the United States by handguns. These figures may lead us to question whether taking toy guns away from children while putting real ones in the hands of adults is the best way to eliminate violence in our society.

A large number of parents who oppose play warfare indicate their objective is simply to discourage a reliance on weapons as the single way to resolve disputes. In their estimate, gun play during childhood can result in a desire for immediate revenge instead of the fair-trial, innocent-until-proven guilty philosophy we expect of grown-ups. This perspective is expressed by Jane, a mother of two preschool boys, who recalls: "After overhearing one of my children tell his cowboy companions he was going to shoot and kill them, I felt compelled to say 'Donnie, you don't mean that.' I reconsidered and thought maybe I should sit him down and explain that when you kill someone they are dead, and they will never breathe again. Then I wondered, if we don't let Donnie play with guns, it might give him the feeling that we are convinced he is so violent he requires different toys from everyone else. Finally, not knowing just what to do or say, I ignored him and went on feeling guilty."

Children and Death

Jane's dilemma is a common one. Perhaps we can reduce the problem by more closely examining just what young children mean when they talk about killing and dying. The concept that death is final comes at about mental age 9. This means that some

bright children may become aware of the finality of death as early
as 7, and slower children not until early adolescence. Before
mental age 9, children deny that death is permanent. To the very
young, death is a reversible process. Whether they play hide and
go seek or cowboys and Indians, all the dead people are expected
to recover quickly and live again. The conventional television
cartoon reinforces this notion when a rabbit falls off the cliff, hits
bottom, and, in keeping with the child's reversible concept of
death, is brought back to life. The same thing happens when
children see a television character die on one program and later
appear miraculously on a panel show. Some time ago, when my
son Paris was 4 years old, we had this conversation:

> *Paris:* Dad, I'm going to dress up like an army man.
> *Dad:* You look just like a soldier. I was a soldier once.
> *Paris:* Why?
> *Dad:* Because the country needed me—we were having a
>   war.
> *Paris:* Dad, did you die?
> *Dad:* No, I was lucky.

For most children, the realization that death is terminal
seems to develop in stages. Between ages 3 and 5, there is a great
deal of curiosity and questioning about death. Unfortunately,
many of us tend to suppress this curiosity. We think it is impolite
for a child to ask old Mrs. Thompson when she is going to die. By
contrast, a century ago it was common for children to witness at
least one deathbed scene, although at the same time information
about sex was withheld from them. Now death seems to have
replaced sex as the subject to be discussed privately among
adults. Yet for the preschooler death is not final; it is like being
less alive. Accordingly, many parents find themselves with a curious child who wants to know where and how the dead continue to live. To be sure, movement is limited by the coffin, but
the dead must take nourishment, and they must keep breath-
ing. The people in the cemetery have a way of knowing what is
happening on earth. They feel it when someone thinks of them,
and they are sad for themselves. Dying therefore disturbs the
preschooler, since life in the grave is seen to be boring and

unpleasant. But mostly it bothers the child because death separates people from one another. And, at this age, a child's greatest fear is separation from parents.

Between the ages of 5 and 9 the child tends to personify death, seeing it as an angelic visitor or a ghost-like character who makes rounds in the night. Counseling psychologist Robert Kavanaugh of the University of California explains that the big shift in the child's thinking from the first stage to this stage is that death is recognized as possibly being final. It is no longer seen as just a reduced form of life. This view of death emerges with increasing personal experiences that suggest that certain separations are permanent. When the goldfish dies, mother buys a new one because, she says, the other is gone forever. Parents know that they cannot guarantee a long life for pets but that they can reduce a child's exposure to televised death. Often the logic of this decision to protect children results in a refusal to let children watch detective programs, a reluctant acceptance of cartoons, and an ambivalence about allowing children to watch the news, which often portrays actual cases of violence or death. In any event, the typical 5- to 9-year-old believes that there are protective measures that can be used to avoid personal death. One child contends "You won't die unless you have bad luck," whereas another argues "My grandfather will never die, because we are taking such good care of him."

Finally, about the age of 9 or 10, children realize that death is not only final but inevitable. It will happen to them, too, no matter how clever they are or how well they take care of themselves. Our time is without precedent in that millions of children around the world are growing up in the midst of death and the threat of destruction. They see death on television with such regularity that war has become their most common fear and in consequence a prominent theme for play. Yet in some ways the young have fewer illusions on the subject than do many adults. Edna St. Vincent Millay once described childhood as "the kingdom where nobody dies." For most boys and girls that statement is true, but only before they reach the age of 9.

Children look to us for answers about death, but our *attitude* is the important response. Youngsters love mystery, and they will adopt our sense of wonder and uncertainty if we express it.

So much of the world is already ambiguous for children. They can live with yet another and final unknown, if only we can. Although many of us will continue to have doubts about the worthwhileness of guns, tanks, and other weapon toys, I hope we don't evade the more important question: how can children who are going to live in a world of frequent conflict be taught to negotiate differences constructively—to express their disagreement with words rather than with weapons?

PARENTS AS JUDGES

There are many playthings various parents feel children could do without. Some dislike military toys because they reflect violence. Others oppose the Evel-Knievel-type stunt cycle, since it could encourage risk taking on bicycles. Similarly, crash cars are thought to sanction a disregard for safety, and of course Kung Fu dolls present karate as a method of resolving conflicts. Parents with these complaints are ambivalent in that they want to purchase toys that reflect their own values, but they also recognize the need for children to make some decisions in order to develop a value system. And where is it more appropriate for children to choose than in the realm of play? Grown-ups can justify making certain decisions on children's behalf, such as whether they are to attend school, whether they will see a doctor, and when it is time for bed. On the other hand, to claim that boys and girls need coherent values and then to deny them choices is unreasonable. So mothers and fathers are naturally bothered about the priority they should give to the feelings of children in the selection of toys.

When parents confront me with this issue, as they often do, I urge them to reexamine their role. I suggest they think of it this way: Instead of declaring your values by choosing the child's toys or by censoring the content of play, enact your values during parent-child play. The imposition of values has less influence than the illustration of values. So, if you don't like war, you can try to include the peacemaker role as a part of the play with toy soldiers. Show your values to your child instead of protecting yourself from having to demonstrate them. It isn't a question of who is opposed to war; almost everyone is. Rather, the issue is how to develop a concern for peace. Unfortunately, some people

teach about peace in the same way they teach about sex—by
never mentioning it.

All of us share the aspiration that either a balance of nuclear
power or international disarmament will rid us of war. But,
although peace means the end of war, it doesn't mean the end of
differences. Because there is a critical distinction between the
fantasy wars of children and the bloody wars of men, it is a serious
error to misinterpret the motives of the preschool soldier. The
readiness to credit children with criminal intention denies them
respect; it also illustrates the need for grown-ups to see favorable
possibilities in a child's choice of playthings.

Certain needs of children may be served by conflict toys and
games. This kind of play offers relief from feelings of powerlessness and dependence, which together account for much of a
child's experience. Surely there is nothing strange about the
desire to control others, especially those who daily exercise
power over yourself. Children delight when they can assert
themselves and make daddy run away or fall down because he's
been shot. Grown-ups often forget that boys and girls realize
themselves through the impact they make on the world. Since
many parents recognize as worthwhile only those strengths that
emerge during adolescence, it follows that little children must
experience power vicariously if they are to experience it at all.
Then, too, conflict playthings offer a safe setting in which to express disapproved feelings, such as anger, fear, frustration, and
jealousy. These are normal feelings that shouldn't be repressed,
but in many homes they are met by punishment, ridicule, or
shame. Danger play also provides an opportunity to repeatedly
confront fearful issues, such as war, death, and injury. Although
these subjects are of universal concern to young children, many
adults try to avoid discussing them and in the process increase a
child's anxiety.

Risk taking requires practice in a low-cost setting. During
danger play children can afford to take chances, to see what it is
like to rebel, to be the bad guy or outcast—risks they dare not try
in their family life. In this connection, it is worth noting that for
some children war play is the only context in which they can
conduct conflict without guilt. Even though parents should teach
constructive methods for settling differences, some boys and

girls are taught instead to feel guilt whenever they oppose an authority figure. For many kids competition needs are fostered by fighting off the mutual "enemy." War play also allows children to experience leadership, to lead and command others as well as to become heroes like their television favorites. Finally, conflict toys and games are enjoyed by the participants—they're fun, a fact that should be appreciated by a pleasure-oriented society.

Instead of placing all our emphasis upon the choice of *what* we allow children to play with, we can recognize that *how* we play with them also has an influence. Otherwise, we overestimate the plaything and underestimate the influence of the player. We cannot fulfill our child-rearing role merely by buying the right toy or disallowing the wrong toy. Our best role is not that of a judge but of a play partner.

We often regret that children tend to believe almost everything they see advertised on television, but our own condition is not much better if we believe everything we read on the package. For example, mere exposure to so-called educational or creative toys will not necessarily yield creative children. The same threadbare notion persisted years ago when so-called great books were to make young readers become great people. We later went through a similar worship of curriculum materials in science education. Recently we have begun to see that the key is not the materials but the interaction between those who are teaching and learning with the materials. Similarly, creativity does not reside in certain toys because of their design but in the interaction between those who play with them. Research in creative behavior and modeling make it quite clear that parents should become play partners with children; they should become participants rather than limit themselves to judging the efficacy of playthings. It is disappointing that people who believe certain toys can actually have a lifelong disabling effect on the personality of their children often find it difficult to believe that they themselves can have any influence by playing with a child. Yet the latter possibility is supported by research evidence, while the former is not.

In my view, we must discontinue judging the content of play. Once we insist that the direction of children's play is our choice and not their own, the young are no longer decision makers. And, in fantasy play, choice making is essential for participation. We can share in the direction of play only if we substitute the role of partner for that of judge. I believe that it is unwise always to interpret the content of children's play as a direct correlate of serious motive. When an actor portrays a killer, we may say the performance was convincing and therefore successful. However, when a pretending child chooses to play this same role, the supposed reasons for becoming that particular character may receive more attention than the performance. It is this cynical way of interpreting the content of children's play that leads to unfair inferences and to the attribution of motives that children do not in fact have. The simple fact is that the motives of children who "kill" each other in gun play are unrelated to the motivations for violent activity in adult life.

Perhaps we should go a step further and recognize the everyday situations in which the humanistic behavior of children actually surpasses our own. Consider 5-year-old Marsha, who decides to give her talking doll to Julie. Certainly this is an act of generosity. However, when Marsha's mother learns about the gift, she sends her to retrieve it, saying "You're too young to give things away. Besides, that doll is almost new, and it cost $8." Two weeks later Marsha is obliged to accompany her mother to the garage, where she has brought together a group of no longer functional household items. Then the little girl is given a lecture about the importance of sharing with others and about how this package of discards from her family to Goodwill will bring joy to poor people.

Forgiveness is another desirable characteristic that can sometimes be seen more often in children than in their parents. Martin comes into the kitchen crying. It seems Peter threw him down too hard while they were wrestling. Ten minutes later the boys are again busy playing as though no tears had ever been shed. But Martin's parents find it difficult to dismiss the episode. Indeed, a week later they are still angry about the visitor's lack of restraint, his negligent parents, and the drawbacks of living in this neighborhood. Despite their own reluctance to forgive Peter and his family, Martin's parents still believe they can convey to their son a quality that is already more prominent in him than in themselves. Occasionally we find parents who so easily hold a grudge that they forbid their child to be with an inconsiderate playmate who has been forgiven by the youngster. In these cases, a child has to regularly announce to a friend: "My dad says I can't play with you any more."

Parents need help in learning how to choose good toys and how to select good television shows, but they also need encouragement and guidance in how to become participants in their children's play. Otherwise they remain locked in the role of judges instead of interpreters and partners. Creative children would have us participate in play rather than serve as censors or judges. We can help them learn to judge for themselves by the example of our participation.

IMPROVING TOY SAFETY

Let us change our focus now from concern about the psychological safety of playthings to concern about their physical safety. Although parents spend a great deal of money on toys, most of them feel overwhelmed by the wide range of choices. In fact, shopping for children's playthings has become such a complex responsibility that parents are unable to do it successfully on their own. At least this was the conclusion reached by Congress when it unanimously passed the Toy Safety Act and directed the Food and Drug Administration to remove and keep from the customer shelves all children's products with electrical, mechanical, and thermal hazards. At first the task seemed impossible. Imagine the manpower needed to monitor an entire industry of 1200 companies that together produce over 140,000 different types of toys and games! There was also the question of means for determining how many people suffer toy-related injuries and for identifying the specific manufacturers involved. A partial solution to these problems was achieved in 1973, when the Consumer Product Safety Commission was established. At the same time Congress authorized a unit known as NEISS, the National Electronic Injury Surveillance System. Each day NEISS receives computer reports from 119 hospitals across the country. The emergency-ward data from these representative hospitals make possible a national projection of toy-associated injuries per 100,000 population.

A high rate of injuries does not necessarily mean that a product should be banned. For instance, taken by itself the number of adults hurt on snowmobiles would suggest that these popular leisure vehicles are unsafe. However, a detailed analysis revealed that in many cases the injured snowmobilers were bar-hopping at the time of their accident and were under the influence of alcohol. Thus, the effort to find the actual causes of snowmobile injury prevented an unfair ban. Sometimes the Commission's follow-up investigations lead to new safety regulations. To illustrate, more than one million bicycle injuries occurred in the United States in 1976. Stunts and collisions with obstacles were found to be the leading causes of accidents, but almost 20% of the mishaps were the result of faulty bicycle design and construction. As a result, the Consumer Product Safety Commission decided that new standards for bicycles should top their priority list of needed improvements. Of course, certain toys are banned without any record of injury. If the CPSC, which has only 800 employees, believes that a toy presents a hazard or that its safety is conceptually in question, a ban will be imposed pending further investigation. Then, when the manufacturer revises a banned product to comply with safety regulations, the ban is removed.

Concern about toy safety centers on the preschool population, as it should, since 2- to 4-year-olds are the ones most frequently injured. Their curiosity and developing physical abilities lead them into everything they can get their hands on. Accordingly, the new small-parts regulation calls for improved toy design so that young children cannot detach pieces they might swallow. In durability tests, toys for players below the age of 18 months must withstand ten drops from 4½ feet and still be safely functional. Toys for players up to 8 years of age must survive four drops from a height of 3 feet. The notoriety given toy injuries and the ban of approximately 1800 toys over the past several years might suggest that the toy industry holds the key to all child safety. On the contrary, many more child injuries are parent-related, such as injuries caused by cosmetics and drugs, drinking-glasses, sharp tables, and grass cutters, as well as bath falls. In fact, NEISS has determined that less than 5% of the reported injuries to children in and around the home are associated with toys. The reasonable conclusion is that one of the safest activities at home for a child is playing with toys.

CHOOSING TOYS

The real key to child safety is collaboration by government, industry, and parents. Until consumers develop better purchasing judgment, they will unwittingly contribute to the dangers in Toyland. Hopefully, more programs in parent education will become available that offer guidance in toy selection and family play. Meanwhile, here are some reminders for parents that may be helpful.

Begin by choosing from the toys that are appropriate for your child's age. Otherwise boys and girls will encounter tasks for which they are unready and participate in situations that produce frustration, insecurity, or unnecessary dependence. Apart from these educational concerns, there is the record of court cases indicating that most play injuries are a direct consequence of improper toy selection. We sometimes forget that a toy that is safe for one child may be dangerous in the hands of an unsupervised and less skillful younger brother or sister. So, instead of the traditional broad age-group recommendation, United States manufacturers soon may be required by proposed packaging standards to specify the minimum age of persons who should play with the toy.

A second guideline is to closely inspect the playthings you purchase. Parents choosing a toy for a small child should make sure that the toy is too large to be swallowed; that it has no detachable parts that can lodge in the throat, ears, or nose; that it won't break easily into small pieces and has no sharp edges or points; that it is not put together with easily exposed straight pins, sharp wires, or nails; that it is not made of glass or brittle plastic; that it is labeled "nontoxic"; that it has no parts that can pinch fingers or catch hair; and that it has no long cords or thin plastic bags if selected for a child under 2 years of age. Ideally, parents would not have to take such precautions; however, the ban of an unsafe toy does not guarantee its removal from all stores. Although retailers are forbidden to sell any products appearing on the banned list, there are over a million toy dealers. The problem of supervision is so large that the government decided in 1975 to discontinue its public list of banned toys. Two reasons brought about the termination: the CPSC realized that it is physically incapable of properly policing all playthings on the market, and many consumers were incorrectly assuming that if a given toy was not on the list it enjoyed what amounted to a federal recommendation. Instead of a negative approach, the agency has shifted to such techniques as consumer testing and a nationwide, toll-free hot line. Hopefully these measures will, in time, adequately inform the shopping public about toy quality and safety.

In general, it is wise to limit selection of toys to name brands. Most of us would not consider buying certain kinds of food labeled "Brand X from Hong Kong" simply because they cost less than domestic products. Yet this same concern for the reputation of a producer is felt less when parents buy toys. Those who witness comparative-drop tests recognize why we ought to avoid cheaper imported toys in favor of safer, domestically pro- duced playthings. Such tests urge the conclusion that nobody has enough money to buy cheap toys. Cheap substitutes can be far more expensive than parents realize. Indeed, over half of all toys on the banned lists are produced by foreign importers, some of whom have ties with American companies. According to David Miller, President of the Toy Manufacturers of America, interna- tional standards are now being negotiated that will offer the widest selection of safe playthings to children throughout the world.

A third recommendation is to change our buying habits— to purchase toys in harmony with a child's development rather than to shower children with objects and games on festive occasions—on birthdays, at Christmas, or when someone re- turns home from a trip. The desired change occurs when parents learn to regard the tools of play as necessities rather than lux- uries. That most parents feel otherwise is shown by the fact that two-thirds of all toys are sold between Thanksgiving and Christ- mas. Few of us do the kind of window-shopping for playthings that we insist on when buying something for ourselves. Instead of actively avoiding the toy department so that the child won't fuss when it's time to leave, we should visit the toy department often without always making purchases. This practice allows a child to let us know the kind of toys he or she prefers. I recall as a boy visiting a particular store half a dozen times before one Christmas. Each time Dad learned that the 8-foot giraffe was my first choice. Naturally, it was too expensive, but Dad got the idea that what I would appreciate most was some kind of large stuffed animal.

As the general public becomes more informed about the worthwhile effects of toys as well as about their potential hazards, they will likely insist that toy sales personnel become more knowledgeable about their wares. As things stand now, the toy department is often the only one in the store in which clerks unashamedly excuse themselves for knowing little about their job and the goods they sell. Since toys should be chosen wisely, it follows that we must somehow reduce the number of uninformed toy salespersons rather than continue the pretext that their ignorance is justified by the nature of short-term holiday employment. This ignorance not only is regrettable; it is unnecessary. Whether the Toy Manufacturers of America will educate an appreciable segment of the sales force who represent them remains to be seen; what does appear certain is that the toy industry is in the best position to bring about the desired change.

Everyone should realize that no law can protect a child completely from all dangers. No industry can guarantee the quality of every item it produces. No federal agency can ensure that hazardous playthings will not reach the customers. But, together with concerned and judicious parents, government and industry can help make play with toys a safer activity—one that brings enjoyment instead of tears.

SHARING YOUR IMPRESSIONS

1. Why do some parents object to children's playing with toy weapons?
2. Identify some needs of children that may be met by conflict toys and games.
3. Give your opinion about letting children choose their own playthings.
4. What do young children mean when they talk about killing and dying?

5. Discuss the issue of whether children should be allowed to bring toy weapons to school for play during recess.
6. Speculate about the influence toys have on a child's psychological development.
7. Give some reasons why the selection of toys should be taken seriously.
8. What help is available for guiding parents when they choose playthings?
9. Suggest some tips for adults who buy toys for children.

REFERENCES AND SUGGESTED READING

Coords, Henry. "Perspectives on Consumerism." Presidential address to the Toy Manufacturers of America, New York, December 7, 1970.

Frymier, Jack. "On the Way to the Forum: Repeal the Second Amendment." *Educational Forum*, Vol. XL, No. 2 (January 1976), 132–135.

Gavitt, Frank. "Some Other Opinions on Toys and Violence." Unpublished memorandum prepared for members of the Toy Manufacturers of America, New York, July 1969.

Kastenbaum, Robert. "The Kingdom Where Nobody Dies." *Saturday Review-Science*, January 1973, pp. 33–38.

Kavanaugh, Robert. "Children and Death." In *Facing Death*. Baltimore: Penguin Books, 1974. Pp. 125–144.

Kubler-Ross, Elisabeth. *On Death and Dying*. New York: Macmillan, 1974. Pp. 1–37.

Levinson, Boris. *Pets and Human Development*. Springfield, Ill.: Charles C Thomas, 1972.

Leviton, Daniel. "The Role of the Schools in Providing Death Education." In *Death Education*, edited by Betty Green and Donald Irish. Cambridge, Mass.: Schenkman, 1971. Pp. 29–42.

Morris, Norman. *Television's Child*. Boston: Little, Brown, 1971. Pp. 14–29.

Sims, Patsy. "How Children Learn What Death Means." *San Francisco Chronicle*, February 8, 1972, p. 20.

Stull, Edith. *My Turtle Died Today*. New York: Holt, Rinehart & Winston, 1964. Pp. 1–14.

Zeligs, Rose. *Children's Experience with Death*. Springfield, Ill.: Charles C Thomas, 1974.

BOOKS TO SHARE WITH YOUNG CHILDREN

Bemelmans, Ludwig. *Madeline*. New York: Viking, 1967. Little children don't understand the causes of illness, but they worry about getting sick. Madeline's girlfriends are the exception, because their hospital visit to see her convinces them that they too should have an operation.

Brown, Margaret Wise, and Charlip, Remy. *The Dead Bird.* Reading, Mass.: Addison-Wesley, 1965. Death is a subject that children wish their parents were more willing to talk about. When several youngsters at play find a dead bird, they reveal feelings about animal death and their ability to cope with it.

Cattaert, Claude. *Where Do Goldfish Go?* New York: Crown, 1963. Children are upset by adults whose reaction to animal death is that a pet can be replaced. When Valerie's goldfish dies unexpectedly, no one is bothered; yet the family is overcome with sorrow when grandfather dies, even though his death was anticipated for years.

de Paola, Tommie. *Nana Upstairs and Nana Downstairs.* New York: Putnam's Sons, 1973. Grandparents are the most likely human relatives to die. Little Tommy has a hard time realizing that his great-grandmother will never come back, except in his memory.

Viorst, Judith. *The Tenth Good Thing about Barney.* New York: Atheneum, 1971. Parents do not want children to feel sad; yet there are times when grief should be encouraged. Barney the cat has died, but his funeral is not a hurried affair, because the mourners intend to think of all the good things he meant to them.

SEVEN

A TIME FOR PLAY

Why should we put children through school? The customary reply is "to prepare them for the world of work," but this answer is hardly sufficient now that the leisure proportion of our lives is beginning to exceed the proportion spent on work, thanks to a longer life span, earlier retirement, shorter work days, and longer weekends. To be sure, we will continue to prepare youngsters for employment, but they also need help in learning how to use discretionary time.

We cannot expect to teach children how to handle the large amounts of free time they will enjoy as adults within the traditional system of 15-minute recesses during the school day. One way to get children ready for the coming four-day work week is to experiment with a four-day school week. Perhaps the weekly calendar for school should be revised to include only four days of formal classes, followed by a day outside of academic study. Fridays could be devoted to helping children learn constructive ways of using extended leisure. This innovation would include encounters with teachers from outside the school—members of the community who have found satisfaction in a wide range of recreational and volunteer activities.

At present we choose a somewhat more protective approach. Mindful that our children are easily bored, many of us anticipate difficulties during the summertime, when school is not in session. Accordingly, we plan a schedule of activities for our sons and daughters that will take up nearly their entire summer. This same recognition of the probable consequences of boredom is used by city officials in defending their proposed summer budgets. Thus, the parks-and-recreation departments of most cities may be expected to argue that, unless they are properly funded, the resulting cutback in youth programs will enlarge the delinquency problem for the police. In effect this amounts to an admission that such programs don't teach people to rely on themselves in coping with extended leisure.

75

TOO BUSY TO PLAY

It's ironic that children are expected to learn the worthy use of leisure time from grown-ups whose work seldom leaves them available for play. Even in their own homes some youngsters are regularly told "I'm too busy now to play with you—wait until later." Of course, this evasion of parent-child play is not a deliberate attempt to frustrate the young; it simply reflects the difficulty most of us have in arranging time for our children. One of the recommendations I am frequently asked to give involves the amount of time parents should spend at family play. It would be insufficient to point out that, since families differ, there can be no single set of guidelines; instead, I advise parents to make their own decision after they have asked themselves the following questions.

How long can I remain interested while at play? There is no doubt about the attention span of children for play. Even a casual observer will notice that young boys and girls often cry when they are obliged to leave the park or playground. To discontinue play is disappointing for them. Adults' readiness for play is quite a different story. Many of us find it difficult to remain interested in pretending for very long. The typical adult beginner can handle only about ten minutes of fantasy play with a preschooler. It is unreasonable for adults to participate beyond the point at which they lose interest, for they will only convey the impression that the activity isn't worthwhile. Rather, when it becomes necessary to withdraw, parents should tell the child: "I think it's time for me to stop now—I can't play for as long as you can." Most parents begin to find enjoyment in imaginative play after a few sessions. As a result, their attention span grows, and they become able to play for longer periods of time.

How important is my influence during play? Some parents believe that play with age-mates is sufficient to meet the needs of children. Mothers and fathers who reach this conclusion don't love their children any less than parents who play with their kids, but they may fail to recognize the benefits that are unique to parent-child play, especially the chance for children to learn how to conduct conflict, to develop their values and vocabularies, to share dominance, and to receive approval for exercising their imaginations. Once informed of these possibilities, parents may still suggest that the amount of time spent with their children is less important than the quality of that time. This excuse does not recognize that, without practice, play between an adult and a child is bound to be of low quality, oriented toward coercion or concession. Moreover, the development of any skill—whether it is in golf, basketball, or imaginative play—requires repetition, which in turn takes time. In short, parents are unlikely to achieve a "quality" relationship with their children unless they invest time in it. Then, too, children often base their sense of worth on both the amount of time and the degree of involvement that parents are willing to devote to their activities. Thus, it isn't surprising that the most accessible parents, those who play the most with their children, are also the ones who have the most appropriate child-rearing expectations and who enjoy the most responsiveness from their children. These people have taken seriously the question "How much time is my child worth?"

How comfortable am I during play? A majority of grown-ups report feeling silly when they first enter the realm of child play. This sense of embarrassment reflects a belief that childhood is the only justifiable time for pretending. Unless their inhibition can be reduced, parents will have less access to imagination than is needed for fantasy play. Whether parents feel uneasy can also depend on how they view the interaction. If the younger player is seen as a competitor whose creative behavior must be surpassed, then the adults will probably undervalue themselves and withdraw altogether. It is only when the child is seen as a partner that the parent ceases to engage in unfavorable self-comparison. In a partnership the strength of each member is to the advantage of both parties. Therefore, during imaginative exchange no one loses, because success is mutual. Actually, parents who feel comfortable at play have learned to teach respect by their example. Essentially, respect means allowing other people's strengths to influence our relationship rather than locking them into a subordinate role by interacting only on our terms. Grown-ups can respect the creative strength of children by sharing dominance with them during play.

Am I willing to set aside a time for play? Many of us seem unable to schedule play. Consider the growing number of people whose employers allow them to work at home. Often these parents are perplexed about how to handle the continual interruptions by their children. On one hand, they feel guilty about not responding to the child's appeals for play; on the other, they are angry because conditions are such that they cannot be productive. Reluctantly, they may decide to go back to the office. One alternative is to set aside a time for play that the child is aware of and can depend upon. Given this intention, a father can say to his 4-year-old son: "I'll be in my study from 9 to 11 and must not be disturbed. But at 11 I'll come out and play with you. If I'm not out when mother says it's 11, you come and get me."

The chance to withdraw is seldom an option for housewives who remain at home with small children. They report a need to be surveillant most of the time and a high frequency of interrupted activity. Some of them learn to alternate their chores with sessions of pretending. Others plan the day so that a child can count on spending a regular play time with mother and a time by themselves with access to her.

A somewhat different problem is experienced by people who have to leave home for work. When they return home tired or late, their tendency is to excuse themselves from parent-child play until the weekend. This decision is unfortunate not only because of the child's continuous need to share intrafamily dominance but also because of the short attention span of parents for fantasy play. A better plan is to amend the family's daily schedule so that two periods of at least ten minutes can be devoted to parent-child play. Parents should be sure that these daily sessions include some of their best minutes of insight and energy rather than their least tolerant moments, their time of fatigue. In addition, they should try to recognize when unscheduled play is necessary. There will be occasions when most every child will make demands or give other clues that extra attention is needed. In such cases a few minutes of play may well avoid punishment or an all-day argument.

What will happen if I avoid family play? Parents differ in the value they assign to conversations with young children. Some of them view the exchange as a delight; others regard it as an unwelcome distraction. Later, however, when the same children reach adolescence, some parents reverse themselves by complaining that they can't get their teenagers to talk to them. Usually this lack of communication is explained as a normal development, a natural change indicating teenagers' greater reliance on peers and their quest for independence. The fact that some parents continue to enjoy access to the feelings of sons and daughters once they become teenagers and continue to be sought after for advice is often interpreted as a stroke of luck. The truth is that at every age we share ourselves most with those who have demonstrated their willingness to spend time with us. For example, psychologist Daniel Brown, who directs the Conciliation Court in Tucson, Arizona, reports a study of 300 seventh- and eighth-grade boys who kept a diary of the time their fathers spent with them. Brown noted that, during an average week, a typical father and son were alone together a total of seven minutes. It seems that parents can establish themselves as a lasting source of guidance only if they regularly take the time to participate in activities that interest their children.

How effective a model for leisure am I? In a society of increasing leisure, a child should observe parents at leisure to learn what adults enjoy. Youngsters cannot do this if parents say "I'll relax later, when you're in bed," or "I'm sacrificing my spare time in order to provide you all the things I never had." What parents can share with children is more valuable than the things they can give them. Certainly happiness is one of our most elusive goals. When we show our children how to achieve satisfaction during adult life, the young are rich, if not affluent, beneficiaries. But if in attempting to provide our family with a higher income we insist on holding two jobs or avoiding the pursuit of our own pleasure in the children's presence, we fail to convey how satisfaction can be attained. In my own profession, I know many teachers who assign themselves too much homework. Usually they see themselves as dedicated persons whose evasion of time with the family is justified by their example of hard work. The fact remains that, unless such parents also illustrate for their children how to find joy and contentment during adult life, the young must discover it by expensive experimentation with immature peers.

There are many parents who live for tomorrow. Perhaps they look forward to the freedom and economic advantage that should come after their children grow up. Some look ahead to leaving the job, to retirement and its leisure options. But, in our anticipation of the future, many of us fail to enjoy our children now, our jobs now, our lives together now. Then, when the date for retirement does arrive, we regret that the children are gone, we resent the loss of our vocational roles, and we painfully face our failure to establish intimacy. To enjoy the future, we must learn to cope with leisure in the present. Moreover, at school and in the home we have an obligation to teach the young how this can be done.

SHARING YOUR IMPRESSIONS

1. Preparing students for life in the future should include an emphasis on leisure. What do you foresee as the most desirable changes in education for leisure?
2. What kinds of concerns do you recommend that the parents of a young child consider when deciding how much time they should spend playing with their child?
3. In your opinion, how much of the school-time schedule should be devoted to education for leisure?
4. In principle, how do you react to allowing fathers and mothers of preschoolers to spend half of their job time at home (with pay) on condition that the time is devoted to parent-child play and other forms of education?
5. Discuss the consequences for the family of children's dependence on television.
6. Think of some recommendations for parents who want to use television as an educational influence.
7. How do you feel about forbidding children to watch certain television programs?
8. What kinds of concerns do you recommend that a faculty consider in deciding how much school time should be devoted to play?

REFERENCES AND SUGGESTED READING

Charlesworth, James. *Leisure in America: Blessing or Curse?* Philadelphia: American Academy of Political Social Science. Monograph 4, 1964.

Joseph, Earl. "Forecasting Non-Linearities in Trajectories toward Alternative Futures." Paper presented to the American Association for the Advancement of Science, Philadelphia, December 1971.

Joseph, Earl. "Education for the Future." Address given at Arizona State University, May 12, 1975.

LeCourtre, R. (ed.). *Leisure Activities in the Industrial World.* Brussels: Van Clé Foundation, 1974.

Munn, Norman. *The Evolution of the Human Mind.* Boston: Houghton Mifflin, 1971.

Marien, Michael. "Higher Learning in the Ignorant Society." *The Futurist*, April 1972, pp. 49–54.

Rojas, Billy. "Futuristics, Games and Educational Change." *Learning for Tomorrow*, edited by Alvin Toffler. New York: Random House, 1974.

Shane, Harold. "America's Educational Future 1976-2001." *The Futurist*, October 1976, pp. 252–257.

Theobold, Robert. *Futures Conditional.* Indianapolis: Bobbs-Merrill, 1972.

Toffler, Alvin. *Future Shock.* New York: Random House, 1970.

Toffler, Alvin (ed.). *Learning for Tomorrow: The Role of the Future in Education.* New York: Vintage Books, 1974.

Williams, Charles. "Inventing a Future Civilization." *The Futurist*, August 1972, pp. 137–141.

BOOKS TO SHARE WITH YOUNG CHILDREN

Blain, Marge. *The Terrible Thing That Happened at Our House.* New York: Parents Magazine Press, 1975. Sometimes the life of a parent outside the home can become so busy that children receive too little attention. In this story, when the little girl's mother starts a full-time job and her father can't play because his responsibilities at home have increased, she decides to question their priorities.

Buckley, Helen E. *Grandfather and I.* New York: Lothrop, Lee and Shepard, 1959. Children need to be with some adults who are not in a hurry. A young boy finds that parents and siblings are in such a hurry that it's hardly any fun to be with them. Being with a grandfather who takes time is quite a different story.

Guilfoile, Elizabeth. *Nobody Listens to Andrew.* Chicago: Follett, 1957. Children want adults to listen when they have something to say. But nobody in Andrew's family has time to hear his report about the potentially dangerous situation upstairs in his room.

Maestro, Betsy. *In My Boat.* New York: Thomas Crowell, 1976. Children should be able to count on having some play time with parents almost every day. The pirate girl in this story tries without success to find a playmate until her father comes by.

Zindel, Paul. *I Love My Mother.* New York: Harper & Row, 1975. Being a successful single parent requires investing a lot of time in the children. One little boy tells about how he and his mother spend time together, their feelings, and the way they handle differences.

EIGHT
PARTNERS IN FANTASY

BECOMING OBSERVERS OF PLAY

Many parents and teachers underestimate the influence they have as observers of children's play. Perhaps this fact helps explain why most of us are poor observers of play. Some people disagree, however, and suggest that we are too interested in observing play. After all, an increasing number of men watch athletics on television so much each weekend that they run the risk of disrupting their marriages. Apart from ignoring wives in favor of "Wide World of Sports," these game-minded fathers are also accused of having a poor influence on their children. The Saturday-Sunday-Monday routine of television football allows little time for family interaction; in some homes, only occasional grunts are heard from the father, who insists on silence except during commercials. Some adults have been warned by physicians against observing sports too much, because, unlike the athletes they watch, the excited fans cannot release the emotion of game stress; as a result they increase their risk of heart failure. Nevertheless, these kinds of circumstances do suggest that being a play spectator is an accepted role in our society.

Given the wide appeal that being a play spectator enjoys, why do we consider the play activity that once occupied most of our time as children and gave us such pleasure to be no longer worth watching? Is observing children's play less satisfying or less important than watching organized athletics? Surely preschoolers want to be watched; their constant appeal is "See me!" "Look" "Watch this!" They gain obvious satisfaction from being observed. Why, then, can't we find the time to look at little boys and girls as they engage in imaginative play, when we will travel miles to watch our preteenager participate in a little-league contest? Why are we so quickly distracted as we witness a 4-year-old at play? Is it because we don't know what to look for, what to find pleasing, how to identify success, what to say about a form of play that has no rules, no hits, no runs, and so cannot be scored? Why is it that I can invite friends to see my 10-year-old son, Steve, take part in a hockey game, but, if I ask them to stop by for half an hour to watch 4-year-old Paris play, they ask "Why? Has he a special trick? What does he do?"

Whatever prevents our becoming serious and regular observers of preschool play, I believe we are lesser guides to young children, lesser parents and teachers because of it. In learning theory there is a law of effect. Simply stated, this law is that behavior that is satisfying tends to be repeated. We know that preschoolers like to pretend; they also desire the approval of their parents. So, when pretending brings parental disapproval, indifference, or inattention, it predictably begins to wane. If, by seldom observing child drama, we give boys and girls the impression that imaginative play is unimportant to us, that original thinking doesn't merit our attention, that fantasy isn't worth watching, that we respect only nonfiction play, then we should expect that the wish for parental affection will lower the priority the child attaches to imagination.

Perhaps our difficulty lies in holding too narrow a definition of "achievement." Many of us agree that creativity will be crucial for adults in the future; yet play, the dominant form of creativity during childhood, receives infrequent respect, is too little observed, and in some cases isn't even allowed. Perhaps we need to shift the focus to ourselves and compare the play encounters we have with children of different ages. Playing games like football and baseball—activities in which motor skill, rules, and judgment have a higher priority than imagination—seems to present little problem for most parents. These types of play please us, and we can spend hours being involved. On the other hand, most of us have trouble spending even a few minutes playing with a preschooler or simply watching him or her at play. Our adult attention span appears to be in question.

By watching children at play we can communicate our confidence in and approval of their ability. By watching them at play we accept them as they are. Conversely, if we ignore their play, they may find it more difficult to like and accept themselves. They must feel they are worth the time for us to bother watching them before they can believe their imaginative play is important enough to continue engaging in.

My advice to parents is this. If you believe in reward, don't underestimate the reinforcing influence of your observation. Since observation requires time, watching represents approval. In my judgment, your time is a far more authentic reinforcement than is verbal praise. To give time requires an investment of oneself, whereas no personal investment is required to momentarily acknowledge a child's appeal for observation by announcing that the play is good or wonderful. Observation is more effective than verbal comment as a form of reward.

In this regard, I am always disappointed by parents who tell me that after their children visit the grandparents they are difficult to live with, because they have been spoiled. I don't think that reaction is a fair assessment of the influence of many grandparents. What in fact often happens is that, when children visit grandparents who don't have jobs, who are able to spend more time with them than their parents are, the grandparents watch the children a great deal and play with them. The children come to expect the same response when they return home. Instead we pronounce their higher expectations of us a fault engendered by grandparents; we say the children have been spoiled.

Actually, one of the best ways to show other persons respect is to watch them do their thing. It follows that, if we avoid spending time in the children's arena of play, we pass up a valuable chance to share power and to acknowledge their strength—in short, to show respect for them. Once again, by "respect" I mean allowing the other person's strength to affect our relationship rather than keeping the other person in the position of a subordinate.

By watching children play, we automatically reinforce the importance of who they already are and of the creativity they own. More of us must learn to value in our children what we would have them retain beyond childhood. The philosopher Montaigne said it best: "The play of children is their most serious business." I propose that we make the observation of play a larger part of our own serious business as parents.

PARENT-CHILD FANTASY PLAY

In addition to being observers of play, parents should also recognize their influence as partners in play. Although the role of partner is more difficult, it can be achieved by anyone who is willing to learn from children. Let's consider some of the desirable and undesirable behaviors that take place during parent-child play.

Desirable Behaviors

Children sustain attention. Many children have a short attention span for adult-preferred activities. For example, boys and girls alike find window-shopping a low-interest activity. Typically, they ask mother to end the shopping well before she is ready to do so. They also exaggerate the amount of time spent shopping. What the children may complain of as having been "a long time" is recognized by mother as having been only a few minutes. We find this relative disability of attention span reversed in the child-preferred activity of play. During play it is the adult who has a short attention span. Most of us have trouble spending even a few minutes playing with a preschooler. When we time the play or play observation of parents with 4-year-olds, the grown-ups generally estimate the duration of their involvement to be three to four times greater than the actual amount of lapsed time.

The great breadth of children's focus during play is usually considered as an indication of short attentive ability. Yet, through observation of 440 children in nursery schools, Burton White's preschool project at Harvard University identified the ability to focus on more than one thing at a time as an asset contributing to a child's competence in dealing with the world. Perhaps the preference of children for a wide focus facilitates an inventive orientation by bringing together otherwise remote ideas. From this perspective it would appear that more parents need to enlarge the length and the scope of their attention in order to participate in fantasy play.

Children delay closure. Parents have a greater need than children do for reaching conclusions, and this accounts in part for parental frustration during play. Whereas the child moves from one focus to another and back again without revealing a need for completion, parents feel tension unless the play themes reach some type of conclusion. Most parents who need play closure also show a preoccupation with rules. They tend to think that, before fantasy play can take place, it is necessary to decide the rules and to define the boundaries of behavior. This press to eliminate ambiguity by determining in advance the limits for players is not part of young children's peer play. The exact age when the change happens has not been determined; however, I am often disappointed in observing 9- and 10-year-olds who find it necessary to spend most of their play time trying to decide about rules. Some teachers regard this daily scene at recess as evidence of the beginnings of democratic behavior; it could also be that the teacher is witnessing the decline of creativity.

Young children's peer play does not require closure. Since no rules are set forth and the reward is continuous rather than terminal, the child is not obliged to complete play. To the child, play is a never-ending and all-important task. Parents who approach fantasy play as though it were a form of competition feel a need to finish one thematic event before starting a new one. That is, their satisfaction lies in the *outcome* rather than in the *process* of play. We live in a world of early deadlines, a period when the time for reaching conclusions and for finishing tasks is continually compressed. Most of us are disappointed with the forces that dictate our accelerated conclusions; yet we impose the same conditions on children when we insist that every play event must have a finish. The more completion-conscious we become as a society, the less likely it is that we will be able to tolerate delayed closure when we meet this characteristic in children. However, the stubborn fact remains that creativity and the ability to delay closure go together.

Children express emotion. It is common for parents who witness excited children simulating sounds for trucks and trains to caution "not so loud." The noise of children's play that reflects the intensity of involvement is sometimes considered an indicator of hearing loss. A more reasonable assessment is that the young train conductors are doing what is required in adult life, and therefore in role playing: shouting above competing engine noises. If a mother were aware of this, she would know how foolish it is to announce in a whisper "All aboard." One mother playing with her child credited herself with blowing up a bridge without making a lot of noise. Much to her dismay, the young play partner continued to cross the bridge—refusing to acknowledge its demolition, since he hadn't heard the dynamite charge.

Granted, there are many families who live in densely populated apartment complexes. Mindful of paper-thin walls and neighbors' complaints, parents in these circumstances feel obliged to minimize the sound of child play. Apart from the restriction that lack of space imposes on play during early childhood, there are serious losses in the possibilities for affective identification when noise, too, is restricted. At age 4 a child is modeling emotion—what the parents feel and how they express their feelings. It's fair to say that grown-ups who suppress or fail to show emotion during play represent poor models of response. Paradoxically, such parents are both less and more influential than they intend. On one hand, parents who neglect to show emotion offer a limited repertoire to their child. Studies by Earl Hoffman at Northern Illinois University have shown that, when tired or uninterested parents dutifully read or tell stories to their preschoolers, the monotonous presentation—as assessed by facial expression, speech inflection, and emotional tone—has a negligible educational benefit for the child. By comparison, parents who read with feeling and express emotion in telling stories to their children register an appreciable impact.

From another perspective, parents who undervalue emotional expression have a great, if unfortunate, influence. When adults invest too little of themselves in situations, their children can adopt the same coping response. For instance, if a parent fails to show fear, grief, or excitement about a play fire, accident, or death, the child may learn this reaction to disaster. Today it is fashionable to blame television for blunting the emotional reactions of children. But to what degree are we as injurious an influence through our behavior during play? To what extent do we, by trying to depress the noise level of children at play or by failing to show feeling during play, contribute to the inhibition of emotional expression? At least there is emotion on television; it cannot always be seen in parent-child play.

Children accept imagination. It is one thing to lack the power to pretend and quite another to be unaccepting of that power in someone else. When 5-year-old Greg wanted to drive his toy truck to Africa to join a safari, his grown-up play partner did not react with enthusiasm. Instead she dismissed the venture by reminding Greg that Africa is across the ocean and that trucks cannot travel by water. Or consider Steven, who didn't feel that his account of every play event had to be plausible. However, his explanation that a man in a crash between two toy trucks wasn't hurt because he wore a brick coat was immediately dismissed by the parent, who wanted to use the occasion to urge the value of safety belts.

An unwillingness to accept divergent thinking shows up in Maria's record. Her mother felt compelled to remove the policeman from a group of toy cowboys because "he doesn't fit." Young Maria perceived the matter differently and so kept the officer in the group on the premise that, since the fort was already surrounded, the cowboys would be unwise to exclude a possible ally just because he wore blue. I wonder if we unwittingly teach children prejudice in the name of classification. Grown-ups often ask preschoolers to decide "Which one doesn't belong in the group?" Usually the choice is among objects, animals, and persons. The intended lesson is that the different should be isolated because they do not belong. If integration is our society's goal, "unlikes" will have to go together. Maybe we can start by teaching the recognition and acceptance of differences instead of insisting that the different be excluded.

The assumption that decline in creativity is genetic or a function of age has been disproven by cross-cultural research. While Anglo-American cultures show a drop in creativity beginning at about age 9, this is not the case in cultures such as those of Western Samoa and the Sikhs of India. It appears that parents and teachers have an important influence in determining the continuity of creative development. In this connection, Paul Torrance, at the University of Georgia, is concerned about the preservation of creativity among children. He has examined the "ideal pupil" concept as perceived by approximately 1000 teachers representing several countries. Each of the teachers from Germany, India, Greece, the Philippines, and the United States was presented a list of 62 student characteristics, all of which were included because of their previous reliability in discriminating between persons of high and low creative ability. The educators were obliged to indicate the characteristics describing the kind of person they wished to see their students become. Conversely, they were to indicate the characteristics they felt ought to be discouraged. All five cultures seem to have values that undermine the growth of creativity. In the realm of "accepting imagination," it was learned that, as a group, teachers in the U. S. sample unfortunately believed that the following characteristics should be discouraged: being intuitive, being a good guesser, regressing occasionally, being a visionary, and always asking questions.

Children accept spontaneity. Most of us have been counseled at some time against interrupting a speaker. The stated reason is that courtesy requires peers to take turns so that everyone has the respect of being heard. For conversations between preschoolers and adults, the rules are even more restrictive. In this relationship, age is commonly believed to bestow a privilege of dominance. There are many homes in which guests can expect to find normally exuberant children comparatively silent during their visit. Such children are less often described as controlled than as well behaved—meaning that they don't question an imposed imbalance of speech. I am unsure how old some children must be before they are accepted as persons in their own home—that is, as individuals whose feelings and thoughts can be expressed at any time without permission.

Certainly we can take pride in the fact that fewer parents than ever before believe that children should be seen and not heard. Still there are a great number of youngsters who hear "Be polite and wait for your turn to talk." That admonitions like these may be an inadequate guide to maturity is shown by the behavior of most elderly people who, like preschoolers, can carry on a conversation speaking and listening at the same time. Next time you encounter an old couple, notice their unashamed manner of mutually talking to you at the same time that they elaborate or disagree with each other. It would seem that those of us between early childhood and old age are the least able to demonstrate this ability. To make our disability an obligation for everyone seems a poor response. Rather, if we cannot listen and speak concurrently, let's learn from the children and the elderly, who can.

Among themselves, preschoolers are not bound by an established order for speakers. When deference occurs at all, it is to those who exhibit a readiness to say something. This basic difference between the rules of child conversation and the rules of adult conversation tends to disturb parents when they begin participating in play. Whereas children find it acceptable for all the players to talk at once, most beginning adult players can accept only one voice at a time. For grown-ups, the custom of taking turns is sacrosanct. Unlike children who interrupt a companion without reluctance, many parents and teachers politely wait for a turn, supposing that, out of courtesy, their child partner will eventually allow them an entry. Observation reveals that open moments seldom happen, leaving some grown-ups to conclude either that their prospect is hopeless or that their child partner needs instruction in etiquette, a lesson in how to behave. Yet the spontaneous nature of play makes the ordering of its expression an impossibility. Therefore, adults must decide what kind of speech they want to encourage—the predictable or the spontaneous. Many early childhood programs produce predictable speech; too few programs aim for spontaneous speech.

Children await reflection. Some parents complain about the noise a child makes during play. When the same child is reflective, they feel uncomfortable about the *lack* of noise. Adults who undervalue deliberation assess its silent process in children as a sign of misunderstanding. Consequently, they often amend their questions or resort to cueing. However well intended, attempts to press a partner for premature answers disrespect his or her pace of decision making, or *cognitive tempo*. The term *cognitive tempo* refers to the speed at which an individual typically processes information, reaches judgment, and solves problems. For example, on the Matching Familiar Figures Test developed by Jerome Kagan of Harvard University, children are asked to choose from six similar pictures one that is identical with a standard. Boys and girls who have an impulsive tempo are inclined to act on their first impression without pausing to evaluate its merit. Thus, they respond quickly but make many errors. By comparison, reflective children take more time to examine the variant pictures. Since they think before acting, the reflective children make fewer mistakes.

The trait of cognitive tempo is evident by age 2 and seems to become stable at about age 4. Tempo appears related to early patterns of interaction between mother and child. At Ohio State University, Ellen Hock conducted a tempo study of inner-city children. The results indicated that a high proportion of low-income children classify as impulsive types.

Perhaps the differential is best illustrated by contrasting how children of different tempos respond to different types of television programs. John Wright examined the content and audience of the programs *Sesame Street* and *Mister Rogers*. These two programs were chosen as extremes, because *Sesame Street* is fast moving, sharp, and brisk. It is geared for the low-income, urban child and incorporates much street knowledge. *Mister Rogers* is slower paced, more gentle, and cuts across the experience of all income groups. On *Sesame Street* there were 18 dialogue shifts per minute, compared to two per minute on *Mister Rogers*. The depth development of characters on *Sesame Street* was assessed as "shallow" and on *Mister Rogers* as "deep." Wright's results suggest that, since impulsive (fast and inaccurate) children tire faster of some stimuli, perhaps they should be taught the same concept by different approaches—the technique offered by the format of *Sesame Street*. On the other hand, *Mister Rogers* may be better for reflective (slow and accurate) children, who can be taught by using highly familiar situations, people, and places over and over again to teach different concepts. In my estimate, however, inner-city children should not be limited to televiewing that appeals to their impulsivity. Success at school requires an ability to reflect, and the need for this ability increases as a student moves up through the grades. For these reasons I favor enlarging the scope of televiewing for inner-city children to include reflective as well as impulsive-oriented programs.

Children share dominance. Most parents can remember overhearing a confrontation between their child and a playmate.

Parents naturally ask "What's the trouble?" Often they are told "Nothing; we're just playing." It seems that children and adults sometimes differ in how they define play. Because we are interested in learning how to play with children, the child's definition of play is important for us. It has been my observation that, in the estimate of children, they are playing with parents only when they share control and dominance.

Perhaps we can better appreciate the play needs of children by examining our own recreational needs. What kinds of games do we consider the most exciting, the most fun to watch? Generally adults agree that they like a close game, one in which the outcome remains doubtful until near the finish. When a football team outscores another 60 to 0, the spectators may be heard to complain that it wasn't a game at all. By this they mean that the imbalance of power eliminates the uncertainty and consequent excitement about who will win. Indeed, when our team runs away with the score, we may even begin to encourage the opposition to score and find pleasure in their success. The pro draft was initiated just so that power would not become the exclusive realm of one team in the league. Sports promoters realize that, whenever power is unilateral, fans will conclude "Why watch?"

Some parents experience a similar motive when they play games with young children. The parents recognize that they are too competent for the child to win the game, perhaps even too powerful for the youngster to feel any satisfaction in playing at all. Thus, in a game of checkers, when the child begins to complain, threatens to quit, or seems ready to cry, the parent must decide what to do. Why do some parents decide they should cheat in favor of their young opponent? Certainly it isn't to teach the child dishonesty. Isn't it to make the child feel powerful? The fact that young children are so often powerless in games oriented toward adult rules means that these are not the best play activities for intrafamily encounter. There is a better and more authentic way to respect small children and become involved in their lives—through fantasy play.

In the Parent-Child Lab at Arizona State University, we decided to run a simple check on the hunch that preschoolers need play with parents in order to share dominance. A group of middle-class, suburban couples were obliged to engage their 4-year-olds in fantasy play for ten minutes each morning and evening. This schedule was followed for a week. During the succeeding week, the parents were instructed to avoid any participation in play. Throughout the experiment, each of the two dozen families kept its own daily record of child misbehavior. As a group, the family records showed an incidence of misbehavior six times as great for the non-play days as for the "child power" days. The fact that when parents played with children there was less misbehavior suggests that certain power needs are met during family play. In addition, we have found that parents who play with their youngsters more often than most other parents have more appropriate child-rearing expectations.

Our lab experience also indicates that the child's need for power and consequent self-assertion has a place in parent-child play. When we ask 4-year-olds whom they prefer to play with, playmates or parents, almost always they choose parents and give as their reason "Then I can be the boss." The possibility of power also seems to explain why preschoolers prefer to play alone with the parent rather than to include a sibling. Older siblings are less able to accept the dominance of younger brothers and sisters, because they have a more narrow scope of power than do their parents. In other words, the fact that preschoolers prefer a less competent partner (like a parent) to a more competent player (like a peer or sibling) suggests that the child's desire for play with parents is partly a desire to redress their imbalance of interpersonal power.

We should acknowledge that it is in the realm of pretending that a small child qualifies as the family's strongest member. Whether the child will continue to value this strength and be respected for it depends on whether parents are routinely involved as play observers, partners, and models. I am often asked by parents "What right do we have to intrude in our child's play?" My shortest answer is that a parent's promotion of a child's self-respect is not a fault but an obligation.

Undesirable Behaviors

All the behaviors we have looked at so far are desirable and can more readily be seen in children than in parents. We turn now to several undesirable behaviors that are common among beginning adult players.

Adults imitate speech. Whenever we don't know what to say or how to act, it is helpful to watch and imitate others of greater experience. Unfamiliar situations often require that we imitate in order to quickly adapt, to remain inconspicuous, or to physically survive. Granting the adaptive merit of imitation, it is wise to recognize as well that continued imitation can prove maladaptive. Unless one moves from only copying the behavior of others to incorporating the process that generates the copied behavior, an incomplete adaptation remains fixed. If, in learning from a preschooler, parents limit their speech to imitative repetitions of what the child says, they unwittingly avoid interaction and hence entry to the arena of play.

Some parents rationalize their imitative speech by suggesting that it provides immediate corrective feedback of a child's expression. This preference for correction over interaction is defensive. Apart from the obvious problem that a child at play is less interested in an echo than in a partner, the possibilities for speech development actually decline. Children improve language more by interacting with persons of greater verbal ability than by listening to an adult replay of themselves. Indeed, by subconsciously imitating adult speech, children recognize our greater verbal ability. It is doubly unfortunate to refuse a child's strength and simultaneously ignore the possibilities of our own. Yet this is what happens when we imitate a child's less mature speech and consequently refuse to give a reaction to his or her imagination. The differing strengths of parent and child warrant a mutual response in order that each party can share the role of teacher and learner.

Adults praise indiscriminately. Children seek recognition, but I believe that what they seek is not so much the recognition of praise as the recognition of acceptance. Because persons who are accepted can remain who they are without risking a loss of affection, they don't have to change to continue being valued. In this sense, acceptance is the greatest reward we can offer children, for they can then retain their imagination in adult life. Although praise is generally well intended, it is often used to shape behavior in ways that deflect a child from normal development. Normal development would be the continuation rather than the decline of creative behavior. If praise sustained creative behavior, schools would not influence its decline, because most teachers spend a great deal of time praising the children. It is when we want to develop initiative, creativity, and problem solving that praise fails us most. To liberate these qualities in people, we need to rely on internal motivation; that is, we need to make people feel they are free of our control.

An observer of play among children will note that children experience the intrinsic satisfaction of play and thus seldom praise one another. Boys and girls attempt to control playmates and playthings, but praise is not their tool; nor does the scope of power include the partner's way of thinking. The praising adult seems oblivious to the intrinsic satisfaction of play and insists on being a judge whose function is to verbally reinforce selected behaviors. If parents found pleasure in play, they would not have difficulty sustaining attention. The law of effect states "behavior that is satisfying tends to be repeated." If parents find play dissatisfying, their lack of satisfaction will usually show up in terms of a short attention span and the use of praise, an extraneous reward system.

Because praising adults are easily distracted from play, they frequently lapse into a pattern of nearly constant praise. Harvey, a 5-year-old, was playing a submarine plot with Jill, his grown-up partner. When Harvey announced they were getting close to an island of monsters, Jill replied "OK, you keep watching the controls." Almost immediately Harvey exclaimed, "Oh-Oh, we're out of gas." Without delay Jill said "Good, keep going." Harvey, who was the only person involved in this play theme, then declared "Good? What do you mean *Good*?" Many children could ask Harvey's question of their distracted parent partners who substitute praise for involvement, who use praise as an excuse for not investing attention or time.

Adults sense embarrassment. Unlike preschoolers, many parents are embarrassed about engaging in fantasy play. Probably this is because most of us were taught to conceal weakness, to avoid situations in which we lack competence. Often the result has been to postpone play with children until their interest includes the nonfiction games that require our skills. Naturally, this background makes us uneasy when educators urge that we engage children in fantasy play. Perhaps our decision rests on how we choose to view the strength of our children. We tend to feel self-conscious about the greater strength of someone when we regard our interaction with them as competitive. Our studies at Arizona State University show that it is better to view the parent-child dyad as a partnership in which the strength of each member is to the advantage of both members—an arrangement in which no one loses, because success is mutual.

Unless parents feel comfortable about the greater play competence of their children, they may severely judge themselves and withdraw. This tendency to unfavorably evaluate oneself as a play teacher occurs even among middle-grade children. Research with fourth-graders who were trained to teach kindergartners vocabulary by using toys and fantasy themes have shown the necessity to enlarge the teachers' usual standard for judging themselves. When play teachers of any age recognize that their tolerance for creativity and their willingness to reduce control are the attitudes that result in student gains, teacher self-evaluation is more satisfactory. For example, the priority put on their imagination and play increased the enthusiasm and eagerness of kindergartners who participated in our cross-age teaching program. Over an eight-week period the percentage of the kindergartners' undesirable perceptions about the teaching/learning process dropped from 47% to 3%. This worthwhile transition suggests that the fourth-grade child teachers achieved a most important lesson; because they believed in creativity, their students became more confident and reliant upon imagination.

The conclusion for parents might be stated as an admonition: don't be embarrassed about your inability as a player. Be embarrassed about your reluctance to learn. Better yet, get down on your knees and play!

SHARING YOUR IMPRESSIONS

1. What do you remember about parents or teachers playing with you as a young child?
2. What kinds of problems do grown-ups have in playing with young children?

3. Speculate about the benefits that are unique to parent-child play.
4. What differences do you see between being a play teacher at home and using play as a teacher at school?
5. How do you react when children destroy something they've made?
6. Recall a childhood experience in which you were the youngest and least capable in a group venture.
7. Suggest some guidelines to be used by adults who wish to educate for creative behavior.

REFERENCES AND SUGGESTED READING

Arnaud, Sara H. "Some Functions of Play in the Educative Process." In *Readings In Educational Psychology: Contemporary Perspectives* (1976-77 edition), edited by Robert A. Dentler and Bernard J. Shapiro. New York: Harper & Row, 1976. Pp. 200-203.

Bronfenbrenner, Urie. *A Report on Longitudinal Evaluations of Preschool Programs*. Washington, D. C.: U. S. Department of Health, Education and Welfare, Office of Human Development, 1974.

Caplan, Frank, and Caplan, Theresa. *The Power of Play*. Garden City, N. Y.: Anchor Books, 1974.

Cass, Joan. *Helping Children Grow through Play*. New York: Schocken, 1973.

Herron, R. E., and Sutton-Smith, Brian. *Child's Play*. New York: Wiley, 1971.

Hock, Ellen. "The Relation of Culture to the Reflection-Impulsivity Dimension." Unpublished master's thesis, Ohio State University, 1967.

Hoffman, Earl. "Prekindergarten Experiences and their Relationships to Reading Achievement." *Illinois School Research*, Fall 1971, pp. 6–12.

Smilansky, Sara. "Can Adults Facilitate Play in Children: Theoretical and Practical Considerations." In *Play: The Child Strives toward Self-Realization*. Conference Proceedings, National Association for the Education of Young Children, Washington, D. C., 1971. Pp. 39–50.

Strom, Robert. "Observing Parent-Child Fantasy Play." *Theory into Practice*, Vol. 8, No. 4, October 1974, pp. 287-295.

Strom, Robert. "Parents and Teachers as Play Observers." *Childhood Education*, January 1975, pp. 139–141.

Torrance, E. Paul. *Rewarding Creative Behavior*. Englewood Cliffs, N. J.: Prentice-Hall, 1965. Pp. 221–234.

Wright, John. "Cognitive Tempo: Matching the Pace of Communication to that of the Child." *Elementary-Kindergarten-Nursery Educators News Notes*, April 1973, .pp. 1–4.

BOOKS TO SHARE WITH YOUNG CHILDREN

Klein, Norma. *If I Had My Way*. New York: Pantheon Books, 1974. Children need to share dominance within their family. Ellie is tired of always being told what to do; so she imagines what things would be like if she were in charge of the family.

Russ, Lavina. *Alec's Sand Castle*. New York: Harper & Row, 1972. Parents can learn from children during fantasy play. When adult relatives take over the building of Alec's sand castle, he goes off by himself to create a better one with a shovel, a pail, and some imagination.

Scott, Ann Herbert. *Sam*. New York: McGraw-Hill, 1967. Children like to play with their parents and wish the grown-ups would pretend with them. Sam's attempts to involve his family in his play are seen by both parents as an unreasonable interruption.

Shecter, Ben. *If I Had a Ship*. New York: Doubleday, 1970. Parents who participate in a child's fantasy play support the development of creativity. When an imaginative boy describes to his mother the presents he will bring her from around the world, she enters into the adventures and encourages him to visualize all sorts of possibilities.

Stover, JoAnn. *I'm in a Family*. New York: David McKay, 1966. As we redefine the role of mother and father, both parties should see themselves as obliged to play with the children. Conversely, in this book children are shown all the other important things parents must do that prevent them from playing as often as youngsters would like.

3

FEARS
AND
ANXIETIES

NINE

SHARING FEARS AND ANXIETIES

SHARING FEARS

The experience of fear is not limited to any one period in life. Children have always been afraid, but the objects of their fears have changed with the times. Fifty years ago, boys and girls reported fearing phenomena like ghosts and skeletons more often than anything else. By contrast, a recent nationwide study of nearly 1000 children in grades three through six shows that the supernatural has been replaced by war as children's most common fear. It seems that many children who observe actual war on television worry about whether the battle will reach their own town. Until they comprehend the political situation, children don't understand how it is that fighting can take place daily in the Middle East but never in California. However, if television has enlarged the prominence of certain fears, it seems to have reduced the effect of others. For example, apart from war, the most intensely felt fears of children today involve natural phenomena such as darkness, thunder, lightning, tornadoes, and floods. The lessening of children's fear of the supernatural may in part be due to the influence of programs such as *Sesame Street*, which depict monsters as endearing and harmless rather than as threatening. Whatever its object, fear has a significant influence on mental health throughout our lives.

To clarify the role parents and teachers should assume in helping youngsters learn to cope with fear, we need to examine our own response to the irrational. It is well known that boys and girls live more with fear than do adults. This difference can be explained in part by the greater access children have to imagination. For them, the day includes more fiction, and sleep brings more nightmares, than we experience. Nevertheless, many parents and relatives are ashamed of fearful children and attempt to banish their fright by denial. For example, I recall taking my preschool son, Steven, to the zoo. Since Steven was fascinated by crocodiles, we spent quite some time at the reptile exhibit.

While we were in the aquarium, another little boy arrived with his family. The youngster was apprehensive and preferred to stay at some distance from the floor-to-ceiling window behind which the crocodiles lay. Taking notice of his fear, the boy's father lifted him up, then held him against the window and announced "See, it's like I told you before; they're locked in, so you have no reason to be afraid." Imagine how confusing it is for a little boy to be told he is not afraid when he really is. His parents, those all-knowing authorities, must know more than he does. Some children thus develop an alienation from their own feelings. They learn to mistrust their senses and rely on other people to tell them what to feel.

Sometimes children encounter an opposite but equally firm denial that their individual experiences are unique. Each of us has heard people say "I know just how you feel." Actually, we cannot know *exactly* how another person feels, any more than we can tell how hard someone else is trying. However, this limitation of what is called *empathy*, or the ability to participate in another's experience, becomes less disturbing when we realize that it confirms our assumptions about being individuals. For parents this means that the fears of children ought to be respected whether they share the same fears or not. Our *acceptance* of other people seems to play a larger role in determining interpersonal success than does our *understanding* of other people. Indeed, if we limit our respect to those people whose experience we understand, the quest for understanding itself becomes an obstacle to successful relationships.

Ridicule is also a common response to fear. But laughing at another's fears does not decrease the fear. Instead, the effect is to lower the individual's confidence in himself or herself. Statements like "There is nothing to be afraid of in the dark" or "It's just a dream and not real" may be well intended, but they still inspire shame for having fears that grown-ups declare to be unwarranted. To laugh at someone's fears or to call a person a "sissy" or a "baby" is to limit the relationship. Children (and adults) whose feelings are ridiculed soon stop sharing their experiences. The tragedy for parents is that they reduce the chance to know their child better and forfeit an opportunity to help the youngster learn to cope with doubts, anxieties, and fears.

The first step in overcoming fear is to acknowledge it. Because preschoolers identify closely with parents, a sound way for parents to reduce the harmful consequences of children's fear is to admit their own fears. A child who is afraid of the dark, of being alone, or of starting school should be assured by grown-ups that fear is a natural reaction and that acknowledging fear does not make one a coward or a sissy. Although parents may insist that there is no danger in the dark, a child knows that Mom chooses not to go out alone late at night and that the doors are locked only at night. A child should not be made to feel ashamed of expressing feelings of fear. After all, adults are afraid of getting old, being alone, losing their hair, developing cancer, taking academic tests, and being rejected by peers. However, adults have an idea of what fear is, whereas children are afraid long before they can comprehend the notion of fear.

The child whose fears are unsuspected or unshared by loved ones bears the added burden of loneliness. Arthur Jersild of Columbia University has suggested "No aspect of a child's experience is more poignant and more deserving of compassionate attention than fears. Also no aspect is more baffling, either to a child himself or those who want to help him." Certainly children should know someone who will hear their doubts and fears without judging them. They will have this experience if parents accept them unconditionally. It should be unnecessary for sons and daughters to repress fear or to feign bravery to gain their parents' esteem.

The way in which mothers and fathers handle their own feelings is also important. Because preschoolers have a strong tendency to imitate their parents' behavior, parents can, by their example, lead children to express feelings honestly or to learn to deny them.

SHARING ANXIETIES

The anxieties of children also deserve attention. By *anxiety* I mean the feeling that goes with anticipating something new or strange. In tradition-oriented societies, people are less often anxious than in places like the United States, where to be uncertain and to encounter the unfamiliar is a common experience. In terms of benefit, doubt and ambiguity are known to stimulate creative behavior. However, when anxiety is excessive, the resulting stress can lead to mental disorder. It is this dangerous outcome of anxiety that we should try to prevent.

The preconditions for experiencing anxiety are essentially the same as for being human. So far as we can tell, animals do not lie awake at night picturing difficulties that make them dread tomorrow. They lack the ability to fantasize that predisposes humans to anticipate every conceivable danger. There are other differences helping to explain why anxiety is peculiar to ourselves. While our so-called instincts are strong, they do not govern our behavior. Then, too, compared to animals, human beings are immature for an extraordinary length of time. Still another factor is that the social environment to which we must adjust is very complex. Finally, because our cerebral cortex is relatively large, it is continuously engaged in imagining about the other human factors. We fantasize about what our instincts of the moment are seeking, what our social clique of the moment will approve, what our competence of the moment will support. As human beings we are always imagining, and during this process we are sometimes alone or helpless. When we find ourselves in all three of these conditions at the same time—imagining, alone, and helpless—then we are in a state of anxiety.

Aloneness is a variable condition. The age and needs of a person determine what is required to feel alone. At a certain age, or because of certain needs, we may feel alone whenever a particular person is out of reach. At another stage of development, or when influenced by different needs, we may feel alone if companions disagree with our opinions. Similarly, over a period of time the same person may feel helpless when facing the tasks of tying shoelaces, figuring subtraction, or reading a foreign language. For anxiety to occur, the conditions of aloneness and helplessness must combine to confront an open imagination. If an imagining person is alone but not helpless, that person may feel disappointed, unhappy, or abused and yet still avoid anxiety. A person who feels helpless but not alone may resent being dependent or even develop a sense of inferiority; still, he or she will not be anxious. If we feel alone and helpless but are able to cushion the effect of our imagination, we may become angry, suspicious, or afraid. Nevertheless, we will escape anxiety. It appears that, short of madness, there are only three ways to avoid being anxious—to be less alone, less helpless, or less imaginative. Since the future will require us to be more creative than ever before, efforts to cope with anxiety should not include reducing imagination but rather focus on the phenomena of aloneness and helplessness.

When anxiety threatens mental health, a person of any age should be referred for psychotherapy. By using one of several mediums, such as play, hypnosis, drugs, dream recall, or free association, the therapist tries to recreate the client's anxieties in a setting where they can be shared. A certain amount of uninterrupted time is regularly scheduled with the therapist. Any self-disclosure during these sessions is considered confidential. Together the guarantee of time and safety urge intimacy. In addition, the behavior of therapists inspires confidence, for they are trained to be good listeners, to remember details, to correct inconsistencies, and to raise reflective questions. Once the images that previously led to anxiety are shared with the therapist, a person may re-experience guilt, shame, doubt, or some other natural reaction, but no longer experience anxiety. For many people the release from anxiety brings therapy to a close. The decision to give further treatment for feelings of helplessness may depend on a therapist's case load and on whether the therapist subscribes to the theoretical views of Sigmund Freud, Carl Jung, Alfred Adler, Carl Rogers, or some other figure of renown.

Being a mother or father predisposes us to certain types of anxiety. Consider some of the situations in which parents feel alone and helpless with their imaginations:

> "The teacher says Ramon is behind in math and that he'll probably fail unless a dramatic improvement takes place. Ramon looks to me for help, but the school expects him to use different methods of computation from the ones I was taught."

> "John has limited athletic ability and sits on the bench unless his team is far ahead. I'm unsure whether to encourage his unrealistic aspirations, suggest he drop out and take up some other sport, or confront the coach about letting everyone play."

"My wife and I have just seen a television report citing the widespread use of drugs among students at Roberta's high school. How can we ensure that she won't get mixed up with the wrong crowd? At the same time, we don't want her to think of us as interfering parents."

"Charles is made fun of almost daily by the neighborhood children, who are several years older. What can I do to lessen his sense of disappointment? What can I do to make the other kids accept Charles?"

"The school counselor informed me that the testing shows Kim has a learning disability. I've had such wonderful plans for her future—things that I never got to do—and now what can I do about my expectations?"

"My husband has worked long and hard to establish a good reputation. But our eldest son, Jim, seems determined to undo all that with his motorcycle escapades. I can't say anything or Jim might leave home."

"I realize that Nancy's classmates won't allow her into their clique unless she has certain kinds of clothes. However, with finances the way they are, I just can't afford to buy such things right now."

"Even though Mary Jo has been warned not to go in the street, I still worry about accidents. There is so much traffic in this neighborhood, and a driver might not see her until it's too late."

"Since our divorce last fall, Tony's father has been telling him things about me that are untrue. I want them to have a good relationship, but Tony is my son too."

"Julie has become much more independent lately, and I've begun to worry. What if she decides not to stay within the family's religion and rejects the values and morals that we hold?"

"People with little children can always get some kind of parent education. But what about me? Now that my boys are in school, how can I remain a competent mother without access to continued guidance and training?"

It seems that nearly all fathers and mothers experience occasional doubts about their fitness for the demands of child rearing. In isolation they anxiously wonder: "Am I too strict, too lenient, too protective, or too naïve? Will I turn out to be a successful parent?"

Teachers also feel alone and helpless in the child-rearing role. Let's identify certain of the conditions that support their anxiety.

> "I worry most about accountability. How can all the children in my room be prepared so they will score at grade level on the achievement tests? If they don't measure up, what will their next teacher and the administration think of me?"

> "My anxiety centers on having to assign grades, to group students by their ability, and to decide on promotions. I am unsure which of the evaluation methods are fair, and I dread handling the aftermath of student complaints."

> "The issue of accountability bothers me a lot. On the one hand I feel pressured by the administration and school board to meet their achievement-test objectives. At the same time I feel bad about not being able to give enough attention to the emotional development of my students."

> "Classroom discipline is a constant problem for me. Many of the students have a record of low achievement, and they qualify as troublemakers. I usually feel alone and powerless against them."

> "This semester has presented me with two anxiety-producing experiences. In September I was involuntarily transferred from the school of my choice as part of the ethnic-balance program. Now I have been assigned to teach all the sixth-graders science, a subject for which I am inadequately prepared."

> "I'm anxious whenever someone comes in the classroom to observe my teaching. Whether it is the principal, another faculty member, or a parent, I get uptight thinking they may misjudge me."

> "There is a high divorce rate in this neighborhood. Each time someone in our classroom has to go through the experience of separation from a parent, I feel miserable, because it's my student and there's nothing I can do to help."

> "I'm under stress because of the administrative pressure to use unfamiliar teaching methods and a new mathematics curriculum with which I basically disagree. My principal has made it clear that being transferred is the only alternative to being involved."

"The differing expectations of parents are my reason for anxiety. Some of them always want more homework, while others complain about not leaving the child enough time for out-of-school activities. During the conferences I'm intimidated by disagreeable parents who feel their child's lack of success is all my fault."

The last comment offers a clue for reducing the anxiety of parents, teachers, and children alike. In a partnership, teachers and parents will feel less alone and less helpless with their important and complementary roles. It is clear that the combination of demands for higher achievement by children and for greater accountability by caretakers will lead to rising anxiety unless the home and school learn to collaborate more.

It is worthwhile to think about how we can provide children better access to treatment for their anxieties. Certainly the prevailing ratio of only one school counselor for every 600 students needs to be improved. But in my opinion our greater effort should center on finding ways to reduce the number of boys and girls who become so anxious that they require counselor care. As a rule, teachers suppose that, because anxiety is the major concern of therapists and counselors, they ought to be responsible for handling student anxiety. By contrast, teachers regard themselves as primarily responsible for creative learning. Actually creative thought and anxiety are related, inasmuch as they are the two poles of a continuum. But they should not be mistaken for one another. According to Richard Jones at the University of California, the methods employed by therapists are intended to reduce a child's sense of aloneness and helplessness, while a teacher's methods are expected to increase the polar opposites, community and mastery. We can diagram the complement of these professions as follows.

$$(\text{Imagination} + \text{Aloneness} + \text{Helplessness}) = \text{Anxiety} \rightarrow \text{Psychotherapy}$$
$$\text{Instruction} (\text{Imagination} + \text{Community} + \text{Mastery}) = \text{Creative Learning}$$

The diagram shows that imagination plus aloneness plus helplessness leads to anxiety, which can be treated and relieved through psychotherapy. At school, instruction combines imagination with community and mastery to produce creative learning.

To the degree that teachers achieve the goal of creative learning, they also help to prevent anxiety. But our rate of success in the classroom can be much improved. The fact is there are many students who feel alone and helpless. They may feel alone because they are new at school, because their parents are breaking up, or because they hold uncommon opinions. Other boys and girls feel helpless because of unfair competition or their powerless role or because they don't comprehend homework. Somehow the uniqueness of each child must be preserved without making the child feel alone. Establishing a sense of community seems vital. Indeed, this may be what schooling in the future will be all about.

We can begin by helping more students feel they belong at school and in regular classrooms. It may be that teachers of the past were more able than ourselves to cope with varying levels of student ability. At least they were obliged to accept a broader range of individual differences. The point is that, unless teachers are trained to accommodate diversity, they develop a need for uniformity. In turn this means they feel uncomfortable with students who deviate from the norm and consider such persons as better off in a segregated class. The unintended result is that fewer classrooms represent a microcosm of our diverse society. When teachers require sameness among students, they convey the impression that anyone whose behavior or achievement falls outside the range of the "normal" or average does not belong in class. Under these conditions, children miss the chance to learn what being a member of a community is all about, especially that it involves accepting differences. Another way to promote feelings of community is by peer teaching, which defines the student role in a less selfish fashion. Children are also less likely to feel alone when they need special help if their teachers do not see themselves as alone. The teacher who sees school as a community feels comfortable calling upon supporting staff, such as the counselor, psychologist, or nurse, when the need arises.

Similarly, we must help students attain a sense of mastery without isolating them. We should be concerned about the growing number of youngsters who are unnecessarily inclined toward cynicism. People who are schooled only for individual competition may limit their adult roles to being social critics.

This choice prevents them from working with others to improve their community, and it denies them the sense of potency that goes with achieving social change. To exert influence in a world of institutions calls for a broader kind of competence than in the past. What is required is not so much our strength as individuals or loners but our readiness for social and corporate action. At present, collaboration is often forbidden in school or even regarded as cheating. Therefore, other students' talents are viewed as one's own misfortune. Only when we have shown students how to achieve mastery through collaboration, to see and appreciate the value of interdependence, have we minimized the chance for them to experience aloneness, helplessness, and anxiety. In this way teachers have an opportunity to prevent the anxieties that therapists would otherwise have an obligation to treat.

SHARING YOUR IMPRESSIONS

1. If you come from a broken home or have friends who do, share some of the adjustments that had to be made.
2. Make some guesses about the anxieties and fears you would expect to be more common among children of divorce.
3. What can parents and children do to help one another through a divorce?
4. How can a divorced parent help children with their feelings of anxiety toward a potential parent?
5. In what ways should parent education be different for single persons who are rearing children by themselves?
6. What do you suppose are today's dominant fears among children? Adolescents? Young adults? Middle-age persons? The elderly?
7. What have you found to be the best way of coping with fears?
8. What are some examples of anxieties faced by most students? Teachers? Parents?
9. What anxieties do you suppose are most prominent among parents who are divorced? Unmarried? Widowed?

REFERENCES AND SUGGESTED READING

Bauer, David. "Children's Fears: Reflections on Research." *Educational Leadership*, March 1974, pp. 555–560.

Croake, James. "The Changing Nature of Children's Fears." *Child Study Journal* 3 (1973), 91–105.

Jersild, Arthur. *Child Psychology*. Englewood Cliffs, N. J.: Prentice-Hall, 1968. Pp. 327–365.

Jones, Richard. *Fantasy and Feeling in Education*. New York: New York University Press, 1968. Pp. 55–86.

Kemp, C. G. *Intangibles in Counseling*. Boston: Houghton Mifflin, 1967. Pp. 81–99.

Loch, Sherry. "Children's Ideas about the Causes of Illness." Unpublished master's thesis, Arizona State University, Tempe, May 1976.

Meares, Ainslie. *Relief without Drugs*. Sydney, Australia: New Century Press, 1974.

Noshpitz, Joseph D. "Phobias." In *Elementary Education Today*, edited by Robert D. Strom and Mary Elizabeth Bell. Washington: National Education Association, 1971. Pp. 137–143.

Parnes, Estelle. "Effects of Experiences with Loss and Death among Preschool Children." *Children Today*, November–December, 1975, pp. 2–7.

Rogers, Donald. "How to Teach Fear." *Elementary School Journal*, May 1972, pp. 391–395.

Sullivan, Judy. *Mama Doesn't Live Here Anymore*. New York: Arthur Fields, 1974.

Temple University Institute for Survey Research. "National Survey of Children: Preliminary Results." New York: Foundation for Child Development, 1977.

Yamamoto, Kaoru. *Individuality: The Unique Learner*. Columbus, Ohio: Charles E. Merrill, 1975.

BOOKS TO SHARE WITH YOUNG CHILDREN

Hirsch, Marilyn, and Narayan, Maya. *Leela and the Watermelon*. New York: Crown, 1971. Little children are easily frightened by the misleading stories older siblings sometimes tell them. Leela's brother has her convinced that the watermelon seed she swallowed will grow inside of her stomach.

Mayer, Mercer. *There's a Nightmare in My Closet*. New York: Dial Press, 1968. Children should be aware that fear of darkness is common among people their age. In this story our hero confronts his nightmare only to find it is timid, cowardly, and very much in need of friendship.

Nixon, Joan Lowery. *The Alligator under the Bed*. New York: Putnam's Sons, 1974. If children cannot share their fears without ridicule, the fears will grow. Whereas everyone else in the family gives a little girl reasons why it is unnecessary to be afraid, Uncle Harry knows about imaginative, not-so-sleepy girls and comes to the rescue.

Stanek, Muriel. *I Won't Go without a Father*. Chicago: Albert Whitman, 1972. Some children of divorce experience anxiety about attending school affairs at which their peers will be accompanied by two parents. Steve doesn't want to go to the open-house night with only his mother, because he will feel out of place among the other, intact families.

Whitney, Alma. *Just Awful*. Reading, Mass.: Addisonian Press, 1971. Children are often more upset than hurt by minor accidents, because they suppose the physical damage is serious. Jim is frightened when he cuts his finger at school, but the nurse has a special kind of treatment.

TEN
A WORLD WITHOUT BULLIES

NEIGHBORHOOD FIGHTS

Our society is very concerned about the mistreatment of some children by their parents. At the same time as we try to eliminate violence within families, perhaps we can become responsive to the more common experience of child abuse by peers. As an example, consider the situation at bus stops. Urban living and school integration have combined to require an increase in busing. At suburban and inner-city bus stops, children of varying ages—often bored and wanting some excitement—daily congregate without adults present. This unsupervised situation promotes bully behavior.

Most parents know the uncertainty that arises when children allege harm at the hands of peers. Depending on the number and physical size of the child's opponents, we are ambivalent about what to do. We are torn between the desire to protect our child and the recognition that we cannot always be bodyguards. Some parents decide that the only alternative is to train the young to protect themselves. Usually this means exposure to some form of judo, karate, or father-taught boxing lessons. An opposite response is to encourage the child to never fight back. Neither of these strategies seems to produce the desired effect. The young boxer often finds that his opponent has older friends who are prepared to avenge the defeat. Meanwhile, the unresponsive, nonviolent child learns that refusing to fight back leads to being called a sissy, which in turn invites even more people to bully him.

Given the undesirable consequences of their first approach, many parents conclude that they should take matters into their own hands and settle things at the adult level. Unfortunately, phoning the enemy's parents is often unsuccessful, because they've heard a quite different account of what has happened at the bus stop. Besides, few parents choose to acknowledge that their child is a bully. Instead, they are likely to suggest "Let the

children work it out for themselves, just as we had to do as kids."
Disappointed, yet more determined than before, the parent who
is trying to be protective may call the school principal and report
the bus-stop dilemma. This procedure assumes that, if the
bully's parents will not act to terminate misbehavior, the school
is obliged to do so. However, the school seldom considers itself
responsible for events that occur outside the gate. The principal
will probably say "This is a neighborhood issue, not a school
issue."

Having exhausted the alternatives they feel are appropriate,
some distraught parents finally resort to driving their child to
school themselves, hoping that, if the bus stop is avoided altogether, the child will no longer feel the need to feign illness in
order to escape peer abuse or react negatively toward the whole
educational process. Certainly this option of driving to school
every day is inconvenient and expensive, but the parents who
choose it consider it essential. An even more desperate attempt
to protect children from threatening peers is the decision to
change schools or even the place of family residence so that sons
and daughters can avoid being victimized.

There must be better ways to eliminate the mistreatment of
children by peers. To begin with, we ought not be deflected by
the argument about permitting kids to abuse each other because
"that's the way the world is"—unless in fact we feel the world
should remain that way. It seems ironic that we even urge the
young to fight their own battles when grown-ups no longer
accept such advice for themselves. Many of the people who live
in apartments and retirement communities have adopted the
security guard as a necessity. An increasing number of adults are
willing to pay for protection so that they can feel secure, so that
they will not be bullied. Do our children deserve less consideration? Should a sense of security belong to adults alone?

No one should be expected to suffer intimidation, least of all
the most defenseless—the very young. If the practice is needed,
the rotation of parent observers at the bus stop is one feasible
form of protection. At the very least, adult protection allows
vulnerable children safe passage to and from school. Moreover,
this method serves to illustrate for everyone that our society
regards children as people who have a right to feel safe, that the

abuse of power will not be tolerated at any age, and that parents have an obligation to promote the safety of children from other families. Until children are educated to treat everyone with respect, we must do the second-best thing, which is to protect boys and girls from their peers who have not learned this important lesson. A serious and related effort involves helping families with school children learn to work together in solving neighborhood problems. Unless programs in parent education achieve this important goal, many boys and girls will live with a continual fear of intimidation. And, lacking the example of parents who cooperate with one another, the young are not likely to achieve an understanding of community obligation.

The magnitude of peer abuse is partially revealed by results from the first National Survey of Children, sponsored by the Foundation for Child Development and reported in 1977. According to Nicholas Zill, director of the study, interviews were held with a scientifically selected sample of some 2200 boys and girls, aged 7 to 11, who represent 18 million youngsters nationwide. More than 40% of those interviewed report having been bothered by older kids while playing outside. A third of them recall being threatened with a beating, and one in four have had possessions taken from them by bullies. As expected, rural children had not experienced as much peer abuse, but there was less variation from inner city to suburb than one might suppose. When the children were asked what they would change about their neighborhood "to make it nicer for kids," the two leading suggestions mentioned were to have more and better places to play and less bad behavior. In the children's own words, "Stop older kids from fighting and picking on little kids."

CONFLICT AT SCHOOL

Not all fighting occurs in the neighborhood. In the 1977 survey just mentioned, 20% of the 7- to 11-year-olds interviewed had at some time or other been in trouble with teachers or principals for fighting. Of those who had fought, 70% were boys. In certain schools, this activity was so prominent it overshadowed learning. For example, nearly one out of three Black students said that, if they had the chance, they would attend some other school, primarily because fighting and fooling around were too prevalent. Many parents cite this problem as a major reason for transferring their children to private schools. Let's examine the usual school response to fighting and see whether some new alternatives might be warranted.

Unlike the bus stop, the school playground is supervised by adults. During recess and the lunch hour, elementary teachers are expected to protect children from abusive peers. This sounds like a relatively simple task, but teachers find it difficult because of the role they assign themselves. The problem begins when boastful children initiate comparisons and arguments. Among little boys the desire for power so often leads to disagreement and fighting that they can hardly be left alone without a reported misunderstanding. Typically, the little girls are quite willing to turn the boys in. It is at this point that the teacher first feels discomfort. Instead of viewing the situation in terms of helping children learn how to conduct conflict, the teacher's usual approach is to decide who is guilty and punish him. If the instigator cannot be determined, the teacher may punish both parties. Here the unintended lesson is that children's conflicts are to be handled by adult punishment rather than by negotiation. Moreover, punishment is not reserved for wrongdoers but is meted out to victims as well. In effect, the adult who trades the role of teacher for that of judge unintentionally exercises an abuse of power. Sometimes the young opponents are offered a chance to reconcile without punishment, providing they do so without hesitation. Obviously, people who are still angry with each other are not emotionally prepared to apologize. If we insist that they apologize, we invite a lie and in effect declare that, in our estimation, being polite is more important than being sincere. By this procedure, we encourage children to develop inauthentic relationships.

What these and similar teacher responses have in common is avoidance of worthwhile learning. Children could learn that anger is acceptable but its destructive expression is not; that disagreements are expected but coercion is not; that tolerable conflict is carried out by words; and that punishment is inappropriate for tolerable conflict. To achieve these more desirable outcomes, teachers would have to abandon their role as judges.

Instead, the children in conflict must judge themselves if they are to develop self-examination and self-control. Certainly the teacher will stop any physical confrontation and separate the parties. But, like angry adults, opposing children need some time apart to reduce anger and to reflect. There should be private places at school for this self-encounter to occur. Later, in the teacher's presence, the two children should hear each other's reasons for anger. The teacher can listen and raise questions while the children talk directly to each other. It is important that the children not talk to or through the teacher as if he or she were the decision maker, the judge. It is *their* conflict, and *they* are responsible for resolving it. Children who engage in this type of process are not led to feel guilty when they oppose others. Instead, in the presence of a concerned mutual friend, they can learn how to accept and express differences verbally without reliance on the abuse of power.

Some elementary educators do not regard themselves as accountable for instruction in how to resolve conflicts. Their position is illustrated by the teacher who only recommends changing the time or place of the battle: "This is not the place to fight—finish it after school." Other teachers express their reluctance to deal with conflict resolution by claiming that it is a job for the principal: "All offenders should be sent to the office, where they will be given a lesson." Still another group exempt themselves from accountability on the excuse that mischievous behavior is just a phase some people go through: "Given time, they'll grow out of it."

It seems that many elementary teachers rationalize why they ought not be accountable for conflict learning. Yet high school teachers are more concerned than ever before about students who are resorting to violence. Across the U. S. in 1976, police were called to investigate over 200,000 assaults by students on one another or on members of the faculty. In many cities the school itself has become a target. Nationwide, the annual cost of school vandalism approximates $500 million. In order to protect the faculty, students, and the schools, more and more communities have reluctantly adopted electronic surveillance, sentry dogs, parent patrols, security guards, and England's practice of housing custodians on the campus. Along with these defense measures a debate is growing over whether teenage lawbreakers should continue to be classified separately as juvenile offenders and be treated with leniency.

In my opinion, a key deterrent to delinquency involves the way peer abuse is handled during elementary school. It seems ridiculous to give young children the impression that they can abuse or mistreat one another until their physical size approximates our own and that only then must they adopt civilized methods for resolving conflict. Since boys and girls lack the maturity to teach one another peaceful means for negotiating differences, the instructional responsibility lies with adult teachers. Schools now identify students with learning disabilities as early as possible to help them succeed; yet we do not follow this line of reasoning where bullies are concerned, even though their misbehavior is easier to detect and the interpersonal problems they will encounter are predictable. Elementary school faculties should acknowledge their responsibility to teach personal-relations skills and in turn take the bully's problem just as seriously as if the child had some other disability that we feel more comfortable in treating. In the final analysis, when elementary educators do not reject violence and teach their students to do the same, they inadvertently support its continued expression.

It would be a mistake to assume that all peer abuse is physical. If we believe that self-concept is important, we ought to recognize'that little children take seriously the names they are called. They believe others see them as they label them. Thus, "Linda thinks I'm a dummy, because that's what she called me." The antique myth "Sticks and stones will break my bones, but names will never hurt me" applies to no one. Indeed, many adults think so much of their names that they would bring legal suit against slanderous peers. Again, should we permit those with the most fragile self-concept to be subject to the greatest abuse?

AN END TO AGGRESSION

Given the complexities of dealing with the abuse of peer power, some parents and teachers decide that the best goal is to eliminate aggression entirely. They express an aspiration like this: "Johnny must not turn out to be aggressive and bad." This way of thinking implies that aggression and hostility are synonymous, that all forms of aggression are undesirable, and that the causes of aggression should be determined and eliminated. Among the theories set forth to explain child aggression, three views particularly emphasize aspects of parent-child relationships. According to one theory, grown-ups generate aggression by creating any situation or relationship that brings the child frustration; to impose frustration and deny aggression is to court disaster. The second explanation stresses *identification*, by which the child models behavior after the parent; thus, the way in which a parent handles his or her own aggression influences the child's responses. The third explanation is that permissiveness in regard to aggression increases the child's tendency to behave aggressively. Notice that all three of these explanations center upon the *environment* and ignore the *biological* bases for aggression—namely, the child's need for separation and independence.

Naturally, I am not suggesting that we should view destructive aggression as good. My point is that, for personality to develop, some show of aggression is necessary; to root its explanation in the environment alone fails to fully account for its occurrence and its potential value. A more reasonable view is that aggression is inborn and will progressively decline in importance as human development proceeds. In other words, there seems to be a relationship between dependence and aggression. To be dependent upon someone or some group implies that they have a certain restricting power, which in turn can produce frustration and aggression. It follows that during childhood, when dependence and inequality are at their maximum, the maximum aggression will likely occur. As children become independent, more separate and differentiated from their parents, overt aggression naturally lessens. At maturity, only so much aggression exists as is necessary to maintain the personality as a separate entity. Furthermore, there will always be at every age level a wide variance among people in terms of their amount of aggressive behavior.

It is unfortunate that aggression is not generally considered as positively related to dignity and maturity when in fact any affirmation of the personality is aggressive. Most people find it difficult to think of aggression as having any meaning apart from hostility. Nevertheless, maturity is characterized by assertion of the personality without hostility or competitiveness. When parents and teachers lack maturity, they hinder a child's development. The less mature an adult is, the less that person can tolerate rebellion in children and the more he or she will require control and obedience. Grown-ups can easily induce the idea that it is wrong or dangerous to verbally oppose anyone else, but this suggestion encourages behavior that is damaging to the personality, because individuality implies opposition and differentiation. Without power there can be no identity; without identity there can be no mental health. Similarly, power and maturity are linked. There is no maturity in powerlessness; nor is there maturity in coercion. Only by encouraging the constructive use of power can we help children achieve both identity and maturity.

SHARING YOUR IMPRESSIONS

1. What do you remember from your childhood about peers who picked on you and how you coped with them?
2. What responsibility do teachers have to the victims of a bully? To the bully?
3. What should parents teach their children to help them deal with those who victimize them?
4. In what ways can siblings and other children help reduce peer abuse?
5. What is it about some children that makes them victims of bullies more often than other children?
6. What are the obligations of neighbors to other people's children?
7. How do you deal with mischievous children in your neighborhood?
8. Think of some ways for reducing the fears children have of their peers.
9. What are your feelings about corporal punishment in the school?
10. Comment on the growing problems of school vandalism.

REFERENCES AND SUGGESTED READING

Adams, Paul, et al. *Children's Rights*. London: Elek Books, 1971.

Bettelheim, Bruno. "Are They So Different?" and "Backyard Jungle." In *Dialogues with Mothers*. New York: The Free Press, 1962. Pp. 90–102, 169–171.

Bloom, Arnold. "Schools Combating Vandalism and Violence." *Inside Education*, March 1976, pp. 12–14.

Dreikurs, Rudolf, and Grey, Loren. *A Parents' Guide to Child Discipline*. New York: Hawthorn Books, 1970.

Elkind, David. *A Sympathetic Understanding of the Child Six to Sixteen*. Boston: Allyn & Bacon, 1971.

Fisher, Robert. *Learning How to Learn*. New York: Harcourt Brace Jovanovich, 1972.

Ginott, Haim. *Between Parent and Child*. New York: Macmillan, 1965.

Gray, Jeffrey. *The Psychology of Fear and Stress*. London: Weidenfeld and Nicolson, 1971.

Lee, Blaine, and Merrill, M. David. *Writing Complete Affective Objectives*. Belmont: Wadsworth, 1972.

Medinnus, Gene. *Readings in Psychology of Parent-Child Relations*. New York: Wiley, 1967.

Montagu, Ashley. *The Anatomy of Swearing*. New York: Macmillan, 1967.

Rachman, Stanley. *The Meanings of Fear*. Baltimore: Penguin Books, 1974.

Temple University Institute for Survey Research. *National Survey of Children: Preliminary Results*. New York: Foundation for Child Development, 1977.

BOOKS TO SHARE WITH YOUNG CHILDREN

Alexander, Martha. *Bobo's Dream*. New York: Dial Press, 1969. All victims agree that it would be a good thing to be protected from bullies. A large mongrel dog tries to take a dachshund's bone until the little one's master intervenes; then Bobo dreams about ways to show his gratitude.

Alexander, Martha. *I Sure Am Glad to See You Blackboard Bear*. New York: Dial Press, 1976. Sometimes imagination makes putting up with bullies more tolerable. When the neighborhood bully steals Anthony's ice cream, he calls on his faithful protector, Blackboard Bear, to help correct the injustice.

Cohen, Miriam. *Tough Jim*. New York: Macmillan, 1974. Bullies are often no match for smaller children if the younger ones stick together. The first-grade costume party promises to be fun for everyone, but then a third-grade bully comes along looking for a fight.

Poulet, Virginia. *Blue Bug and the Bullies*. Chicago: Children's Press, 1971. For some boys and girls, each school day means having to evade a bully. The blue bug is faced with a variety of bullies and must think of ways to get away from them.

Wells, Rosemary. *Benjamin and Tulip*. New York: Dial Press, 1973. Not all bullies are boys. Every time Benjamin passed Tulip's house, she threatened to beat him up; and she did just that until he came up with an unexpected truce.

ELEVEN

IMPROVING OUR
EXPECTATIONS

CHANGING EXPECTATIONS

Our ideas about parent education have changed. Until recently the issue was limited to what a husband expected of his wife. In the past a woman's concept of success was less ambiguous than it is now. Even if she didn't agree with the expectations, a mother knew what attributes were required to be seen as successful. Certainly she could not aspire to having more than one role during the years when her children were growing up. That the children needed her the most was obvious. After all, she was the parent endowed with intuition and feeling, those "uniquely feminine" characteristics that were thought to be essential for child rearing. Since nature was supposed to equip girls for their role in life, it seemed appropriate for them to receive less formal education than boys, whose occupational success depended upon training. The net result of the traditional division of labor within families was a limitation of the spheres of influence of both parents. It seems ironic now that many men actually believed that the perfect mate was one who would always see her husband as more intelligent and more able than herself.

Present attitudes offer a sharp contrast to the expectation that a good spouse is an ignorant one. Indeed, the alleged intellectual disparity between husband and wife has been recognized in West Germany as a cause of marital distress significant enough to merit the establishment of recuperation centers called Mother Schools. Most of the women who come to the 104 branches of the West-German Mother Schools report suffering from nervous strain. The program emphasizes self-understanding and self-improvement and includes instruction in how to read the news and discuss current events. In 1976, the organization spent $10 million to help 90,000 wives, many of whom confessed that their nervousness began when their husbands stopped communicating with them by declaring "There is no use talking to you—you don't understand a word that I am saying."

There have also been changes in the financial responsibilities expected of mothers. Whereas in 1920 employed females generally were single and came from the lower class, most of the women employed now are married, and employed women represent all socioeconomic groups; over two-thirds of them have child-rearing obligations in addition to their jobs. Under these conditions, it is not surprising to find a generalized discontent among mothers who feel that their share of the family work load has become excessive. Accordingly, fathers are being urged to reexamine their own role and the customary division of family responsibilities—to reconsider whether child rearing and other domestic tasks ought to be shared by both parents.

THE EXPECTATIONS OF ABUSIVE PARENTS

At the same time that men and women are beginning to modify stereotypic expectations of each other, they are also coming to recognize an obligation to learn more about their common role as parents. Recognition of the teaching potential of the home has created a new demand for parent education. This movement is not confined to helping families whose overall influence is considered deficient. An increasing number of programs and guidance measures, such as the Strom Parent As A Teacher Inventory, are intended to assist the already competent parent. Indeed, we are becoming convinced that education in child rearing is a good idea for almost everyone and that it should begin long before a person becomes a parent. Accordingly, the United States Department of Health, Education and Welfare has recently developed a curriculum for use in high schools to improve the competence of teenagers as prospective parents. These sorts of efforts reflect our decision that in the future it will no longer be sufficient for mothers and fathers to casually consider what they expect of themselves as teachers. Neither can their expectations of boys and girls be left to discovery. In short, there is a growing national mood that we cannot permit ourselves to be uninformed where child rearing is concerned.

Unfortunately, there is evidence that some families have

expectations that prevent normal child development. For example, the teenage parents who were studied by a Pennsylvania State University professor not only expected too much too soon from their infant children but also slapped, shook, and otherwise abused their infants for failing to meet these inappropriate demands. For three years, Vladimir DeLissovoy obtained information on the marital adjustment of 48 couples, all of whom lived in small towns or rural areas of Pennsylvania. The group was of average intelligence, with a mean IQ of 100. Most had left high school to marry; 46 of the 48 girls were pregnant at the time of their marriage.

To find out what the young couples knew about developmental norms, several questions were presented separately to the wives and husbands during home visits. At the time of inquiry, most of the couples already had a child; seven couples had children between 6 and 9 months of age. Each of the questions called for an answer stating the age in weeks at which a child can be expected to demonstrate certain types of behavior—for example, "How old do you think most babies are when they sit alone without any support?" In this manner expectations were determined for the ages at which babies smile, take their first step, speak their first word, and achieve other behaviors.

Let's examine the expectations of the fathers, whose own ages averaged 17 years. They thought babies would be toilet trained for bowel and urine control at 24 weeks (the norms for these achievements are about 65 and 130 weeks, respectively). According to the fathers, babies should be able to sit alone at 6 weeks (the norm is about 28 weeks), speak their first word at 24 weeks (the norm is about 52 weeks), and recognize wrongdoing at 40 weeks. By comparison, the mothers, whose ages averaged 16 years, were slightly more realistic. They supposed bowel training would be possible at 26 weeks and that the baby should be able to sit alone at 12 weeks, speak the first word at 32 weeks, and recognize right from wrong at 52 weeks. In order to put these results in perspective, the same questions were raised with a group of unmarried seniors attending the same rural high schools. The scores of boys and girls in this unmarried group were nearly identical to those of the married group.

If ignorance about developmental norms does not by itself

differentiate abusive parents, then what emotional factors account for their unreasonable expectations? In general, it seems that abusive parents were themselves denied a sense of being cared for during infancy and childhood. When they become parents, such people usually conclude that their own long-standing unfulfilled needs deserve higher priority than do the desires expressed by their children. This kind of thinking calls for a role reversal in the typical obligations of parent and child. Contrary to the popular impression that infants have a right to be dependent and to make demands, abusive parents feel it is the child who should be responsive and accede to the demands of grown-ups. Even the initiative for loving rests with the child, who should show affection by being compliant, neat, and quiet. When boys and girls are unable to satisfy parental demands for mature behavior, the usual result is adult anger and violence. Some children are beaten; others are stabbed or burned. According to the Pennsylvania study, abusive parents are able to justify repeated mistreatment because they assume youngsters are capable of adult motives and behavior. This is why an enraged father can preface the beating of his 7-month-old son by saying "He's been asking for this all day." Similarly, the entire population of mothers interviewed by DeLissovoy indicated that they regularly spank their babies for "misdeeds."

THE BATTERED CHILD

Although a generation has passed since we first acknowledged the "battered-child syndrome," many people continue to believe that the incidence of such cruelty is greatly exaggerated and is probably confined to families with mental illness. After all, what normal mothers or fathers could be so inhuman to their own offspring? Yet the fact is that in 1976 alone more than 150,000 youngsters in the United States were seriously mistreated by adults. According to figures compiled by the National Center for Child Abuse and Neglect, 3000 of these boys and girls were hurt so badly they died. David Gil of Brandeis University reports that about 48% of child abuse is done by mothers, 39% by fathers, and the remainder by relatives and parent substitutes.

The elimination of child abuse is a worthwhile but complicated task. To begin with, most victims cannot protect themselves, for they are under 12 months of age. These are the most demanding yet defenseless and nonverbal children. Although older boys and girls could describe the suffering they endure, most of them are reluctant to do so because of fear. When parents bring the injured party to a hospital or clinic, the story they tell seldom includes an admission of how the child actually was hurt. Given the limited information that troubled families provide about themselves, it seems imperative for outside informants to act on a child's behalf. Consequently, all physicians and most teachers are now required by state law to inform the proper authorities whenever they have reason to suspect child abuse. Informants are immune from any civil or criminal liability unless the report is made maliciously.

Our improved means for identifying victims have been accompanied by a change in attitude toward their parents. In the past a case of alleged abuse was usually considered closed once there was evidence of mistreatment. Since the accused men and women were presumed to be severely disturbed, the single solution was to take the children away. We now realize that most abusive parents lack impulse control and that they can be helped and need not lose their family. Professionals have found that in 10% of the cases separation of the child from the parents is still the only way to ensure a youngster's physical safety. However, for the remaining 90%, family rehabilitation can be effective. Parents can learn to comprehend and redirect the anger that ordinarily triggers abuse. They can become competent in child care and accepting of the parent role. Given these prospects, Congress passed the Child Abuse Prevention and Treatment Act in 1974, making $65 million available to develop programs for dealing with the increasingly difficult problems surrounding child neglect.

INFLUENCE OF THE EXTENDED FAMILY

One innovative approach to child abuse is taking place at the Extended Family Center in San Francisco. At this "home away from home," isolated parents are offered the resources of an extended family. The service that abusive parents need the most but receive the least is periodic relief from child care. To meet this need, the center offers free day care. The use of day care for abused children is a new and promising alternative. From the parent's standpoint, the chance to do something without the children and yet be sure they are being looked after is most gratifying. For the professional staff, day care is seen as a protective safeguard as well as an opportunity to teach children about successful relationships. At first the children typically distrust the teachers, abuse younger peers, and demonstrate that they don't know how to set limits on their behavior. Limit setting is a crucial but difficult objective for abused children to achieve, because they come from families that demand unquestioning obedience in a manner that prevents children from learning to control themselves. In time most of these boys and girls develop a confidence in their teachers, become more able to see worthwhileness in other people, and begin to develop the sense of trust they will need to establish intimate relationships.

A second objective of the Center is to develop the parents' reliance on one another. To appreciate the benefit of this extended family, we must bear in mind that abuse is episodic and usually occurs during times of family stress. Money problems, work dissatisfaction, even something as unrelated to the child as the failure of a kitchen appliance can precipitate abuse. As a rule children become the target for violence because parents do not perceive any other outlet. However, if parents can call each other, talk when they are angry, and feel comfortable about disclosing negative emotions, their aggression is redirected and loses its destructiveness. In order to help parents become more open about problems and better able to share feelings with other members of the extended family, two special consultants are on the staff. What makes this pair special is that they were once abusive parents themselves. These consultants fulfill a vital function in developing trust and communication between the parents and staff.

The counseling procedures in the extended-family program are another departure from tradition. Instead of an exclusive focus on group-therapy discussions about domestic problems, parents also undergo a form of occupational therapy generally reserved for the physically and emotionally handicapped. The unique value of occupational therapy for abusive parents is that it permits an assessment of their psychological functioning while giving them a satisfactory learning experience. Thus, when craftwork is used as a diagnostic tool, the process reveals characteristic aspects of the parent's development, such as the ability to complete a project, difficulty in relating to authority, lack of self-confidence, and willingness to try new tasks. Periodically the therapist holds individual conferences with parents so that they can understand their gains and identify areas in which they need to improve.

The San Francisco experiment is instructive in several ways. Its form of operation suggests that family rehabilitation ought to include day care for parent relief and child training, emotional support through an extended-family system, and guidance by means of occupational as well as group therapy. This broad approach has demonstrated that abusive parents can improve their expectations and become adequate models for children. Based on the success achieved thus far, there is reason to hope that if better parent education is made available for greater numbers of troubled families, more children can remain safe while in their own homes.

SHARING YOUR IMPRESSIONS

1. Describe a neglected or abused child whom you have known.
2. Make some guesses about what the adults involved in child abuse have in common. Then suggest some ways to minimize child abuse.
3. Children sometimes announce that they're going to run away from home, but until recently parents seldom did so. How do you account for the reported rise in missing mothers and fathers?
4. In your opinion, how does lack of communication between parents affect their children?
5. Recognizing from current statistics that divorce is a reality in the lives of many elementary school children, what should the schools be doing to help children understand something about the causes and meaning of divorce?
6. Parent education now focuses almost exclusively on pre-

school. Give some reasons for supporting the education of parents at other levels of a child's development.

7. Parent education is still in the formative stage. How should it differ from the education of certified teachers in terms of content and procedures?

8. Give some examples for the assertion that the U. S. is becoming an anti-child society. Then provide some reasons for being optimistic about the future of today's children.

REFERENCES AND SUGGESTED READING

Bernard, Jessie. *The Future of Motherhood.* New York: Dial Press, 1974.

Broeck, Elsa. "The Extended Family Center." *Children Today,* March-April 1974, pp. 2–6.

DeLissovoy, Vladimir. "High School Marriages: A Longitudinal Study." *Journal of Marriage and the Family,* May 1973, pp. 245–254.

De Mause, Lloyd. "Our Forebears Made Childhood a Nightmare." *Psychology Today,* April 1975, pp. 85–88.

Gil, David. *Violence against Children.* Cambridge: Harvard University Press, 1973.

Keniston, Kenneth. "Do Americans Really Like Kids?" *Childhood Education,* October 1975, pp. 4–12.

Kerby, Alvy. "Preventing Child Abuse." *American Psychologist* 30 (1975), 921–928.

Sandra. "An Abusive Parent Tells Her Story." *Caring,* Fall 1975, pp. 3, 4. Published by the National Committee for Prevention of Child Abuse, Chicago.

Spinetta, J. J., and Rigler, D. "The Child-Abusing Parent: A Psychological Review." *Psychological Bulletin* 77 (1972), 296–394.

Straus, Murray. *Family Measurement Techniques.* Minneapolis: University of Minnesota Press, 1977. Pp. 1–80.

Strom, Robert, and Slaughter, Helen. "Measuring Childrearing Expectations Using The Parent As A Teacher Inventory." *Journal of Experimental Education,* Summer 1978.

U. S. Department of Health, Education and Welfare. *Homestart and Other Programs for Parents and Children.* Washington, D. C.: Publications No. (OHD) 76-31089, 1975.

U. S. Department of Health, Education and Welfare. *Child Abuse and Neglect Research.* Washington: D. C.: Office of Child Development, May 1976.

Van Dusen, Roxann, and Sheldon, Eleanor. "The Changing Status of American Women: A Life Cycle Perspective." *American Psychologist,* February 1976, pp. 106-116.

BOOKS TO SHARE WITH YOUNG CHILDREN

Klaus, Robert. *Leo, the Late Bloomer.* New York: Windmill Books, 1971. Children are better off when parents accept their individual paces of development. Father is concerned about Leo's growing more slowly than his peers, but his mother urges patience, since she sees him as a late bloomer (and he is).

Noonan, Julia. *The Best Thing to Be.* New York: Doubleday, 1971. Parents who don't compare their children with one another make it easier for boys and girls to be themselves. Jonathan thinks of lots of ways he could be seen as special, but in the end he decides that being himself is best.

Skorpen, Liezel. *Charles.* New York: Harper & Row, 1971. Parents' responsibility goes far beyond merely providing children a place to live. Charles, the teddy bear, finds that just belonging to someone is no guarantee of happiness and that life becomes worthwhile only when one's caretakers set appropriate expectations.

Young, Miriam. *Peas in a Pod.* New York: Putnam's Sons, 1971. Parents who make themselves available to their children get to know them better. The father and son in this story choose to involve themselves in activities that urge both of them to share personal feelings.

Zolotow, Charlotte. *The Quarreling Book.* New York: Harper & Row, 1963. All parents have bad days, and as a result even the children can be adversely affected. Mr. James' problem is passed on to his wife, who in turn neglects the children.

TWELVE
THE MYTHOLOGY OF RACISM

In our society, Blacks, Chicanos, Puerto Ricans, and American Indians, among others, share a fear of rejection and a dream of social equality. Obviously, these fears could decline and the dream come true if the dominant culture would only abandon all racial prejudice. I do not intend to underestimate the difficulty of changing stereotypic expectations that have developed over many years. But I know it is possible for such expectations to be set aside once their origins are understood and seen to be unfair. For this reason, I am going to trace some features of the mythology about race to which most Whites have been exposed. This is the story of only one minority group—not the whole story, but a part of it that most of us know too little about.

THE PLANTATION BIAS

As a point of reference, look back at the Southern plantation culture and the influence its bias still has on Whites today. The adoption of slavery and the destruction of the Negro life-style were accompanied by both controversy and guilt. While abolition movements were succeeding in other parts of the world, slavery was embraced in the American South largely because the practice seemed economically and politically necessary. An important psychological adjustment for the Southern White involved a reconciliation of his economic need to exploit the Negro and the conflicting but natural need to perceive himself as a good person. This emotional accommodation was made possible, as are most such accommodations of incompatible values, by invention. That is, a new image of the Negro was created; he was for the first time endowed by fiction rather than by God as a subhuman being, whose natural inferiority justified servant status and allowed Whites to see themselves as benevolent caretakers.

Thus, one dimension was established. A group of enslaved people could be looked upon as subject to different rules and standards of conduct from those that governed real people; these were "niggers." To be sure, the new image did not correspond with fact, but the necessity of the untruth was that without it Whites would have found it emotionally unbearable to continue the practice of slaveholding.

It is also relevant that Puritanism was a dominant influence when the South was being developed. Because psychology, psychiatry, sociology, and anthropology had yet to be known, the interpretation of almost all behavior had a religious reference. Sin was considered a serious matter, the devil a real adversary, and the wayward self an inner enemy who had to be beaten down or exorcized lest one lose one's soul. Unlike the town-populated North, where there was a rapid decline in Puritan dominance and the attendant anxiety about hell and punishment in the after-life, the Southern plantation culture, consisting of widely separated families, retained the Puritan persuasion. Although they met in church, plantation families had, beyond the religious arena, little social interaction that would have allowed them to relax their mutual fears of damnation and the consequent practice of self-recrimination.

To complicate matters further, the plantation culture's White males became admirers of English knighthood. With Sir Walter Scott's *Ivanhoe* as a guide, the men modified their clothing to emulate the English gentry. As self-styled knights, these Southern cavaliers wore lace, plumose hats, and swords, and they rode horses without regard to the distance they had to travel. To support their desired self-image as hot-blooded, virile, chivalrous, and gallant heroes, the men fantasized their women as being delicate, chaste, magnolia-scented, in need of protection, respectable beyond belief. It is hard to imagine a more effective design for marital incompatibility. Whenever he was so inclined, the would-be knight could sustain his stereotype by leaving the house and visiting the slave quarters across the yard. That many Whites had illegitimate children by Negroes is well known. The historian Arnold Toynbee asserts that George Washington caught cold while on a sexual visit to his Negro quarters and that—although the fact is never written about in official biographies—this cold precipitated the illness that caused his death.

If any doubt remains concerning the sexual habits of plantation owners, a pertinent question should dispel them: Where have all the mulattos come from? Among American Negroes, how many African phenotypes have you seen? Since the proportion is very small, two possibilities exist: either there were many active White males—since White women were unavailable to African slaves—or there was a handful of White males whose sexual activities were beyond belief. Someone of Caucasian stock living in the South impregnated large numbers of Black females. In addition to children, these unions gave rise to the White mythology that one was not really a man until he had sexually taken a Negro woman.

Not surprisingly, this pleasure-principle reasoning undermined the White husband-wife relationship. For, as children began to appear in the slave quarters who resembled neither their mothers nor any of the males purchased to breed them, there was but one plausible source of paternity. The growing number of mulattos could be accounted for only in a way that left White women with hatred for the Negro and disgust for their own men. This circle of discontent was completed as the White man experienced his wife's natural rejection and the press of guilt imposed by prevailing religious values. Torn between what was considered moral behavior and what was known to be satisfying behavior, many men chose alternately to indulge and to rebuke themselves. To worsen the situation, the slaveholder's wife not only was unable to terminate her husband's extramarital relations but also had to accede to the persuasion that Negro women made the best mothers and therefore ought to be surrogates responsible for child rearing.

There was little that the Blacks could do, either. If the master or his son elected one's daughter or wife for his amusement, no recourse was open to the Negro male—except to dream, and translate the dream into folk songs. In the "Blue Tail Fly" chorus we hear "The master's gone away." The Black male had to deny his compulsion to protect the cherished female and could only feel a frustrated impulse to retaliate. Simultaneously, his daughter or wife would submit to sexual abuse knowing that neither she nor the menfolk could oppose the injustice without jeopardy.

FEAR OF REJECTION

Racist attitudes did not terminate with the Civil War, the Emancipation Proclamation, the Plessy-Ferguson case, or any of the subsequent Supreme Court desegregation decisions. As Whites migrated from the defeated South in search of improved economic opportunity, their prejudice toward Blacks was shared with persons who did not know Blacks themselves. Bear in mind that the appearance of Jim Crow in the North came *after* the Civil War and *before* the large-scale northern migration of Blacks during the first World War.

It is ironic that the fiction image of Negroes became dominant for Europeans—men and women new to this country who had never seen Negroes. In their native lands of Poland, Sweden, Russia, and Germany, there were no traditional attitudes toward Blacks. Yet, after only a brief time in the United States, Polish-Americans, Russian-Americans, Swedish-Americans, and German-Americans revealed a high degree of racial prejudice. This readiness to undervalue an entire subpopulation is best understood as a response to the anxiety experienced by many immigrants, especially those concerned about frequent allegations that they were not really Americans—that is, not native-born—and therefore not as worthwhile as the native. For the newcomers, unable to change their place of birth and hence their position as hyphenated Americans, the most feasible defense was to regard Negroes as a still lower population, a beginning base for favorable self-comparison. European immigrants, whatever their lack of facility in English, however low their income, however different and unaccepted their folkways, could at least lay claim to being White—an advantage of pigment only, but one seemingly worth the announcement.

One might suppose that the price of civil war and the memory of its victims would bring a decline in anti-Black bias. Since not more than 3% of the Blacks could read, their freedom was not to be feared as an economic or political threat. It was, instead, a psychological threat. The slave with whom one had sought sexual intimacy, the "subhuman" to whom one had entrusted the task of child rearing—this savage was loose; quite naturally, the White vision of Black freedom involved a projection. By *projection* is meant the common defensive mechanism whereby characteristics belonging to oneself are attributed to others; thus, projection is the practice of condemning in others unadmitted and unacceptable parts of ourselves. And so, concurrent with emancipation, a new Negro image emerged; the Black was one who attacked White women.

Remember that the slaveholder experienced the cold response, the withdrawal and rejection of his wife, owing to her knowledge of his extramarital relations. He had also sensed that the not-quite-human females—those whose refusal would have meant great jeopardy—did not seem frigid in his company. In comparing his sexual encounters, the White naturally wondered how his unresponsive wife might behave sexually were she with one of the "savages" rather than himself. This fiction completed the projection on which many of the thousands of post-Civil-War lynchings in the South were based—namely, an allegation of sexual advances by Negro men toward White women. ("He looked at her with the intent to rape!")

Sex remains a more powerful aspect of White racism than most of us care to acknowledge. It is expressed by the challenge "Would you want your sister to marry a Negro?" The fact that one's sister has the freedom to say yes or no never enters the racist's mind. What does obsess him is the knowledge that, historically, the White man has sexually exploited the Black female at will. And now there is psychological fear of retaliation. When lynchings did take place, the Negro was beaten, tied to a post, emasculated, and then burned alive—these barbaric abuses at the hands of people who saw themselves as proper citizens of the time.

UNDERSTANDING THE BLACK ASSESSMENT

Today, overt expressions of hostility toward Blacks are less common. However, the subtler forms of bias that remain in schooling, housing, and employment practices seem even less tolerable to Blacks than the earlier, physical atrocities. The militant stand by Negroes in recent years has puzzled some Whites who have not recognized that discontent is likely to be highest when misery is bearable, when conditions have so im-

proved that equality seems almost within reach. As he studied
the conditions leading up to the French Revolution, Alexis de
Tocqueville was impressed by the fact that in no period following
the 1789 uprising had national prosperity been so extensive as
it was during the two decades preceding the revolution. The
famous historian was forced to conclude that the French found
their position more intolerable as it became better. The same
circumstance may affect Black people; their life has improved
in recent years, but now they finally can envision the time of
equality as sufficiently close to want to hasten its arrival by both
violent and nonviolent pressure. During the confrontation period of the late 1960s, comedian Dick Gregory made a speech
before the students at Wesleyan University. He summed up
the bitterness and threat of civil war as follows:

> America ain't nothing but a cigaret machine now;
> you can't communicate with her. You know if you're
> running through the airport and put 40¢ in a cigaret
> machine, pull it and you don't get cigarets, that's a funny
> feeling when you can't talk to that machine.
> You go up to the ticket counter and say, "I just put
> my money in the cigaret machine." The girl says, "Look,
> I work for TWA; I just write tickets; I have nothing to do
> with that machine . . ." You go back to the cigaret
> machine and there is a little message there to tell you
> what to do if you blow your dough. "Welcome to Hart-
> ford, Conn. In case of problems with this machine, call
> Dick Jennings in Kansas City, Mo."
> Now you hear the last call for your flight and you
> stand there looking at that cigaret machine that you can't
> relate with and that's got your 40¢ and your flight's
> leaving, so you do the normal thing—you kick the
> machine. Pow! You didn't get no money, but you see the
> dent in it and feel pretty good.
> You go on down and get your plane feeling mellow.
> But let me tell you something, when you kicked that
> machine, if it had kicked you back, you would have
> cancelled your flight and taken the thing outside and torn
> it up in little pieces.
> America is a cigaret machine to us. We didn't put
> 40¢ in to get something that was going to make us
> sick—we put 400 years of our lives in that machine to get
> something that was going to make us well, and we didn't

get nothing and we went to every ticket counter and they
kept sending us to Kansas City. So in the form of Detroit
and Watts and Chicago and Hough, we kicked that
machine and in the form of the national guard and the
state police that machine kicked us back, and we're going
to do the same thing you would. We say, cancel the
flight, Charlie, we're going to tear this machine apart.

The potential for racial violence remains, but there has been
a favorable change. To be sure, we still face in the street, at the
high school, and on the college campus a number of humanists
who declare themselves unwilling to allow further anti-Black
prejudice. Thankfully, they perceive affirmative-action policies
as a better alternative than violence. However, in spite of noble
intentions, those who look upon the racial crisis as a civil-rights
struggle take too narrow a view. For most Blacks today, the
major obstacle to full citizenship is neither civil rights nor political franchise; it is economic equality. Indeed, if every barrier to
fair employment vanished immediately, all the cumulative barriers to equal opportunity would remain. The employment of
Blacks would not suddenly increase in proportion to job open-
ings, because they would lack the educational requirements for
available work positions. It is this inability to take advantage of
whatever possibility the law guarantees that defines the nature
of the problem after enactment of the historic civil-rights legislation. Although elimination of discrimination is a prerequisite for
equal opportunity, it is not sufficient; educational competence
must be achieved before economic equality can be realized.

If education is one of the means by which economic freedom
can become a reality for Blacks, more attention should be given
to the schools in which such learning is to occur. Unfortunately,
some Northern advocates of better education for Blacks in the
South seem unaware of where the greater number of Blacks
reside. More Negroes now live outside the Southern states than
within them. By contrast, at the beginning of World War II,
three of four Negroes in the U. S. lived in the South. The extent
of Negro movement out of the South and into the cities of the
North is shown by this statistic: it is estimated on the basis of
current population trends that in the 1980s the majority of the
population of seven out of ten of the country's largest cities

will be Black. These cities are Detroit, Cleveland, Baltimore, Chicago, St. Louis, Philadelphia, and Washington, D. C. Perhaps we see the withdrawal of urban Whites to the segregated suburbs of these same cities and the rising incidence of unemployment among Blacks as separate statistics. But for the Black they combine to spell "unwanted."

If this evaluation were ever in doubt, our experience with Title VI of the Elementary-Secondary Education Act would have confirmed the matter. Essentially, Title VI deals with enforcement of integration. Initially, almost all of the court cases were in the South; only a few were in the North. The present figures show litigation to be generalized throughout the nation. Although this resistance was forecast, few people expected that there would be major cities in which the majority of school-age White children would desert the public school system. Yet the fact that private-school enrollments have soared since enactment of Title VI is hardly a coincidence. Instead, it represents a prejudice of such enormous dimension as to fault anyone who suggests that his or her region, state, or even city is free of anti-Black bias. At this point even desegregation enthusiasts privately admit that things look more bleak than when their movement first began in 1954. And, depending on how the question is asked, the polls show that from a quarter to nearly half of all Black parents now oppose the busing necessary to create a racial balance in the schools.

THE URGENT ALTERNATIVES

Two factors require more widespread understanding. On the one hand, there is a need to recognize that the economics of automation are unaffected by color. Because Blacks are generally less educated than Whites, they are the first affected by the unemployment caused by automation. Since the need to exploit the undereducated does not exist in an automated society, Blacks find themselves not so much oppressed as unnecessary, not so much abused as ignored—unwanted and without identity. We cannot assess precisely the cost of self-denigration on the part of millions of unemployed Blacks, but we can be sure that it far exceeds the gain from civil-rights legislation. And we should realize that Negroes are a weather vane for the future in that their experience will become common among undereducated Whites as well. The longer we hesitate to confront the meaning of human dignity in an automated society, the more an increasing number of non-Blacks will feel the frustration that Blacks now feel. As more Whites join the ranks of the unemployed, the fiction that Blacks lack jobs because they are lazy can be maintained only with a new claim that some Blacks are being born White. So long as the focus is solely on civil rights, Southern bigotry moved North, and racial strife rather than on generalized economic dislocation, the proper emphasis will not be given to important questions about the economic ideology that justifies prevailing patterns of production and consumption—the merits and demerits of our philosophy concerning the distribution of wealth.

That we have not learned to adjust to a society of abundance is clearly shown by the level of sharing. Sharing seems foreign to us; most proposed benevolence encounters legislative resistance. Perhaps John Kenneth Galbraith of Harvard University was correct in asserting "An affluent society which is both compassionate and rational would no doubt secure to all who needed it the minimum income essential for decency and comfort." To document that we are a people proficient in reasoning, in being rational, is easy; to show that we are a compassionate people is difficult. The truth is that, had education provided affluent Whites with compassion, had our learning given all of us a sense of relatedness with all others in society and a consequent feeling of responsibility for their well-being, we would by now have resolved the welfare and racial crisis. Instead, because the process of education increases the ability to rationalize, we seem remarkably able to accept the existence of slums as well as the abuse and injustice faced by those who must live in them.

After spending years attempting to improve the education of low-income students, Ernest Melby of Michigan State University announced "It has begun to dawn on me lately even our grandchildren will have to do the same thing unless we change the education of the advantaged, the affluent, the White middle-class in such a way that they will not tolerate poverty, slums and racial injustice." I share Melby's perception that education of the advantaged is perhaps our greater problem and that it must be improved simultaneously with inner-city education. We have erroneously supposed that to make people literate is to make them human. The problem is that, without compassion, learned people sustain injustice, tolerate slums, and reject the less fortunate. As long as being advantaged essentially means being selfish, being reluctant to share affluence, being unconcerned about and unwilling to help others, for that long there will be a disadvantaged population.

SHARING YOUR IMPRESSIONS

1. What are some of the ethnic prejudices you were led to believe as a child?
2. Disclose some of the racial prejudices that are still with you.
3. Compare the ethnic prejudice of your children or students with that of boys and girls when you were growing up.
4. Share your thinking about busing as a means to achieve racial balance within schools.
5. What do you see as the best ways for helping children to grow up without racial prejudice?
6. What are your feelings about the worthwhileness of boys and girls having playmates of different races?
7. Identify some of the nonintellectual factors that influence academic success. How has each of these affected your own education?

REFERENCES AND SUGGESTED READING

Allport, Gordon. *The Nature of Prejudice.* Palo Alto, Calif.: Addison Wesley, 1954.

Bernard, Jessie. *Marriage and Family Among Negroes.* Englewood Cliffs, N. J.: Prentice-Hall, 1966. Pp. 1–25.

Bloomberg, Warner. "Prejudice and Its Antecedents." Address to the Racine, Wisconsin, Public School Teachers, March 17, 1967.

Galbraith, John Kenneth. *The Affluent Society.* Boston: Houghton Mifflin, 1958.

Gregory, Dick. Excerpts from a speech of April 1968 to the students at Wesleyan University, reprinted in *The Ohio State Faculty Peace News,* April 8, 1968, p. 4.

Hunt, Chester. "Patterns of Minority Group Adjustment." *The Educational Forum,* January 1975, pp. 137–147.

Hunter, William. *Multicultural Education through Competency-Based Teacher Education*. Washington, D. C.: American Association of Colleges for Teacher Education, 1974.

Melby, Ernest. "The Community School: A Social Imperative." *The Community School and Its Administration*, October 1968, pp. 1–4.

Scott, Sir Walter. *Ivanhoe*. New York: Heritage Press, 1950.

Staples, Robert. *The Black Woman in America*. Chicago: Nelson Hall, 1973. Pp. 35–72.

Strom, Robert. "Education: Key to Economic Equality for the Negro." *Journal of Negro Education*, Fall 1965, pp. 463–466.

Toynbee, Arnold. "Peace, Power, Race in America." An interview by J. Robert Moskin. *Look*, March 18, 1969, p. 26.

BOOKS TO SHARE WITH YOUNG CHILDREN

Alan, Sandy. *The Plaid Peacock*. New York: Pantheon Books, 1965. Some people begin to experience social rejection early in life because of their skin color. The young peacock in this story illustrates how victims of prejudice often respond with courage.

Beim, Jerrold. *Swimming Hole*. New York: William Morrow, 1951. All boys and girls should learn that their color does not make them any better or worse than anyone else. Because Danny is Black, he is left out—until the kids recognize that what makes you a better person is how you treat others.

Clifton, Lucille. *All Us Come Cross the Water*. New York: Holt, Rinehart and Winston, 1973. Teachers and parents should encourage children to feel proud of their racial origins. When Miss Willis asks her students to stand according to what country their family comes from, several Black boys are confused; so they try to trace where their ancestors came from.

Gorey, Edward. *Sam and Emma*. New York: Parents Magazine Press, 1971. Learning to value ethnic differences is essential for growing up in a multicultural society. Until she gets a valuable lesson, Emma always criticizes anyone whose habits or appearance are different from hers.

Udry, Janice May. *What Mary Jo Shared*. Chicago: Albert Whitman, 1966. Family pride can be an effective shield against racial prejudice. Mary Jo, a Black child, finds that bringing her father to school for show-and-tell is a good idea.

4

MODELS
AND
OBSERVERS

THIRTEEN
LIVING WITH CONFLICT

There is an old saying that "what you don't know won't hurt you." Many parents still live by this notion. For them, being a good parent means providing a conflict-free environment for children. Accordingly, they feel obliged to hide their conflicts behind closed doors so that their children will be unaffected. However, the fact is that young children are greatly affected by the unknown. During early childhood, imagination is more active than at any other stage in life. At the same time, preschoolers understand little about causation, what makes things happen. Because they daily encounter so many situations and events that defy their comprehension, it is natural for them to substitute fantasy where they lack information. By this process little children frequently enlarge their misunderstanding of parental conflict and assign themselves blame they don't deserve. Too many children believe that they are the cause of their parents' dispute when in fact they're not even being discussed.

Children's unnecessary guilt is not the only consequence if parents conceal their differences. When children are not allowed to witness the disagreement of grown-ups at home, they are deprived of a model for conducting conflict. Because they don't learn conflict resolution from their family, some children must rely on immature peers, who have little of value to teach them. This is a disastrous tradition, because it leaves youngsters totally unprepared for the demands that a conflict culture will make of them. Understanding how to accept and express differences is absolutely essential to the growing-up process in a diverse society, and its learning cannot be left to chance.

VIEWS OF CONFLICT

Until recently, the general tendency in most cultures has been to take a dim view of conflict. Faith systems, utopias, government, and social sciences all present this impression. Most religions regard salvation as a state of rest in which there are no unsatiated needs, no basic grudges or grievances. Similarly, the visions of earthly paradise that we call utopias usually start from the premise that everyone is essentially alike. According to this simplistic model of human experience, social structures can be designed to ensure universal satisfaction. Although we know that people tend to be unique, changeable, and inconsistent, those who construct utopias are seldom influenced by the diversity of human beings. In politics, conflict is acknowledged, but attempts are often made to terminate it as soon as possible. One method is to get rid of the opposition, perhaps by defining them as dishonest, subhuman, or as enemies, so that they can be distrusted, segregated, or even killed. Then there is the more refined, democratic way of permitting those with whom we disagree to organize themselves as a party and then proceeding to ignore them, since they are eliminated culturally by being out-voted. Again, in all the social sciences, from the emphasis on what happens inside a person to studies dealing with the human condition at the international level, the basic views have often been that people try to escape from conflict and that conflict is necessarily bad.

Norwegian researcher Johann Galtung, at the University of Oslo, points out that both the social conditions today and the forecasts for tomorrow urge us to look at conflict differently. The fact is that we are going to have more conflict in the years to come instead of less. In the first place, there is a worldwide breakdown of homogeneity. Until now the idea has been that people living in the same territory should be of the same kind—ethnically alike and, in more modern terms, members of the same nation. But the tendencies toward mixture are increasing much faster than ever before. A rising number of people identify with more than one country because they have a foreign spouse, have studied abroad, have lived overseas, or perhaps have worked for an organization with offices throughout the world. Then there are the international groups and ideological associations that bridge national borders. All these dislocations of classical patterns of loyalty are growing rapidly, and they make the way of structuring large-scale conflict less obvious. To make matters even less clear, we are witnessing a global mass migration toward centers of urban development. The net result is that people on almost every continent will increasingly find that their neighbors look different from themselves and act differently as well.

The second reason we can expect increasing conflict stems from the rejection of coercive management. All over the world, institutional dictatorship is being challenged as underdogs unite. Organized groups bring the power of their cohesion to bear against the traditional power of authorities through direct confrontation—in prison, by inmates; at universities, by students; in factories, by labor unions.

Another reason we will experience more conflict lies in our relationship to the future. For both nations and individuals, there is great uncertainty and at the same time a sense of new possibilities. Because of technology, it appears to be more in our power to shape the future than ever before. However, as technology makes a greater range of goals possible, we are forced to decide on what goals ought to be achieved and on the order of their importance. In this context a distinction between morality and intelligence perhaps no longer has merit. Already many of the social issues we are expected to resolve invite a contradiction between our feelings and our thinking. For example, we can choose to protect the environment or abuse it, to feed the hungry or neglect them. People disagree about the goals we should pursue, the changes that should be made and the priorities that deserve to be adopted. Particularly in democratic countries, where diverse opinion is acceptable, there is bound to be continuous conflict.

VIEWS OF CONFLICT RESOLUTION

In addition to the world breakdown of homogeneity, the erosion of institutional power, and our new relationship to the future, certain traditional ways of resolving conflict are breaking down. One customary method of dealing with conflict has been to repress it, partly by denying that it existed, partly by not discovering it. This expedient seems less possible in an open society, where many social scientists are allowed to make the society transparent; if we do not see a conflict, they will describe it to us. Once ritual was a useful technique, but our technological society has left ritual behind. Wars have moved toward the prospect of total annihilation, but we have made little progress in preparing ourselves for nonviolent alternatives.

Yet there is also reason to be optimistic about meeting the challenges arising from increased conflict. At the University of Michigan and at University College in London, a science of *conflictology* is emerging that draws on insights and techniques developed in the social sciences, from psychology to international studies. Schools are expected to gain much from this new science. Almost every investigation that has been conducted regarding teachers' despair and low morale highlights their concern about discipline—how to control students or to avoid conflict. A disagreement between students and teachers has usually been interpreted in terms of deviance rather than growth. It is relevant to observe that until recently critics outside the school accounted for most of the pressure to change education. Today, however, students are considered an influential group. Young people no longer assume that their objections to the school need to remain private; nor do they believe that dissatisfaction with the educational process can best be expressed by dropping out. Instead, students now prefer to negotiate as a group with teachers, administrators, and boards of education about the conditions they judge to be inappropriate. The science of conflictology can help all the parties to such encounters be more successful.

Another promising development involves new curricula. The teaching of history is a highly indirect form of conflictology that gives students an insight into conflicts of the past but not of the present. Because technology will allow us to shape some aspects of the future, there may be much conflict over which plans are most desirable. To bring about the best tomorrow, training in the design of alternative futures should begin during childhood. Some elementary schools already offer courses in futurism. Students in these courses are urged to go beyond the problem-solving ethic of looking for fault, limitation, and weakness. They are encouraged to think about the possibilities for our future, to consider many life styles and environmental options. "There are two sides to every issue" is usually an understatement in a heterogeneous society. Gaming as an educational experience also deserves mention. It is used in business and industry for recruitment, training, and promotion. Through certain kinds of simulated games, students can learn how to solve conflicts without having to suffer the consequences of a real-life situation.

Many educators are realizing that, rather than sending children involved in a conflict to the principal's office and relying on the administration to settle all student and faculty differences, the parties themselves should be brought into the task. In order for the benefits of conflict management to occur, we need to legitimize self-assertion without imposing guilt, withdrawal, or apology. Since conflict affects us all, conflict management belongs to everyone. It is unfortunate that some self-proclaimed experts in human relations are people who regularly avoid conflict, press guilt upon others for engaging in conflict, and lead people to believe that the emotional expression of opposition describes persons of limited intellect. Certainly, if we seek collaboration among neighbors of different cultural backgrounds, we should expect conflict. If we ask people to be honest about their feelings, we should anticipate conflict. If we educate children to assert their individuality, we should expect the expression of divergent thought. These natural forms of conflict contribute to human development.

"Children need to know much more than they learn now about coping with conflict." When this goal is stated in general terms, it may seem vague or overwhelming. However, when we divide the goal into a larger number of manageable tasks, a better picture emerges of what conflict learning is all about. In addition, some lessons the school should emphasize and other lessons should be learned at home. In both settings, the way for parents and teachers to begin is by choosing the objectives they are willing to pursue. For example, the goals presented here each deserve consideration; taken together, they outline the ability to live successfully with conflict.

Recognizing that people who love each other may conflict

Learning to share things and to take turns

Learning to express differences without resorting to coercion

Learning to assert oneself without feeling regret

Learning to accept role changes without guilt

Realizing others have the right to work without being disturbed

Recognizing that respect for personal property reduces conflict

Realizing that helping others may involve conflict (not watching or standing back)

Learning to substitute verbal for physical response

Learning to accept changes in other people

Developing an ability to compromise

Learning how to compete and how to accept losing

Learning to stand alone if necessary

Learning to live with uncertainty

Learning that self-conflict is necessary for moral behavior (conscience)

Learning that self-conflict is necessary for self-respect

Learning that creative behavior and ambiguity go together

Learning how to conduct conflict without loss of status or affection

Learning that conflict can provide alternatives

Recognizing conflict as an opportunity to learn about others

Learning to tolerate a variety of views

Accepting the possibility that some conflicts cannot be resolved

Learning to listen to the feelings and opinions of others

Learning how to analyze a conflict situation

Learning to share dominance, to cooperate

Learning to cope with the unfamiliar

Learning to accept authority

PARENT MODELING

Given the kind of training most parents received in school and at home, they are naturally reluctant to assume the role of models for conflict. Part of the reluctance to teach ways of dealing with conflict arises from the hope that the future will be devoid of international conflict, a time of world peace. Certainly, most everyone wants peace. But, while peace means the absence of war, it will not bring an end to differences or conflict. Rather, peace means learning to accept differences and placing reliance upon the constructive forms of conflict—negotiation, discussion, and collaboration. Recently, more parents have begun to see that the conditions for interpersonal conflict are maximized in our society of increasing leisure, ethnic diversity, and urban crowding. They also recognize that schools are trying to encourage individual differences rather than to eliminate differences and that, since the resulting conflict can support learning, we ought to appreciate its constructive potential.

Yet the feeling of incompetence makes even these parents

unwilling to become conflict models. By their own admission, they just don't know how to constructively work out their own differences and are therefore unable to teach what children need to learn. That many adults require greater learning in how to live with differences is apparent. One has only to note the size of domestic-court dockets or the incidence of litigation between neighbors to confirm that withdrawal is still the dominant reaction to disagreement. Increasingly people are turning to the single subpopulation that has been schooled in conducting conflict. Rather than learn to resolve our own conflicts, it is easier to announce "My lawyer will speak for me."

The most unfortunate result of these common reactions is that they effectively prevent us from growing up, from developing respect for others. One criterion for a mature relationship is that the other party is seen as a separate person whose perceptions and judgments should be honored when they vary from one's own. Given this recognition, perhaps we should abandon the view that the good parents are those who conceal disputes from children and lead them to believe that life is essentially free from frustration and conflict. A better approach is to follow several guidelines for helping children live with conflict. First, we can recognize that self-assertion is a healthy way to achieve identity and that it is essential for making ourselves known. Unlike coercion, which is the imposition of our will upon others, self-assertion is simply the statement of how we see things and what we stand for. Only through this kind of self-disclosure can intimate and lasting relationships be developed. Secondly, we can recognize the relationship between creativity and conflict resolution. Children need to retain their ability to see many possibilities in a situation if they are later to do well in resolving conflict. This is not so much a matter of our teaching them as it is of our accepting and encouraging their early preference for divergent thinking. If we invite boys and girls to self-disclose and to continue using their creative talent, they will also learn from our behavior why acceptance is an integral feature of conflict resolution.

SHARING YOUR IMPRESSIONS

1. How did your parents feel about conducting conflict in your presence when you were a child? An adolescent? Now?

2. How do you feel about arguing or expressing differences with another adult in front of your children or students?
3. Why do you suppose so many of us tend to fear interpersonal conflict?
4. We seldom view the conflict of children in terms of possible benefit. Identify some types of conflict that youngsters experience, and consider how these encounters can support personality development.
5. Which goals of conflict learning seem more possible to reach in the home? On the playground? In the classroom?
6. How can parents and teachers help young children better understand the place of conflict in human relations?
7. In what ways do the changes resulting from technological advances stimulate conflict? How might this kind of conflict contribute to emotional growth?

REFERENCES AND SUGGESTED READING

Bach, George, and Wyden, Peter. *The Intimate Enemy.* New York: William Morrow, 1969.

Cuber, John, and Harroff, Peggy. *Sex and the Significant Americans.* Baltimore: Penguin Books, 1968.

Dedring, Jaergen. *Recent Advances in Peace and Conflict Research: A Critical Survey.* Beverly Hills, Calif.: Sage Publications, 1976.

Ekman, Paul, and Friesen, Wallace. *Unmasking the Face.* Englewood Cliffs, N. J.: Prentice-Hall, 1975.

Fromm, Erich. *The Anatomy of Human Destructiveness.* New York: Holt, Rinehart and Winston, 1973.

Galtung, Johann. "Conflict as a Way of Life." *Progress in Mental Health: Proceedings from the Seventh International Congress on Mental Health*, edited by Hugh Freeman. London: J. & A. Churchill, 1969.

Gelles, Richard. *The Violent Home: A Study of Physical Aggression between Husbands and Wives.* Beverly Hills, Calif.: Sage Publications, 1974.

Lederer, William, and Jackson, Don. *The Mirages of Marriage.* New York: W. W. Norton, 1968.

Nesbitt, William. "To Simulate or not to Simulate." *Intercom*, Summer 1974, pp. 2–11. Published by Center for War-Peace Studies, New York.

Raths, Louis, Harmon, Merrill, and Simon, Sidney. *Values and Teaching.* Columbus, Ohio: Charles E. Merrill, 1966.

Strom, Robert. "Educating Teachers for Collaboration." *Educational Leadership*, January 1971, pp. 373–376.

Sullivan, Judy. *Mama Doesn't Live Here Anymore*. New York: Arthur Fields Books, 1974.

Sarraillon, Carol. "Battered Women: A Major Problem with Few Solutions." *Interaction*, April 1976, pp. 11, 14.

Yankelovich, Daniel. *The General Mills American Family Report 1974-1975: A Study of the American Family and Money*. Minneapolis: General Mills, Inc., 1975.

BOOKS TO SHARE WITH YOUNG CHILDREN

Mayer, Mercer. *Boy, Was I Mad!* New York: Parents Magazine Press, 1969. Learning to forgive and forget makes for better mental health. This story shows how natural it is for all of us to get mad and why most of us can't stay that way for very long.

Supraner, Robyn. *It's Not Fair*. New York: Frederick Warne, 1976. Sibling rivalry can upset parents for years unless they learn to cope with it. When the family always sides with little brother Andrew, his big sister decides there must be some way to achieve justice.

Udry, Janice May. *Let's Be Enemies*. New York: Harper & Row, 1961. The best relationships are ones in which people express their feelings honestly. John plays with Jim a lot and doesn't want to lose their friendship, but sometimes it's necessary to protest Jim's behavior.

Zolotow, Charlotte. *Big Brother*. New York: Harper & Row, 1960. Some parents unreasonably expect brothers and sisters always to get along without conflict. The big brother in this story delights in teasing his little sister, but then she helps him discover other ways to enjoy being around her.

Zolotow, Charlotte. *The Hating Book*. New York: Harper & Row, 1969. When people are angry with each other, they should realize that it isn't the best time for them to talk. After her daughter argues with a friend, mother wisely suggests letting some time pass and then trying to talk again.

FOURTEEN
HEROES IN THE SCHOOL

Everyone dreams of becoming a hero, but for most of us the opportunity never seems to arrive. Instead we can only wonder whether public acclaim would go to our heads or leave us unaffected. Teachers, however, are a notable exception. Because of their jobs, they can count on being models, heroes, and objects of infatuation. Nevertheless, when confronted by a student who seeks an intense emotional attachment, teachers are typically puzzled about how to react. The usual question is "Should I be flattered or express disappointment or just try to ignore the student?" In order to decide what to do about infatuation, it is helpful to understand the reasons that account for its occurrence among students.

Being attracted to the teacher is a normal experience for children between ages 5 and 7. During this period boys and girls are reducing their dependence on parents and quite naturally transfer some feelings of affection to the teacher. A somewhat different motivation initiates the attachment that is likely to occur in junior and senior high school. In order to break childhood ties, an adolescent needs to find emotional gratification outside the family. Since girls begin the maturing process earlier than boys, male teachers are more often the subject of teenage infatuations.

Whatever the student's age or sex, a strong attraction to a teacher does not necessarily mean that the teacher is an unusual or inspiring individual. Unfortunately, some teachers—particularly if they lack emotional satisfaction in their own lives—may reciprocate the intense feeling of an admirer by flirting, spending extra time with the student, or exempting the student from class assignments. Regardless of how favoritism is shown, it can interfere with the learning of an entire class. Youngsters are sensitive; when they feel the teacher is neglecting them in favor of one or two students ("teacher's pets"), they resent it and commit themselves less to learning.

The decision to ignore a student admirer may be well intended, but this also invites the student to fantasize, to distort the relationship by misinterpreting the teacher's motives. A better approach than saying nothing is to confront the student kindly and without embarrassment. The teacher can explain the infatuation as being a normal expression of strong needs that he or she respects. At the same time, the teacher should point out how this attachment can interfere with learning and encourage the student to make education his or her major concern until affection can be found in a more realistic way elsewhere. An honest discussion about feelings of closeness gives the teacher an opportunity to put them into proper perspective and to help the student move toward satisfaction in other avenues of school life.

Parents often wonder what to do when they see an adolescent daughter or son developing an infatuation for a teacher, especially one who doesn't seem to know how to handle the situation. It may be tempting to offer disparaging remarks about the teacher and then point out why such a person is undeserving of anyone's admiration. However, this tactic is seldom effective, and it forces the young person into a defensive role, thus making the infatuation even more difficult to give up. Parents can help most in this situation by encouraging their son or daughter to invite friends of both sexes to the house and to go with mixed groups to school functions and community events.

THE TWO CULTURES

Some models, of course, are not classroom teachers. Here the importance of nonacademic and extracurricular activities deserves attention. I was disappointed when in 1975 the city of San Francisco announced that it would solve its schools' budget-deficit problem by declining to offer physical education for the ensuing year. Ordinarily, when an austerity move is taken, it begins with a scaling down of the offerings in art, music, or physical education. Perhaps the most saddening aspect of the San Francisco case was the response of other teachers in the school system. They might have decided to forego some proportion of their regular salary so that the physical-education instructors could be retained. But in general their reaction was one of relief that the cut did not include science or reading or whatever they taught. By their silence these teachers gave the impression that they too saw little merit in the subjects that do not prepare one for a job.

We should remind ourselves that the school has two cultures—one *expressive* and the other *instrumental*. According to Robert Havighurst, a University of Chicago educator, the instrumental culture is made up of those activities that lead to the skills, knowledge, and values that are stated as goals of schooling. A student participates in the instrumental culture for the sake of obtaining or achieving something outside of and beyond the process of study and learning—to be promoted, to be praised by the family, to get a diploma, to become a doctor or an engineer. The school consists in part of a set of instrumental procedures that produce an individual who is a reader, mathematician, or master of a foreign language. On the other hand, the expressive culture at school includes those activities that students take part in for the sake of the activity itself rather than for some purpose beyond the activity. The games children play at recess, intramural athletics, art, music, and so on are all part of the expressive culture.

Although the expressive culture sometimes involves the learning of knowledge and skills, these outcomes are generally not as important as they are in the instrumental culture. Children can enjoy singing in the chorus, working with clay, or playing volleyball without acquiring much knowledge or skill. The criterion of success is not so much how well they can do as it is how much they enjoy doing it. To be sure, the instrumental culture sometimes has expressive impact—for instance, when a student learns to enjoy reading or performing science experiments or doing multiplication and will do these things for their own sake. Conversely, there is an instrumental undertone to most expressive activities. But students usually distinguish the expressive from the instrumental culture. Since most students can succeed in the expressive culture, where there is not such rigorous and explicit competition, it follows that this realm is especially good for teaching values. In this context some youngsters can learn to appreciate school, to become committed to learning, to value successful participation in the expressive as well as in the instrumental culture. Then, too, even the parents with little formal education can take part in the expressive aspects of school without embarrassment.

There are various combinations of success and failure in the expressive and instrumental cultures of the school. The social and intellectual development of a student depend on his or her particular combination of successes. A high level of success in both cultures is characteristic of the good student who also finds satisfaction as a social leader. A high instrumental/low expressive combination describes the bookworm who is socially invisible but does well at scholarly pursuits. A low instrumental/high expressive combination defines the mediocre student who still is able to obtain satisfaction at school because of participation in extracurricular activities. There are young people whose interest in athletics or band is the only incentive for staying in school. It is foolish to tell such persons that unless they maintain a "B" average on the instrumental side they can no longer take part in the expressive realm. Finally, a low instrumental/low expressive combination represents the students who can find no satisfaction or reward in the school. Often these youngsters decide to quit formal education as early as legally possible.

Through a creative use of the expressive culture, the school can become a place of satisfaction for more children, and it can teach certain values more effectively as well as improve performance within the instrumental culture. A dramatic illustration of these possibilities was recorded a few years ago in New York City. The setting was Junior High School 43, located in a slum section of Harlem. About 50% of the student body were Black, and nearly 40% were Puerto Rican. The most successful half from the entire school population of 1400 were selected to participate in the Higher Horizons project. These students had a median IQ of 95 and were, on the average, a year and a half below grade level in reading and mathematics. Instead of increasing the amount of time these students spent on math or reading by eliminating the so-called "frill" areas of education, an opposite approach was taken. That is, a number of motivating influences from the expressive culture were introduced to increase satisfaction with school and desire for learning. The boys and girls were brought to sporting events, concerts, and movies. They went to parks and museums and on sightseeing trips.

Follow-up studies showed that the project members who entered senior high school graduated in substantially greater numbers than had those from the same junior high school in pre-project years. Furthermore, 168 of the graduates went on to an institution of higher education, compared with 47 from the three classes preceding the experiment. It seems that the expressive activities gave rise to some important value changes in the experimental group that in turn led to improved performance in the instrumental culture. Findings like these ought to cause more of us to take the extracurricular, the nonacademic, the expressive aspects of schooling far more seriously than we do. That students in higher education sense this need is made obvious by their increasing enrollment in noncredit classes such as belly dancing, bicycle care and repair, blackjack, indoor gardening, Hatha yoga, non-loom weaving, occult science, self-hypnosis, photography, macrame, beginning water color, and Scottish country dancing.

A HIERARCHY OF NEEDS

We turn now to what models can do for those who admire them and choose to act as they do. Models are in a unique position for influencing others to adopt a life-style balanced between instrumental and expressive involvement. The necessity of such a balance for each of us can be demonstrated in terms of mental health.

According to biologist Robert Ardrey, human beings have three innate needs, all of which demand satisfaction. As shown in the diagram, our highest need is for identity, the opposite of anonymity. Below identity is stimulation, the opposite of boredom. Security is the lowest need; if it is unfulfilled, the result is anxiety. Our society may be without precedent in enabling the largest proportion of a society's people to achieve security and the smallest fraction ever to attain identity. This massive failure to ensure our highest need can be explained in part by unemployment due to automation, by the nature of jobs in large, impersonal organizations, by unfair competition in schools, and by life in overcrowded neighborhoods. Whatever the reasons, identity has eluded millions of anonymous beings for whom there is no rank, no territory, and no sense of significance.

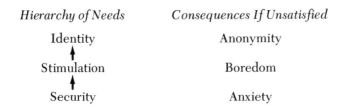

Hierarchy of Needs	*Consequences If Unsatisfied*
Identity	Anonymity
↑	
Stimulation	Boredom
↑	
Security	Anxiety

Achievement of security and release from anxiety presents us with boredom, the psychological process least appreciated by social planners. We are only beginning to see something of the chaos that a bored society can produce. Of course, massive boredom could not exist if we were other than a technological people with little chance to preserve identity. The knowledge that we have influence and are respected is the appeal of identity. Among animals this need is met by territory or social rank. But for ourselves, imprisoned by affluence and anonymity, stimulation appears to offer the only escape from boredom. It is more than coincidental that shock and sensation have arrived at the same time in most industrial countries. The frustration of boredom triggers a high growth rate for pornographic pictures, fantasy drug trips, adolescent sexual adventures, casual adultery among the married, nudity on the stage and screen, petty theft by affluent burglars, topless and bottomless attractions, music to assault the senses, violence for kicks, and street vocabulary by literary figures. All these and other nuances provide stimulation for the members of bored societies who have nowhere else to go to escape boredom.

In certain of the economically poor nations, people must settle for the security-anonymity combination. But in the United States we are committed to enabling individuals to achieve identity. We need not give up this goal, but there may be good reasons for reconsidering the path to identity. During recent years the prevailing view has been that, in order for more people to feel they are important persons, we must create an increasing

number of awards, trophies, and titles. Although this approach
has in some cases met the need for recognition, in other cases it
has made the quest for recognition insatiable. I believe that there
is a more promising alternative. We can make identity possible
for a greater number of people by removing the barriers to their
involvement in the expressive culture. Our government has
begun to support this view and is serving notice that girls will no
longer be denied access to team sports. Title IX of the Elementary and Secondary Act also calls for making instrumental music
available to students who seldom participated in the past because
parents could not afford it. These and other legislative efforts to
reduce the scope of sex and economic discrimination are commendable. But even laws that guarantee equal opportunity will
not greatly increase participation in the expressive culture so
long as youngsters are led to exclude themselves. And this is
precisely what happens when they are taught to regard the
outstanding performers of an activity as the only ones who deserve to participate.

The use of a restrictive standard for determining who is
worthy to participate begins early. It can be observed among the
very young in little-league sports. Similarly, within the classroom, teachers feel obliged to "find out what the student is good
at and encourage tasks calling for that particular strength." In
effect, the message is that everyone ought to limit themselves to
those leisure pursuits in which they excel. It follows that, unless
students are identified as having extraordinary talent in athletics,
music, or art, they should withdraw, because the quality of their
performance will not support a favorable self-impression. Under
these conditions it is no wonder that many children reluctantly
conclude "I like spending time in this way, but I'm not good
enough to continue." Thus they give up certain activities that
could have provided them with life-long satisfaction.

Adults often experience the same pressure to subordinate
enjoying an activity to achieving competence in it. To illustrate,
four "good" golfers are waiting behind the first tee for the couple
ahead to begin play. As it happens, the couple are not avid
golfers, so each of them drives the opening shot just a short
distance. The waiting foursome then wonder aloud "What are

they doing here?" as if to say that the only people who belong on the golf course are highly skilled players. The less serious persons who want to play for fun ought to reconsider and become spectators. As spectators they can watch the expert few and perhaps in the process experience at least a vicarious sense of identity.

It has taken a while to learn an important lesson, but we now know that in the future identity cannot be reserved for persons of uncommon achievement. Adult models have a special obligation to bring about the necessary transition. Parents who are anxious about the occupational futures of sons or daughters may not recognize the need for a balance of academic and expressive activities. Consequently, they often urge the school to reduce or give up expressive offerings. In turn, when teachers are held accountable for scholastic attainment only, other important aspects of a student's personal development are neglected. By encouraging all students to participate in the expressive culture for fun, we can help them develop self-esteem and avoid boredom.

SHARING YOUR IMPRESSIONS

1. Recall some of the social fears you had as a teenager.
2. What are some worries that bother the adolescents of both sexes? What are some concerns that are more common among boys? Among girls?
3. Make some suggestions for parents and teachers about ways to help teenagers who lack self-confidence.
4. Try to recall who your heroes were during adolescence.
5. Who are the heroes of adolescents today? What qualities do these heroes represent?
6. What is the function and importance of heroes during childhood? Adolescence? Adult life?
7. How can parents deal with a youngster's hero worship, especially when they disapprove of the hero's values?
8. Describe a personal observation of student infatuation with a teacher.
9. Comment on the influence extracurricular activities have on students in the upper elementary and high school grades.

REFERENCES AND SUGGESTED READING

Ardrey, Robert. *The Social Contract*. New York: Dell, 1970.

Berman, Sidney. "Crushes: What Should You Do about Them?" *Today's Education*, December 1969, pp. 12–15.

Branden, Nathaniel. *The Psychology of Self Esteem*. New York: Bantam Books, 1971.

Fromm, Erich. *Escape from Freedom*. New York: Holt, Rinehart and Winston, 1964.

Goldman, Ronald. *Breakthrough*. London: Routledge and Kegan Paul, 1968.

Havighurst, Robert. "Overcoming Value Differences." In *The Inner-City Classroom: Teacher Behaviors*, edited by Robert Strom. Columbus, Ohio: Charles E. Merrill, 1966. Pp. 41–56.

Howsam, Robert. *Now You Shall Be Real to Everyone*. Washington: American Association of Colleges for Teacher Education, 1976.

Jourard, Sidney. *The Transparent Self*. Princeton: Van Nostrand, 1964.

Langdon, Grace, and Stout, Irving. *Homework*. New York: John Day, 1969.

MacKinnon, Donald. "Maslow's Place in the History of Psychology." *Journal of Creative Behavior*, 6 (1972), 158–163.

Maslow, Abraham, *The Farther Reaches of Human Nature*. New York: Viking, 1971.

Morris, Desmond. *The Human Zoo*. New York: Dell, 1969.

BOOKS TO SHARE WITH YOUNG CHILDREN

Anglund, Joan Walsh. *The Brave Cowboy*. New York: Harcourt, Brace & World, 1959. Children should be encouraged to imagine themselves as heroes. This little boy's many adventures in the Old West include meeting up with Indians, rattlers, and buffalo.

Cohen, Miriam. *The New Teacher*. New York: Macmillan, 1972. Teachers can be worthwhile heroes for children. All the first-graders are anxious about the substitute who will take over for their teacher when she goes on leave.

Lexau, Joan M. *Me Day*. New York: Dial Press, 1971. Children of divorce sometimes identify the absent parent as a hero. Rafer believes his birthday will be spoiled because dad no longer lives at home, but the boy underestimates his mother's sensitivity.

Rowe, Anne. *The Little Knight*. New York: Lothrop, Lee and Shepard, 1971. Children need to realize that courage and compassion do not depend on a person's physical size. Only the littlest knight is brave enough to enter the cave and confront the fearsome dragon—who turns out to be sad and lonely for friends.

Shortall, Leonard. *Tony's First Dive*. New York: William Morrow, 1972. Recreation teachers who are not part of the school system often become heroes. Tony was reluctant to take swimming lessons and had some unpleasant experiences before an interested lifeguard earned his confidence.

FIFTEEN

LEARNING TO TRUST
TEENAGERS

The fear of being an unsuccessful parent is common. Most of us try to do a good job, but doubts and anxieties arise whenever we hear reports about the growing incidence of drug taking, venereal disease, and juvenile crime. It isn't strange, therefore, that couples who are newly married struggle with the question "Do we want to take the risks and assume the responsibilities that go with having a family?" Insofar as risk is concerned, there is much evidence that success as a parent is still not only possible but likely when mothers and fathers establish and maintain a close relationship with their children. If would-be parents suppose it probable that in time their daughter may become an unwed mother, a drug addict, or a fugitive from the law, they are discounting their role as potential models in her life. In effect, they acknowledge that peers and the media will have a dominant role while supposing that the home will be without influence. On the contrary, many studies show that parents are the primary influence during early childhood and that, depending on the continuing relationship, their prominence as models may be sustained or lost.

If a person concludes "I'd have to do a lot to be a successful parent; therefore I'm unwilling to assume the role," his or her reluctance is warranted. Many mothers and fathers believe that bringing up children today requires more parental involvement than it did only a few years ago, whether in an intact family or in a single-parent home. In the past the extended family, including grandparents, uncles, aunts, and cousins, helped with child rearing. Moreover, a sense of *communal* obligation for the well-being of youngsters was more common. Whereas neighbors used to know one another better and felt comfortable in offering advice to other people's children, the tendency now is to regard parents as the only proper source of correction and non-institutional guidance. Accordingly, parents reason "If our daughter doesn't turn out right, we will be considered at fault."

Before we examine the ways in which parents reveal their feelings about adolescent accountability for behavior, we should consider a little further the role that goes with being a neighbor. A sense of obligation in this sphere is what people are lacking when they argue "We don't have any children, so don't blame us for the sad state of youth." This self-exemption from favorable influence shows up when we see someone else's children in need of help and excuse ourselves from responding with "Why should I bother? After all, they're not my kids. It's up to their parents to look out for them." Certainly the decision to avoid having children is unrelated to our responsibility as citizens. Any of us can choose to be childless—or, as some couples prefer to call it, child free—but we cannot elect to belong to a society and yet remain unconcerned about its other members. Contrary to tradition, boys and girls can no longer be seen as the personal possessions of their families. In an urban, mobile society all grown-ups are responsible to some degree for the safety and direction of the young.

SONS AND DAUGHTERS

There is a long-standing dispute over whether girls or boys are the most difficult to bring up. There is no doubt, however, about which sex parents prefer their unborn child to be. Consider a recent national survey conducted by Candida and James Peterson of Northern Illinois University. They were trying to find out how widespread the effect of the feminist movement for sex equalization had been. One indication, the researchers thought, would be whether people's preference for male children had changed over the years. This would probe an area of sex discrimination that most people were totally unaware of and that might affect a child even before birth. The Petersons compared their findings with those of a similar survey made 20 years ago. The results showed that 90% of men and 92% of women wanted their firstborn to be a boy, compared with 93% of men and 90% of women in the earlier survey. When asked about the preferred sex of an only child, 81% of men and 64% of women wanted a boy, compared to 92% of men and 66% of women in the original study. The most striking difference over two decades was the decline in men's preference that an only child be male. Perhaps this decline may be attributed to economic factors. Men are no longer the only breadwinners; daughters as well as sons are now commonly employed.

Whether the parents of teenagers still agree with their original sex preference is unknown. However, any professional who works on a regular basis with the parents of high school students has been exposed to their anxieties about daughters. The availability of contraceptives, increasing peer pressure for intimacy, and the presence of drugs combine to make girls more vulnerable than in the past. Parents vary in the kind of sex education they offer adolescents. Some mothers are able to answer unashamedly all of a daughter's questions and at the same time to help develop the needed sense of responsibility. Unfortunately, another group of mothers contend that it is best to warn girls, to tell them about men and "what they're after."

Things are not much easier for fathers when they try to tell sons about the facts of life. Clearly, sex education is a task that parents need more help with than they have been given. It is time to acknowledge that children have more misconceptions about sex than about almost any other subject. Boys, especially, get most of their information from older peers who pretend to know more than they actually do. Since it's not cool to admit ignorance, older boys usually make up answers to preserve their image of being well informed and experienced. The results of this kind of peer teaching are disappointing. Nevertheless, the situation can be expected to continue for as long as youngsters remain afraid to ask their parents for information about sex and parents feel uncomfortable supplying it.

One promising alternative is the growing number of short sex-education courses designed for separate mother/daughter and father/son pairs. For example, the Mesa, Arizona, YMCA focuses its course on the needs of fifth- through eighth-graders. During the initial session, a number of exercises are used to improve communication. For example, a mother is obliged to tell her daughter about a feeling she has experienced, and the daughter tries to repeat it back. The mother then realizes how easy it is to be misunderstood where sex is concerned. In later sessions a pediatrician talks about sexual functioning of the body, contraception, and venereal disease, and then takes questions from the parent/child partners. Guilt feelings about sexual practices such as masturbation and premarital sex are considered. Various clergymen are brought in for one session to express their views on the moral implications of sexual behavior. Chip O'Hern, the project director, reports that the reason most frequently given for liking this educational method is that in a group setting it is less embarrassing for both parties. The course does not push particular sets of moral standards. Instead, the attempt is to present fact rather than myth, to promote further family discussion, and to offer young people new questions to think about.

Regardless of the approach to sex education, all parents find that sooner or later what adolescent girls and boys want most is to be trusted. Since trusting someone requires that we relinquish control of their behavior, we can claim to trust only those persons who are allowed to reach their own conclusions and make their own decisions. It follows that parents fail to trust when they regularly insist on deciding for teenagers. Moreover, without trust there are fewer chances for the development of wise decision making.

SIGNS OF TRUST

Some parents are oblivious to their lack of trust if it takes any form other than accusation. To them it does not appear inconsistent to tell their daughter "We trust you, honey, but we can't say the same for your friend Dick." Much to their surprise parents may find that an adolescent interprets this remark to mean "We don't trust *your* choice of companions." And it is true that some of us would prefer to pick our daughter's boyfriends for her. But we cannot; besides, a close examination might reveal that the criteria we would use are no more worthwhile than her own.

Another expression of trust involves respect for the privacy of adolescents. Unfortunately, some parents wish to make their trust contingent upon their daughter's self-disclosure. In practice, this usually means that she is expected to provide some kind of narrative when she returns from a date. Predictable and disappointing consequences follow this approach. For one thing, the teenager's feeling of romance disappears when it is interrupted. A college freshman remembers "Many times I would have liked to have come in quietly from a date and gone right to bed so I could make the spell last a few more minutes. But not a chance. I had to pass by the kitchen and the living room, where my father and mother both would be waiting, always with questions, comments, and advice." On some occasions, girls may decide that they are unwilling to substitute a discussion with parents for the self-encounter they feel should follow a date. As it happens, parents sometimes misread their daughter's reluctance to tell them everything and suppose that her failure to report means that she has something to hide.

Interrogation often disqualifies parents from the role they most desire, that of confidants. It is true that teenagers commonly feel a need to express in words the mysterious impulses and sensations they experience, but in most cases the listener they choose is someone about their own age with similar feelings. So, bosom friends share everything. Of course, they may frequently whisper to keep the communication private. The longing to verbally express secret thoughts also accounts for another phenomenon of adolescence—namely, the keeping of a personal diary. Obviously, an inexperienced pal cannot fulfill the guidance function of a mature parent, but, as teenagers see it, neither can mothers or fathers who lack trust. This impression underscores how trust and sharing go together. If parents withhold their trust from children, the young will in turn refuse to share what is happening in their lives. Since the outcome is a decline in family intimacy, everyone is poorer when parents lack trust.

There is a great difference between telling a daughter or son "I don't trust you" and saying "I am afraid for you because . . . ." Surely the fears of a parent deserve to be heard, while to announce trust is seldom necessary. According to teenagers, the number of parents who lack trust is very large. This decline of trust in our children and in our society coincides with the growth of cynicism. Cynicism always prevents trust. Rather than describe people who still trust each other as being naïve, it is important for each of us to determine whether we have lost the ability we once had to see the best in other people. For example, students in my classes sometimes ask "Just how honest should a teacher be?" I find that what they really mean is "Under what conditions is dishonesty justified?" Usually this is indicated by the second part of their question: "Do you realize what would happen if I were to be honest with all students, parents, colleagues, my husband—everyone? It would be disastrous." People who frequently contend that they would like to be honest if the cost were not so great are in effect making it known that most of their perceptions are negative—that they undervalue many of the people with whom they associate and therefore regard dishonesty as necessary to prevent the dangers that would follow a disclosure of their feelings. On the other hand, optimistic teachers or parents do not fear the cost of honesty about feelings, because they tend to value people and to see them, the world, and their own circumstances in terms of possibilities rather than limitations. In this respect they resemble very young children, whose preference for looking at life in an intuitive way provides them with a nearly constant optimism and sense of trust—the bases on which mental health depends. In many families, parents need to recover a sense of trust if they are to experience the respect of their adolescent children.

SHARING YOUR IMPRESSIONS

1. As an adolescent, how were your dating intentions judged by your parents? By other adults?
2. Compare the worries of parents who have adolescent daughters with those of parents who have sons.
3. If you could have children "made to order," what qualities and characteristics would you want your child to possess?
4. What effect has the pill had on parent fears about adolescent sexual behavior?
5. Comment on the possibility of a collaboration between home and school to provide sex education.
6. Provide some examples for your opinion on whether the level of parental trust has changed in recent years.
7. How can parents demonstrate their trust to teenagers?

REFERENCES AND SUGGESTED READING

Bardwick, Judith. *Psychology of Women.* New York: Harper & Row, 1971. Pp. 47–69.

Calderone, Mary. "SIECUS, The Sex Information and Education Council of the United States." *SIECUS Newsletter*, New York, 1974.

Deutsch, Helen. "Puberty and Adolescence." *The Psychology of Women.* New York: Bantam Books, 1973. Vol. I, pp. 94–152.

Dinitz, Simon, Russell, R., and Clarke, A. "Preferences for Male or Female Children: Traditional or Affectional?" *Marriage and Family Living*, 16 (1954), 128–130.

Evans, Wayne. "Mind Altering Drugs and the Future." In *Education for Affective Achievement*, edited by Robert D. Strom and E. Paul Torrance. Chicago: Rand McNally, 1973. Pp. 191–199.

Fromm, Erich. *The Revolution of Hope.* New York: Bantam Books, 1968.

Keller, Suzanne, and Lindberg, Siegwart. "When Parents Can Choose—Which Sex Will It Be?" *The Futurist*, October 1972, pp. 193–196.

Lanouette, William. "Should We Have Kids?" *The National Observer*, April 10, 1976, pp. 1, 14.

Neubeck, Gerhard. *Extramarital Relations.* Englewood Cliffs, N. J.: Prentice-Hall, 1969.

Peterson, Candida, and Peterson, James. "Preference for Sex of Offspring as a Measure of Change in Sex Attitudes." *Psychology*, May 1973, pp. 1–3.

Pomeroy, Wardell. *Your Child and Sex.* New York: Dell, 1974.

Roberts, Robert. *The Unwed Mother.* New York: Harper & Row, 1966.

Strom, Robert. "The Psychosexual Significance of Puberty." *Psychology for the Classroom.* Englewood Cliffs, N. J.: Prentice-Hall, 1969. Pp. 388–406.

Williamson, Nancy. *Sons or Daughters: A Cross Cultural Survey of Parent Preferences.* Beverly Hills, Calif.: Sage Publications, 1976.

BOOKS TO SHARE WITH YOUNG CHILDREN

Kruss, James. *The Zoo That Grew.* New York: Platt and Munk, 1968. As a society becomes more interdependent, the need to trust other people grows. Harry's parents gave him a farm, which he turned into the friendliest zoo in the world.

Lexau, Joan. *Finders Keepers, Losers Weepers.* Philadelphia: Lippincott, 1967. Older children are sometimes trusted as babysitters. Amanda's brother was supposed to be watching her, but, when she lost mother's frying pan and another girl claimed it, the trouble began.

Moore, Lilian. *Too Many Bozos*. New York: Golden Press, 1960. One way parents demonstrate their trust is by allowing children to become responsible for a pet. Danny Drake wants a dog more than anything, but convincing his mother isn't easy.

Sonneborn, Ruth A. *The Lollipop Party*. New York: Scholastic Books Services, 1967. In many families children arrive home from school before either of their working parents. Mother isn't in the apartment when Tomas gets home from kindergarten, and his high school sister must leave him to go to work.

Zion, Gene. *The Plant Sitter*. New York: Harper & Row, 1959. Children can benefit from taking care of a friend's possessions. Tommy is being trusted to take care of neighbors' plants this summer, but, when they grow large, he is faced with gardening problems and a grumbling father.

SIXTEEN

THE FUTURE OF GRANDPARENTS

People who express an interest in learning about the future sometimes overlook the fact that their own aging is tomorrow's most predictable event. What each of us thinks about growing old can determine whether our perspectives of the years to come are favorable. Moreover, children who don't spend time with elderly people are missing a valuable source of guidance. For these reasons, I make the following remarks to children by way of urging them to spend time with the elderly.

Some children know what it's like to be left out because they're considered too young. Being left out can happen to the oldest people as well. We call these people the elderly. Like yourselves, the elderly don't like to be left out. And they won't be, if we get to know them and understand their important place in our lives.

Most young children don't know much about the elderly, but you have a lot in common with them. For instance, you like people to listen when you tell about things that have just happened. The elderly like people to listen when they tell about what happened a long time ago. You like to ask many questions; the elderly like to have children ask about their opinions. You like to listen to stories; the elderly have many stories to tell. You like to be watched while you play; the elderly like to watch children. Both of you—the young and the old—have a special ability to listen and talk at the same time.

But what you don't have in common is even more important. As children you are the most imaginative and the most optimistic of all people. The elderly are the most grown-up, or, as we sometimes say, the most mature. These are good reasons to get together. You should allow yourselves to know elderly people, so that they can help you grow up. And it's important that they get to be with someone like you to fulfill their responsibility to society. The elderly people in your life may be grandparents, neighbors, or people at church. What matters is that you spend time together. If parents arrange for this opportunity, all of us will benefit.

Although most children and old people are willing to test the value of my recommendation that they meet, young parents usually want a more detailed explanation before they are willing to get the polar generations together. Accordingly, it is important for them to learn what is happening to elderly people today, how the role of grandparent has changed, and the consequences of this change for all of us.

BECOMING A BURDEN

People have always wanted to live a long life, to be respected, and to decide for themselves how to use their time. In certain ways this common dream is becoming more attainable. Already there are 22 million people in the United States who have reached age 65. This is about as many as are under the age of 6. For most of the elderly, leisure has replaced employment. However, their need for self-respect remains unmet, largely because our traditional view of dependence has not been revised to accommodate the implications of an increasing life span.

People's ideas about dependency vary according to the cultures in which they have been raised. Unfortunately, most older Americans have been led to see their normal dependencies as an indication of moral weakness, a sign of regression, or a reason to die. These negative interpretations are underscored by results from a study of self-esteem among elderly people in San Francisco. The criterion they most frequently cited for self-evaluation was independence, or at least lack of dependence in any sphere of life. Statements by the 435 participants had an almost frantic quality when they referred to the need for preserving autonomy in order to maintain self-respect. In their words: "It's very important that I not become a burden to my family." "I was taught to stand on my own two feet, to take care of myself." "I'll starve before I take any charity and lose my pride."

It seems that most elderly people have learned to equate self-respect with independence and failure with dependence. Accordingly, they are at war within themselves. During their earlier role as parents, they insisted that their children learn and practice self-reliance. As a result, the current generation of middle-age adults tends to believe that dependency, except in young children, is weak, immoral, and un-American. Yet these same advocates of independence, if they live long enough, will really need other people. This situation represents a serious discontinuity in our society that does not exist in many other cultures. In effect, the self-concept and even the physical survival of older people are threatened by their continued commitment to the values of an individualistic society that no longer has a place for them.

Apparently, one of the key developmental tasks an aging person must face is learning to accept dependency. However, since it is unreasonable for someone to abandon lifelong values without support, the necessary adjustment will involve the rest of society too. A number of changes are in order if we are to allow the elderly their need for independence while at the same time helping them to gradually accommodate dependence. In general terms, this transition will require that people of all ages, including children, recognize the rights and obligations of later life.

We can begin by enlarging the range of legitimized dependency to fit the longer life span. Whereas a baby born in 1900 had a life expectancy of only 47 years, today's children can expect to live about 72 years or more. Yet our society continues to sanction only those dependencies that occur relatively early in life, such as infancy, childhood, and pregnancy. Surely it is now appropriate to add aging to these developmental stages, each of which is predictable in terms of occurrence, timing, and approximate duration. Of course, crisis-related dependencies such as illness, divorce, or death are seldom predictable. But for either type of dependency, our practice has been to regard the period as temporary and to expect that it will be followed by a resumption of independent activity. Obviously, this philosophy of living was developed before the phenomenon of retirement became common; yet it continues as a dominant influence. Given the time limit we impose on periods of dependency, old age is considered a legitimate reason for assistance only if it is of relatively short duration. Those who are uncooperative about "dying on time" are perceived by their children and themselves as burdens.

During the past generation, our society has accepted a rationale that justifies the neglect of older people—namely, that, left to themselves, the elderly can escape the status of burdens. It is well known that children in the U. S. are encouraged to pursue happiness and to honor their obligations toward spouse and children. But, unlike many other cultures, our society allows adults to ignore any responsibility for their aging parents. Since our culture is strongly oriented to the future and the present, services granted us in the past do not bind us to the provider for very long. This means that parents are expected to take care of their children, who years later will reciprocate by providing for their own children instead of also giving back to the parents. Although some families do take care of older parents, Social Security and Medicare were enacted largely because many individuals are unwilling to do so. Fewer than 20% of the old do not have adult children. Certainly most of us would be insulted by the suggestion that our motivation for bearing children was that they could care for us in later life, even though, in other times and places, this was an accepted practice. Now children are planned so that parents can have the satisfaction of watching them grow into self-reliant persons. Few people today anticipate that their children will have to look after them in the future. The value has thus been developed that, while caring for children can be a pleasure, caring for elderly parents is not a pleasure. So we are bound to the old neither by direct cultural demand nor by the feeling that we can sustain a mutually rewarding relationship with them.

THE RETIREMENT VILLAGE

Because being a burden inconveniences the older person's adult children and lowers self-esteem, it can be predicted that, the stronger the desire for family respect, the greater the older person's motivation to remain independent. Under these conditions, it is not surprising that approximately 85% of the elderly choose to live elsewhere than with relatives—twice the population of elderly who lived alone in 1950. It seems ironic that, at the same time that there are more old people, they are more alone. Often the cost of their decision to manage on their own is extreme loneliness, but it is nevertheless considered appropriate

by the women and men who strive to retain their cherished ideal
of independence. Bear in mind that the chances that your marriage partner will precede you in death are five times greater if
you are a woman than if you are a man and that less than 1% of
elderly widows remarry. In addition to the debilitating effects of
loneliness, some older people adopt a preference for isolation.
To be sure, isolation guarantees privacy, and it enables one to
avoid unpleasant encounters, but isolation also increases vul-
nerability to accidents, illness, malnutrition, and despair. These
are high prices to pay for the knowledge that the less attention
an older person demands, the greater the pride of that person's
family.

Unable to live comfortably with their families, many older
people are choosing instead to live among peers. As a result, the
number and size of retirement villages have grown rapidly since
1960. In Arizona alone, the aging population has risen over 80%
during the past decade. Most younger adults believe that life in
an age-segregated community, such as the Sun City or Leisure
World communities in Arizona, must be uniform and dull.
However, a nationwide survey conducted by the University of
California Gerontology Center reveals that most older people in
the U. S. prefer to live in a community inhabited largely by
people their own age. To account for these contrasting perceptions, we must bear in mind the loss in roles, norms, and reference groups that accompany aging.

During childhood, boys and girls are encouraged to "act
your age." What this advice implies is that, at least for the initial
stages of life, there are relatively predictable sets of expectations.
But once beyond adolescence the scarcity of our knowledge of
normal human development forces us to substitute our occupation or educational setting and the relationships required there
as a normative base of expectations for our behavior. Still later,
when age dictates retirement, many individuals find themselves
for the first time lacking a guide or reference group for their
behavior. To be without norms is to be alone in the worst sense,
since one does not know the proper criteria by which to evaluate
oneself. This is especially critical during later life, when what
little one has learned about aging supports fear. Thus, to be old
and to lack norms is to wonder: "Do other people my age have

the same problems with their bodies? Am I different or about where I should be for someone my age? Am I healthy or sick?" For many of the elderly, the need to use a physician as a substitute source of norms is shown by their high frequency of office visits where there is no evidence of organic disease.

For certain people, the consequences of role and norm loss can be fatal. This danger was first recognized almost a century ago by the French sociologist Émile Durkheim, who set out to determine what causes people to take their own lives. When his analysis was complete, Durkheim suggested that the major cause of suicide is intense loneliness, coupled with a lack of clear expectations resulting from a marginal social position. We know from more recent research that suicide is often the consequence of a loss of roles, a loss of norms, and a loss of reference groups. It is more than coincidental that suicide rates beyond adolescence show a larger increase after age 60, especially among men, than for any other age group. Marv Miller of the University of Michigan studied all the cases of older White men who took their own lives in Arizona between 1970 and 1976. The results point to role and identity losses at retirement as having a significant influence. It was also learned that physicians and relatives must become better able to detect and respond to signs of desperation. For example, Miller observed that three of every four suicide victims in metropolitan Phoenix had visited a physician within a month before death; 60% of the victims presented verbal or behavioral clues to their family. But these indicators either went unrecognized or were not taken seriously.

If normlessness leads to self-destructive behavior, how can we compensate for the inevitable loss in roles that people will continue to experience upon retirement? Sociologist Irving Rosow at Western Reserve University contends that age-segregated housing is the answer. He argues that older people in this country are disadvantaged by their lack of roles and normative expectations. Because they have few recognized functions and fewer norms to guide their conduct, one way for increasing norms is to deliberately create an age reference group by means of residential concentration. In bringing the elderly together, the retirement village can be valuable for socialization into old age and for the development of age-appropriate expectations.

THE ROLE OF THE ELDERLY

Whether the elderly live alone or in a retirement complex, what matters most is how they assess themselves and the consequent importance they attach to their lives. Two factors usually combine to threaten favorable self-concept. One is the anticipation of becoming a burden; the other is a retreat from obligation. In the first instance, the condition of becoming a burden actually means involuntary assignment to a social status that is lacking in what can be termed *role reciprocity*. Lack of role reciprocity amounts to being seen as having nothing to offer others in return for their care. Obviously, if because of age an individual is defined as having nothing of value to trade, then any claim that person makes on others is evidence of dependency. This is indeed expecting something for nothing. And given our culture's emphasis on self-reliance, anyone making a claim for dependency can expect to suffer persistent guilt.

To escape this dilemma, we must realize that whether a class of people are believed to have something of value for exchange is largely a matter of cultural definition. Some cultures believe that the elderly can and should contribute to society. Researchers in Ecuador, Hunza, and the Caucasus have tried to determine why people in these places often live much longer and remain more vigorous than in most modern societies. In the estimate of Soviet gerontologist G. E. Pitzkhelauri, who has studied some 15,000 persons over age 80, the persons who stay well the longest and think most highly of themselves are those who remain active in serving society. Similarly, in primitive cultures the status of the aged depends on serving the younger members in exchange for subsistence and protection. Unless disabled, the elderly are assigned certain tasks and therefore have something of value—by cultural definition—to trade. It is important to note that both parties view this arrangement not as unilateral dependency but as a mutually rewarding relationship.

The reciprocal-role concept appears to be successful in nonindustrialized societies, but can our society learn to incorporate the talents of its elderly? I believe that the answer depends on how deeply committed we have become to a youth-oriented way of life. If we continue to be frightened by the prospect of old age and by the possibility of being out of touch with the times, then we will agree that it's best to banish the elderly. Conversely, if the elderly are not to be heard or taken seriously, they will leave us in even larger numbers for an exclusively peer-oriented arrangement. If we see aging as just another social problem, we will welcome this migration to retirement villages. If we believe that the young can avoid spending time with the old and still understand the past, still learn what benefits maturity can bring, and still prepare themselves for their own aging, then the elderly can be said to have nothing of value to offer us. In fact, within a youth-worshipping society, the elderly can be regarded as superfluous people, and as such they may be expected to stay out of sight.

On the other hand, if we can see human development as many other cultures do, then we can view life as concluding with a final sense of integrity, a sense of wisdom, and a mature philosophy of living that deserves to be shared. If we can look at life in this way, as a total rather than as worthwhile only during its initial stages, then we can make the shift from a youth-oriented society to a humanistic society, a society in which we value people for themselves instead of placing a premium on their age. Then the elderly will be honored, and we can belatedly begin to profit from their experience. That many of the retired want to remain active is illustrated by the response to a recent appeal by the Sun City hospital for local volunteers. Although only a few persons were needed, the number of residents who volunteered was more than 1200.

At the same time as we alter our evaluation of the elderly, many of them will need to change their view of themselves. In particular, they must recognize that retirement does not signal the end of responsibility to society. Unfortunately, many retirement communities do not support the mature intentions of their founders, especially when it comes to the need to continue being useful. Instead, some of them have become places in which people are led to abandon their sense of obligation in favor of a constant pleasure schedule. In my judgment, this phenomenon is an overreaction to the elderly person's disengagement from the labor market. During the occupational years, we stress the idea that only a job will validate self-importance. Later, as retirement approaches, the financial independence to do what one pleases is considered the key to future self-regard. The fact is that at every age, however long we live, our obligation to others is what generates their respect for us. As more of the elderly abandon the claim that they don't owe anyone anything, the younger members of society must decide what it is the old can give us and which roles we will entrust to them.

The need to enrich life at the same time as we try to prolong it is reflected by the formation of senior-citizen groups. One example is known as RSVP, an acronym for the Retired Senior Volunteers Program. Men and women who take part in this nationwide, federally supported organization believe that retirement should not signal the end of their responsibility to society. Instead, the participants want to learn how to cope with free time, how to retain a sense of pride in themselves, and how to enjoy rather than resent the years that remain. RSVP attempts to place senior volunteers where their talents can be shared with other people. While serving on the Board of Directors for RSVP in Phoenix, I noted that most of the participants have in common a history of volunteerism. During their younger years, these people experienced a sense of obligation and satisfaction as they worked without pay on various community projects. For them it seemed natural to devote even more time to such worthwhile activities once they retired. On the other hand, retired persons who reject a chance for community service usually report feeling that it is unjust for them to do any work without getting paid. As a rule these folks spend their retirement years in a state of discontent, claiming they *would* be happy if only society allowed them to remain on the payroll of some employer.

Some among the elderly have learned better than the rest of us that there is more to life than having a job, controlling others, and winning in the marketplace. More than any other group, the elderly have been able to reduce their pursuit of competition in favor of our society's secondary values, which have been around for just as long: conservation instead of acquisition and exploitation, concern for others instead of dominion over them, cooperation instead of self-seeking acclaim, and self-acceptance instead of a continual struggle for status. These are the behaviors they have to offer and also the ones we desperately need. Therefore, I hope that teaching the young is one of the first tasks we will expect of the elderly. By taking this step, we acknowledge that mature influence has a place in the education of children and that older people have an obligation to share themselves. The question is not "Can the old still learn?" but "How can we ensure that they share with us what they already know?" In one of her poems, Edna St. Vincent Millay said "Life must go on. I forget just why." We can change this impression for many of the elderly by bringing them back into our lives and in the process gain something ourselves that cannot be found elsewhere.

SHARING YOUR IMPRESSIONS

1. What are some of the ways in which your grandparents influenced your life as a child? As an adolescent? How do they influence your life today?
2. Tell about the retirement experience as you know it from personal observation.
3. Look ahead to your own retirement. What are some of the concerns you have about getting old?
4. Comment about the merits and disadvantages of living in a retirement community.
5. What advice do you have for families who anticipate having aging grandparents move in with them?
6. What assets can today's grandparents contribute to society, and which roles should we entrust to them?
7. Propose a plan by which the very young and the elderly could be with each other more often than is now the case.
8. What is the likely future of grandparents in our society as it relates to their social significance and self-concept?

REFERENCES AND SUGGESTED READING

Atchley, Robert. *The Social Forces in Later Life*. Belmont: Wadsworth, 1972. Pp. 177–198.

Baltena, Gordon, and Wood, Vivian. "The American Retirement Community: Bane or Blessing." *Journal of Gerontology*, April 1969, pp. 209–217.

Bengtson, Vern. "The Sociology of Aging." In *Aging: Prospects and Issues*, edited by Richard Davis. Los Angeles: University of Southern California Andrus Gerontology Center, 1973. Pp. 56–67.

Burgess, Ernest. *Retirement Villages.* Ann Arbor: University of Michigan, Division of Gerontology, 1961.

Clark, Margaret, and Anderson, Barbara. *Culture and Aging.* Springfield: Charles C Thomas, 1967.

Drought, Alice. *The Elderly Arizonan.* Phoenix: Governor's Task Force on Retirement and Aging, 1976.

Durkheim, Émile. *Suicide.* London: Routledge and Kegan Paul, 1952. Pp. 2–48. (Originally published in 1897).

Harris, Louis. *The Myth and Reality of Aging.* Washington, D. C.: National Council on Aging, 1976.

Kalish, Richard (Ed.). *The Dependencies of Old People.* Ann Arbor: University of Michigan Gerontology Institute, 1969.

Kalish, Richard. *Late Adulthood: Perspectives on Human Development.* Monterey, Calif.: Brooks/Cole, 1977.

Leaf, Alexander. "Every Day Is a Gift When You Are over One Hundred." *National Geographic*, January 1973, pp. 93–119.

Mead, Margaret. *Blackberry Winter.* New York: William Morrow, 1972.

Miller, Marv. "Suicide among Older Men." Unpublished doctoral dissertation, University of Michigan, 1976.

Powell, Judith, Banta, Patsy, and Click, Lalia. "Getting Strokes from Older Folks: An Experience in Intergenerational Sharing." Paper presented to the National Association for the Education of Young Children, Anaheim, California, November 12, 1976.

Rosenfeld, Albert. "Prolongevity: The Extension of the Life Span." *The Futurist*, February 1977, pp. 13–17.

Rosow, Irving. *Social Integration of the Aged.* New York: The Free Press, 1967.

Streitfeld, Elaine. "Young and Old Together." *Social Policy*, November/December, 1976, pp. 100–102.

BOOKS TO SHARE WITH YOUNG CHILDREN

Buckley, Helen E. *The Wonderful Little Boy.* New York: Lothrop, 1970. Getting the elderly and the very young together can benefit them both. The grandmother in this story has a special way of knowing exactly how to respond to her grandson's needs.

Moore, Lilian. *Just Right.* New York: Parents Magazine Press, 1968. Many elderly people find that moving at retirement time is hard to do. Farmer West is ready to retire, but selling the farm proves difficult when each potential buyer wants to upset the ecological conditions he has worked a lifetime to protect.

Skorpen, Liesel Moak. *Mandy's Grandmother.* New York: Dial Press, 1975. Children should recognize that elderly people are not all alike. Mandy expects her grandma to be just like those in storybooks, but it doesn't take long to find out that she is unique.

Snyder, Agnes. *The Old Man on Our Block*. New York: Holt, Rinehart and Winston, 1964. All children should get to know some elderly people, regardless of whether the old are members of their family. Three children befriend an elderly neighbor, who is able to share and enjoy many activities with them.

Wahl, Jan. *Grandmother Told Me*. Boston: Little, Brown, 1972. Grandmothers are often excellent storytellers. This one sees all sorts of things that her grandson just misses seeing—like a troll with a wheelbarrow and the singing lion who lives in the green woods.

5

IDENTITY AND
SELF-CONCEPT

SEVENTEEN
BEYOND SEX ROLES

Long before children compare themselves to other children intellectually, they recognize sex differences. Depending on the interpretation provided by grown-ups, boys and girls move toward their own expectations for normal development or are deflected from this larger goal in favor of sex-role behavior. No one can estimate the social cost of tying self-concept to a single criterion or stereotype. However, it is apparent that the need for humanism, sensitivity, self-assertion, creativity, and a host of other emerging survival values has less to do with sex than with maturity. By insisting upon a different realm of experience for males and females, we rob both of a richer life. I will try to explain why all of us must step outside traditional sex roles if we are to become mature as persons.

FUNCTIONS OF PERCEPTION:
SENSATION AND INTUITION

According to the Swiss psychiatrist Carl Jung, each of us has available several functions by which to orient ourselves. Sensation is our first means of contact with the outside world, the function by which we become aware of concrete reality. For individuals who prefer to perceive primarily by sensation, there is a tendency to experience things only as they are, without reliance upon imagination. Because such persons find the world of actuality a sufficient source of experience, they seldom wonder about the inherent mystery of situations. What counts most to them is the strength and pleasure of sensations alone. Since even the same stimulus may arouse a different sensation at different times, it follows that sensual experiences are illogical; they lack reason and reliability.

The second way we can become aware of the world is by intuition. Jung suggested that intuition is a perception of realities that are unknown to consciousness and that arrive indirectly via the unconscious. In every situation, intuition works automatically to help us see the possibilities that we could not discover by sensation. Whereas someone whose preference is sensation focuses on the facts as they are, on what is presented to the senses alone, the individual preferring intuition is future oriented and consistently emphasizes the possibilities of an idea or situation.

To many teachers, the mental process of intuitive children appears to operate in reverse. After all, the conclusion is reached before the premises. But an intuitive person's inability to retrace the steps that led to the correct answer does not indicate that he or she is cheating or is just a lucky guesser. Instead, the steps connecting premise with conclusion were taken by the unconscious. Rather than requiring children to abandon their use of intuition because we do not comprehend how intuition works, the training of such persons should include ways to test the hypotheses produced by intuition. Whatever it takes to sustain the intuitive orientation of children should be encouraged, because, without access to this function, a person is separated from the ability to envision future possibilities.

FUNCTIONS OF JUDGMENT:
THINKING AND FEELING

Remember that the two perceptual functions of sensation and intuition are irrational; that is, their conclusions are reached outside the realm of reason. However, two other functions by which we encounter experience—thinking and feeling—are rational; they follow established rules of judgment. People who prefer to judge by thinking reach decisions through a logical analysis of objective data. Reliance upon thinking as the basis for judgment allows one to discriminate impersonally between truth and falsity. Typically, it is the children who prefer to judge by thinking who are catered to most at school. Education has emphasized intellectual development as the most desirable form of adaptation to reality. Naturally, this preference leads us to favor the thinking child. Because teachers are gratified by minds that resemble their own, and because parents take pride in academic achievement, considerable attention is given to strengthening only that function that is already a particular child's strongest. Unnecessary family sacrifices are commonly made so that bright

children can accelerate the development of their thinking function. Sometimes the result is competent thinkers whose selfish-
ness and lack of sensitivity render them unsuccessful in day-to-
day relationships. For the sake of mental health, superiority of
one function should not be based on the repression of the remaining functions.

People who prefer to judge by feeling choose how they will
behave by giving primary consideration to subjective values.
Their judgment discriminates between what is valued and what
is unimportant. Feeling is not a kind of emotionally muddled
thinking shaped by sentiment alone, as some persons who prefer
to judge by thinking are apt to assume. Rather, feeling is a
rational function governed by laws of relationships that we
choose to embrace and that in part have been determined for us
through social evolution. Feeling is the function by which values
are weighed and either accepted or refused. Concerned primarily with people and human relationships, those who prefer to
judge by feeling maintain an ordered scheme of things, a hierarchy of values to which they adhere.

All of us know people whose feelings we trust. These people
can be counted on in an emotional situation to behave in keeping
with some established set of values. There are other people on
whom we would not wish to rely in an emotional circumstance.
Given the important place feeling occupies in our daily relationships, it is easy to see why the child who prefers this mode of
judgment is so favorably regarded at home. These two differing
criteria of being able to relate successfully and being intellectually able often account for the contrasting evaluation that parents
and teachers hold of the same child.

There is a naïve notion that learning to think requires education but that learning to feel does not. Yet it may be as difficult
for the thinking type of child to feel as it is for the feeling type
to think. The struggle for the thinking type is not confined to
clarifying values or expressing feelings but includes actually
experiencing them. This is why sensitivity training and the encounter movement began—to help thinking-oriented persons
develop their weak function of feeling. Many businesses and
individuals are coming to recognize that their success depends
on human-relations training that cannot be left to chance. Ac-

cordingly, the scope of education must go beyond learning to judge by thinking; it should also include the affective, moral emphasis of learning to feel.

Every person has encountered some experience through each of the perceptual and judgmental functions. Sensation establishes what is given; thinking enables us to recognize its meaning; feeling tells us its value; intuition points to the possibilities. All of us sense and intuit, think and feel. Nevertheless, an individual's preferred mode is often sufficiently clear to allow placement within a scheme of classification. Thus we can say that, in terms of perception, a particular person is more sensation-oriented than intuitive and, in terms of judgment, prefers feeling to thinking.

MALE/FEMALE SEX ROLES

Basing his conclusions on clinical observations, Jung went a step further and declared that men and women differ in the functions they choose to rely on. To elaborate this distinction, Jung introduced the notion of male and female sex roles that our society seems to have accepted as a guide. As shown in the diagram, thinking was considered primarily a male activity, whereas intuition was thought to be the exclusive province of women. As a feminine characteristic, the show of feeling has been permitted girls of any age but for the same reason has been denied to boys. You can see that, by imposing stereotypic sex roles on children, we reduce the kinds of experiences they can encounter. When boys are led to believe that only the sissy is open to feelings, plays with nurse's kits, batons, and jacks, or is interested in household affairs, certain aspects of potential are off limits. Similarly, when girls feel that it is wrong for them to play with doctor kits, erector sets, model trains, and soldiers or to be interested in exploration and experimentation, their creative growth is hindered.

Culturally Determined Sex Roles	Functions of Perception	Functions of Judgment
Male	Sensation	Thinking
Female	Intuition	Feeling

Some children may not have a chance at home to play with toys typically considered appropriate for the opposite sex. Therefore, it is important for elementary teachers, most of whom are women, to allow and encourage this type of play at school. Unless boys and girls are permitted to decide for themselves the kinds of toys they will play with, they can hardly be urged to pursue career opportunities that are new for members of their sex. Then, too, more women teachers who advocate equal-participation rights for girls ought to recognize the influence of their personal example. Consider how seldom little girls ever see women teachers on the playground engaged in playing basketball, flying airplanes, or shooting marbles. Teachers can also call upon older children to sanction cross-sex-role play. The example of older boys and girls taking part in activities usually judged as right only for the opposite sex represents a powerful influence. Finally, teachers can support the needed change in attitudes toward sex roles by encouraging girls' role playing as female doctors and pilots as part of the curriculum in career education.

The impoverishment of experience that results from traditional sex-role expectations provides us with an important clue regarding creative personality. The question involves whether creative persons are more receptive to dimensions of experience usually considered appropriate to the opposite sex. On several measures of sexual identification by interest patterns, creative males studied by psychologist Donald MacKinnon at the University of California gave more expression to the so-called feminine side of their nature than did less creative men. It is important to note that, while the creative males scored relatively higher on femininity, they did not, as a group, present an effeminate appearance or increased homosexual interests. In fact, they scored very well on a measure of masculinity. What their elevated scores on femininity seem to mean is that creative men are not so completely identified with the traditional masculine role that they deny themselves access to ways of learning usually associated with the so-called feminine side of personality.

This inference is corroborated by male performance on the Myers-Briggs Type Indicator, an instrument designed to show, first, whether a person prefers to perceive the world in a factual, realistic way or in terms of inherent imaginative possibilities and, second, whether the individual prefers to arrive at decisions by logical analysis or by appreciating subjective value. MacKinnon prefaces his findings with the estimate that, in terms of perception, perhaps 75% of all men in the general population classify as sensation oriented, with a focus on what is factual and immediate. By contrast, 90% of the creative persons assessed by MacKinnon and his colleagues classified as intuition oriented —that is, not bound to the present but manifesting instead a future orientation, with an emphasis on what may be rather than on what is. These results lend support to the assertion that, in order for men to be creative—or, for that matter, religious—they need to exhibit intuition, a characteristic long considered reserved for women.

Although highly creative people are alike in preferring intuition to sensation, they differ from one another in their preferred means of judgment. As we've seen, we can say that a person judges or evaluates experience primarily with either thought or feeling, thought being a logical process aimed at an impersonal analysis of the facts and feeling a process of appreciation that bestows on things a personal and subjective value. Whether a creative person prefers to judge by thought or by feeling is less related to creativity as such than to the type of material or concepts with which the person deals. Artists and novelists ordinarily show a preference for feeling, while scientists and engineers show a preference for thinking.

PERCEPTION VERSUS JUDGMENT

All of us also choose between perception (sensation or intuition) and judgment (feeling or thinking) in dealing with the outer world. In this choice, perception is defined as *becoming aware* of something; judgment entails *reaching a conclusion* about things. Of course, everyone perceives, and everyone judges. Perception determines what is seen, and judgment determines what one does about it. We cannot use both judgment and perception at the same time, so we alternate; yet each of us has a dominant process. On the Myers-Briggs Type Indicator, highly creative persons show a strong preference for perceiving. Indeed, the more perceptive a person is the more creative he or she tends to be. While a judging person emphasizes the control and regulation of experience and tends toward an orderly, planned life, the perceiving individual is inclined to be more flexible, spontaneous, and receptive to experience. A preference for perception also describes both young children of any culture and the general population among uncivilized people. However, whereas intuition for the primitive serves to generate lifelong superstitions that are reinforced by elders, the grown-ups in civilized societies require children to transfer their reliance to functions of judgment.

The success of education rests largely on maintaining a proper balance between perception and judgment. On the one hand, all of our mental processes depend on perception. Inadequate perceiving results in poor thinking, inappropriate feelings, and diminished interest in life. Given this consequence, we cannot afford to depreciate the intuitive preference of young children by presenting them with a curriculum that honors only judgment. On the other hand, we should acknowledge that an education focused on perception alone will not provide a better life. Once social problems have been identified by perception, the judgmental functions enable us to respond. This sequence of perception and judgment deserves careful consideration. Before individuals or groups can determine which options are best, they must first generate the options. In short, problem solving requires us to engage the irrational functions prior to being rational.

INTROVERSION/EXTROVERSION

A final aspect of our individual orientation to experience involves whether we direct perception and judgment primarily upon the outer environment or upon the world of ideas within. This attitude preference between what Jung called extroversion and introversion affects the direction and subject of thought. Of course, no one is limited exclusively to an inner or outer world, but strong preferences do exist.

The direction of thinking for extroverts is generally outward, corresponding to their prime interest in relating with people, events, and things. At their best when working with others, they keep our business and social life going. Almost always in good stead with the world, their confidence and readiness to socialize discourage withdrawal when disputes arise. Instead they seek to persuade others about the value of their position. Introverts are less influenced by the environment and appear to withdraw and focus their concentration on inner, subjective factors. They prefer solitary pursuits to group endeavors and reflection to activity. Introverts are at their best when working alone or in small, familiar groups. They prefer quiet tasks to noisy ones, and independent judgment is more important to them than generally approved opinion. Predictive statements about introverts or extroverts become more precise when matched with their preferred functions of perception (sensation/intuition) and judgment (thinking/feeling). Using this principle of combination, some 16 separate personality types emerge. To be sure, Carl Jung's scheme does not take into account all human diversity, but it goes far beyond the traditional view that there are only two kinds of people—male and female.

In studies at the Institute of Personality Assessment and Research at Berkeley, California, two out of three creative subjects reveal a tendency toward introversion. This ratio invites us to inquire how a teacher's own extroversion/introversion preference can influence relationships in the classroom. There are some introverts who expect all of their students to work independently and without noise most of the time. A somewhat opposite condition obtains when an extrovert teacher insists on nearly constant group interaction. Even the pace at which students are expected to proceed may depend on a teacher's attitude. Since introverts choose to submit ideas to inner evaluation before they react, it usually takes them longer to respond. It is erroneous, although common, to view the deliberation of an introvert as a sign that the person is stupid.

In the extreme case, a student's overall assessment can be determined by a teacher's attitude preference. I have visited schools where low marks could reasonably be forecast for any child with an attitude preference different from that of the teacher. Thus, in one grade an introverted girl might be judged as a dreamy and withdrawn individual whose reluctance to participate in groups is a sign of insecurity. In the subsequent grade, the same girl may be seen as a sensitive and creative youngster who has a sense of independence. The parents of a child like this one may wonder what changes took place in her to bring about the dramatic reversal of evaluation in only a year. Actually, the opposing verdicts on her ability reflect the willingness of one teacher and the reluctance of another to respect introversion.

REVISING OUR EXPECTATIONS

Our society has begun to revise its traditional expectations for men and women. The women's-liberation movement is perhaps more responsible for this gain than any other group. Nevertheless, we cannot assume that the equalization process is complete. The effort to minimize sex roles is more complicated than just allowing people more choices. Today, if a woman elects to be a mother, she will be reminded of the campaign to lower birthrates. Seen from this view, pregnancy requires an apology rather than a proud announcement. For the woman who already is a mother and housewife, there is a good chance that she will incorporate the belief of those who claim that her role implies vegetating, being incompetent, and living behind the times. In self-defense, she may denounce employed mothers of young children as selfish and unwise parents. In turn, the employed mother may have guilt feelings for allowing her child to be raised under the influence of someone else's values during the most impressionable period of development. Whenever her son or daughter gets a poor school report, has trouble relating to peers, or experiences illness, the employed mother might feel both guilt and doubt about whether her employment was the cause.

Even the mother whose children are grown lives with the prospect that, whatever her role change, it will be interpreted as a defeat. To remain unmarried is yet another guilt-producing choice. One can argue that, since rearing children is the most important task in any society, it deserves greater respect and increased male participation. There are also good reasons for improving day-care and preschool facilities. Certainly the concern about population growth urges us to eliminate the traditional stigma attached to people who elect to remain unmarried. Independently of these lesser social corrections, however, a more fundamental change appears due. For the sake of mental health, we can no longer simultaneously advocate greater choice for women and at the same time attach unnecessary guilt to their every option.

Men can also venture from their customary role if the changes do not require self-depreciation. An example of how parents influence this choice early in life comes from a study by psychologists Dorothy and Jerome Singer. They conducted a year-long series of meetings with mothers of young children to learn how family television habits might be improved. It was learned that many mothers who favored the traditional feminine orientation perceived Mister Rogers as being too effeminate and therefore an inappropriate male model for their sons to watch. Apparently, these parents could not distinguish between homosexual behavior and gentle humanity. A considerable effort was necessary to persuade them that the contempt they felt toward homosexuality was irrelevant to the thoughtful and quiet approach Mister Rogers uses when teaching children. The feelings of relatively liberated women were not much different. Many of them expressed the same belief that their son's development could be distorted if they were not exposed to aggressive and vigorously active male models on television. The Singer research team concluded that, if women's liberation in the ideal sense is to become a reality, women must pay more attention to accepting gentleness in their own sons and to preparing them for more of the sensitivity and tenderness that in the past was considered feminine.

More of us should learn to accept sex-role changes. Yet there is another and perhaps larger obstacle to which we must attend. In an age of increasing specialization, the dangerous tendency is to sponsor development of a single function in lieu of the complete person, whatever the sex. To overcome this tendency, education and success should be redefined in terms of a balance of the human functions of perception and judgment. Only then will boys and girls encounter experience in ways that up to now have been denied them.

SHARING YOUR IMPRESSIONS

1. Describe some of the sexual expectations you have been subject to at home and at school.
2. How have the concepts of masculine and feminine changed since you were a child?
3. Why do you suppose that "tom boys" (girls) are more socially acceptable than "sissy" boys?
4. Speculate about the influence on a child when parents hold differing expectations.
5. What alternatives can a teacher or parent offer the child whose peers call him a sissy?
6. Suggest some ways of eliminating sex-role stereotypes in our society.
7. Try to remember some misconceptions about sex that you were encouraged to believe as a child. In each case suggest how your parents could have been helpful.

REFERENCES AND SUGGESTED READING

Adell, Judith, and Doyle, Hillary. *A Guide to Non-Sexist Children's Books*. Chicago: Academy Press, 1976.

Fordham, Frieda. *An Introduction to Jung's Psychology*. Baltimore: Penguin Books, 1964. Pp. 29–46.

Friedan, Betty. *The Feminine Mystique*. New York: Dell, 1965.

Gamm, Marie. "Pay for Wives?" Melbourne, Australia: *The Age*, October 29, 1975, p. 18.

Kaplan, Alexandria, and Bean, Joan. *Beyond Sex Role Stereotypes: Readings toward a Psychology of Androgyny*. Boston: Little, Brown, 1976.

Keppelman, Murray. *Raising the Only Child*. New York: New American Library, 1976.

Koch, Stephen. "The Guilty Sex." *Esquire*, July 1975, p. 53.

Lopata, Helena. "The Life Cycle of Role Involvement." In *Occupation: Housewife*. London: Oxford University Press, 1971. Pp. 29–72.

Lynn, David. *The Father: His Role in Child Development*. Monterey, Calif.: Brooks/Cole, 1974. Pp. 5-12, 140–166.

Maccoby, Eleanor, and Jacklin, Carol. "On the Origins of Psychological Sex Differences." In *The Psychology of Sex Differences*. Stanford, Calif.: Stanford University Press, 1974. Pp. 277–348.

McGinley, Phyllis. *Sixpence in Her Shoe*. New York: Dell, 1964.

Montagu, Ashley. *The Natural Superiority of Women*. New York: Macmillan, 1968.

Myrdal, Alva, and Klein, Viola. *Women's Two Roles*. London: Routledge and Kegan Paul, 1968.

Pomeroy, Wardell. *Your Child and Sex*. New York: Dell, 1974.

Singer, Dorothy, and Singer, Jerome. "Family Television Viewing Habits and the Spontaneous Play of Preschool Children." *American Journal of Orthopsychiatry* 46 (1976), 496-502.

Sullerot, Evelyne. *Women, Society and Change*. London: Weidenfeld and Nicolson, 1971.

Wickes, Frances. *The Inner World of Childhood*. New York: New American Library, 1968. Pp. 128–155.

BOOKS TO SHARE WITH YOUNG CHILDREN

Freedman, Russell. *Animal Fathers*. New York: Holiday House, 1976. The role of the father is changing to include more responsibility for child care. Many boys and girls suppose baby animals are cared for only by mothers, so this book shows how certain animals could not survive without help from their fathers.

Levy, Elizabeth. *Nice Little Girls*. New York: Delacorte Press, 1974. School teachers influence sex-role behavior by the kinds of activities they encourage. When Jackie insists on trying certain experiences usually reserved for boys, her teacher calls for a conference in which the parents support Jackie.

Schlein, Miriam. *The Girl Who Would Rather Climb Trees*. New York: Harcourt Brace Jovanovich, 1975. Children may experience family pressure to behave in accord with traditional sex roles. Melissa doesn't want to hurt anyone's feelings, but she'd rather climb trees than play with the doll her family thinks is more appropriate.

Young, Miriam. *Can't You Pretend?* New York: Putnam's Sons, 1970. Little children at play reveal their sex-role training. Chris and Cathy have trouble playing together, because neither of them is prepared to pretend roles they feel fit only the opposite sex.

Zolotow, Charlotte. *William's Doll*. New York: Harper & Row, 1972. Parents who want to support creativity should allow their children to depart from traditional sex roles during play. William's request for a doll was met by family ridicule—except for grandmother, who understood that William needed a doll to practice being a father.

EIGHTEEN
THE RETARDED CHILD

In his novel *Anna Karenina*, Leo Tolstoy remarked "All happy families resemble each other; each unhappy family is unhappy in its own way." Tolstoy may have been wrong about happy families, but certainly every family faced with the presence of a retarded member must find its own way of coping with the special problems it experiences.

More than 6 million people in the United States are mentally retarded. Together, these children and adults account for 3% of the general population. What makes them intellectually different may be defective genes, accidents during pregnancy, birth injuries, childhood illnesses, deprived environments, or a host of other causes. Regardless of the expert view of what caused a particular child's condition, the parents involved sometimes prefer to adopt a religious explanation. Some believe, for example, that they have been chosen by God to bear a special burden; others are equally convinced that God is punishing them, that their child is a result of someone's sin. My purpose is not to persuade those who hold unscientific beliefs about retardation to abandon them. Instead, it seems more appropriate to discuss some expectations parents of retarded children may wish to revise. In particular, the difficult goals of identity and achievement deserve consideration as they apply to retarded children.

SCHOOLS FOR EVERYONE

The tendency of our society has been to suppose that there is a correlation between intelligence and feeling, that the more intelligent we become the more humane our behavior will be. Naturally, if intelligence generates feeling, then by definition the least intelligent experience the least feeling. The difficulty with these assumptions is that retarded people do in fact have affective needs; and, unless we recognize that mentally retarded children have feelings, we will not provide them with the kinds of learning that the self-esteem of any person depends on: that I am respected, that I am important, that I am a person. These learnings should not be made contingent upon the ability to read or the completion of some type of job training. If we recognize that the retarded, like everyone else, need a favorable self-impression, we cannot then establish the most demanding conditions for its attainment by this segment of society.

The expectations of a society are reflected by its schools. Certain educators believe that to survive in a complex world requires considerable intelligence and that persons who are mentally retarded can at best be tolerated until they reach school-leaving age. This pessimistic view overlooks the fact that most people today work within a more narrow range of competence than people could ever afford before. Indeed, in some ways previous generations lived in a much more complicated, if less technical, environment. Ordinarily, men and women of the 20th century are too generous in evaluating their encounter with complexity. Apart from ignoring the rate of mental illness among the so-called intelligent population, we forget our daily use of television, refrigeration, automobiles, and a host of other conveniences that most of us do not remotely understand. Nevertheless, certain futurists would have us believe that in order to get by in a technological society the coming generations must reach ever higher levels of intelligence. Given the existing range of intelligence in the general population, it is apparent that to hold uniformly high expectations of everyone will pose a dilemma. Therefore, various schemes are advanced under the banner of eugenics by which some children would be "deselected" from birth. Alternatively, they would continue to be looked upon with remorse, thus sustaining the myth that only the intelligent are persons.

To better understand the school response to the challenge of educating the retarded, we might examine how teachers feel. Most teachers care about mentally retarded children but regard themselves as inadequately prepared to help them. Even the most diligent persons can become discouraged when they fail to see progress. They state it this way: "He can't do the grade-level assignments, and I can't forsake the others just to teach him; so it's best that he be placed in a special class where there is a lower pupil/teacher ratio." This move seems reasonable, except that it results in the elimination of an equally critical ratio—that of normal to retarded children. If the retarded students are separated from normal peers for the sake of better learning, the normal population is in effect prevented from learning how to accept people who are different. Studies have consistently shown that segregation leads to fear of the atypical population. When the retarded are isolated, they remain so. It is this cost of social exclusion by others that overrides whatever cognitive benefit the retarded may gain from segregated classes. This is why what was intended as a safe, special-education environment free of competition is often recognized later as the means that ensures social rejection of retarded persons by the general population.

A better approach, called *mainstreaming*, allows mildly retarded children to remain with normal classmates through much of the school day. About 75% of all retarded persons fit the "mild" classification, based on IQ scores within the 50–70 range. Unlike the other 25% of mentally retarded individuals, whose condition is referred to as severe (0–29 IQ) or moderate (30–50 IQ), the mildly retarded can, with help, be expected to hold a job, marry, and function responsibly in the general society. When mainstreamed, they leave the class only for certain subjects that are taught by special educators. This arrangement avoids isolation and recognizes that we cannot prepare children for life in a culture of diversity if the atypical are segregated in the schools.

Obviously, the definition of who should be educated outside the regular classroom also defines the nature of the educational setting within it. Throughout the greater part of the industrialized world, expert opinion now places greater emphasis on expanding the capacity of ordinary schools, teachers, and classrooms to accommodate a wider range of children than on expanding the segregated provision for students categorized as handicapped. As Willard Abraham, professor of special education at Arizona State University, puts it: "We will not let regular classroom teachers and school administrators off the hook. They are in all this with us and cannot give only lip service to 'individual differences,' 'take the child where he is,' and other clichés we have lived with too long."

There is, of course, some resistance to mainstreaming. If

schools insist upon uniform expectations for achievement, the emphasis is on teaching the retarded to become more like everyone else. If, however, the goals of special education are broadened to obligate the normal population, the focus changes to helping everyone learn to accept and to honor differences. The transition to this kind of learning, which essentially concerns personality development, will not be easy for an institution that has built its reputation primarily by supporting cognitive development. But it must be done. The assumption that learning to read will result in responsiveness to the needs that one reads about lacks support. In fact, we are finding that it can be quite the other way around. Lacking any exposure to the retarded, people can come to regard their obligation as consisting of reading about the retarded rather than accepting them. A large number of normal people consider knowing facts about the cognitively disabled to be the extent of their responsibility. To their knowledge must be added a sense of obligation if they are to fully mature as persons.

GUILT AND IGNORANCE

So long as the families of retarded children are concerned about public opinion, all of us are involved in their lives. Thus, a larger problem than what we expect of the retarded is what we expect of ourselves. Surely our compassion ought not be so meager that we find a humane response difficult. Otherwise we may find it possible to agree that both the particular family of a retarded person and the world in general would be better off if he or she did not exist. From there it is only a short step to the justification of a population ceiling for any deviant subgroup. These decisions about who has the right to life will depend upon our values, our morals, and our definition of what it is to be a person.

The sister of a retarded adolescent expresses the dilemma of many people when she confides "I really loved him, but it wasn't like loving a person." Does her remark mean that only the normal are persons? Can we love as people only those whose intelligence will approximate our own? Granting all the virtues that are manifest in families with a retarded member—the affection, patience, sacrifice—the fact that they sense embarrassment and feel shame about the person's level of development indicates their unwillingness to abandon social norms as a proper set of expectations. This unwillingness is not an indictment of the family, but overcoming it is a precondition of the success of mentally retarded persons.

The tragedy is not that we feel ashamed about mental retardation but that we experience shame for the wrong reason—for someone else's behavior rather than for our own. The shameful thing is not the retarded person's variance from normal intelligence; it is our rejection of that person for being different from ourselves. Viewed in this way, guilt is attached to *our* behavior, which we can change, rather than to the retarded person's ignorance, which we can do less about. The difference is important, because the benefit of guilt always requires that guilt be focused properly. Guilt should end when misbehavior is altered. To experience guilt indefinitely is self-destructive. Thus, the issue is not limited to the question of how we can help the retarded by special education but extends to the larger question of how we can change ourselves to accept them as persons. In order for children to accept one another, they should have an adult model who can live with differences. This condition is more likely to prevail if teachers are trained to see value in diversity.

HANDICAPS FOR NORMAL CHILDREN

In a sense, most of us are slow learners, as is indicated by the time it takes us to become mature. There is a good chance that in the future maturity can be realized earlier if, during childhood, students learn to value people independently of their cognitive achievement or physical condition. The task of educating normal persons to accept those with handicaps has already begun. At Monash University in Melbourne, Australia, Pierre Gorman and his associates are working with several age groups. The parent participants, equally divided in terms of parents who have normal children and parents who have handicapped children, meet regularly in a single group to discuss their individual reactions toward people with various disabilities. The information gleaned from these sessions is being used to develop curricula for parent education. Designing curricula for youngsters is another aspect of the program. Gorman maintains that what most students learn at school about the handicapped is often unrealistic and usually takes the form of collecting money or materials for donations. Instead, the Monash plan calls for students to participate in several basic activities throughout the formal schooling process.

First, to ensure that children understand the significance of impairments, simulated impairments are arranged for each of the elementary students so that they can experience the resultant disabilities. For example, after being blindfolded, a kindergartner is obliged to locate specific objects that have been scattered about the floor. Students may be asked to walk for a certain distance or length of time with a marble placed inside one shoe. By actually using wheelchairs, hearing aids, walkers, and other assistance devices, students become more aware of their functions and limitations. A second activity involves visits outside the school to meet with persons whose handicaps may not be represented in class. These directed discussions are important for several reasons. The conversations often reveal student attitudes that teachers should take into account when planning for individuals. Then, too, the handicapped have an opportunity to explain how the attitudes of normal people affect them personally.

In addition to the visitation and simulation experiences, the Monash team have developed multimedia lessons for social studies that give students at all grade levels a chance to increase their familiarity with the problems of handicapped people. They hope that, by means of this continuous orientation over the entire school career, the prevailing attitudes and behavior of students toward impairments and disabilities will improve. In turn, the revised outlook of these students is expected to make possible more extensive integration of handicapped persons into the general community.

Most of us will eventually encounter some handicaps. It can be predicted that a certain proportion of normal children will acquire impairments or disabilities, whether through accident, illness, increasing age, or changing social conditions. Furthermore, some normal children will become parents of handicapped boys and girls or employers of impaired workers. These are ample reasons why learning to accept differences should become an identifiable element of the school curriculum. The innovation is essential if individually and collectively we are to convey a sense of worthwhileness to those who are unlike ourselves.

There are good reasons for expecting a dramatic improvement in educational opportunity. President Carter's commitment to human rights is one factor, but even more important is Public Law 94-142, which has been called the educational bill of rights for persons with handicaps. What makes this 1975 legislation remarkable among federal education laws is its duration; it is intended to serve the nation's schools in perpetuity. The need for reform is illustrated by the fact that currently more than one million children are excluded entirely from public schools and that appropriate educational services are withheld from more than half of the eight million children who are handicapped (defined as mentally retarded, hard of hearing, deaf, speech impaired, visually handicapped, seriously emotionally disturbed, orthopedically health impaired or suffering specific learning disabilities).

The "bill of rights" is scheduled to be implemented in phases nationwide. Some of the significant elements deserve recognition:

- A free public education will be made available to all handicapped children between the ages of 3 and 21 by 1980.
- For each handicapped child, there will be a written, individualized educational plan that includes all goals and expected services. This plan is to be jointly developed and agreed upon by the school, the home, and, if possible, the child.
- Access to education within a regular classroom is guaranteed unless the person's handicap is such that services cannot be properly offered there.
- School placement and other educational decisions concerning a handicapped child will be made only after consultation with the child's parents.
- Parents can examine and challenge all relevant records bearing on the identification of their child as being handicapped and on the kind of educational setting in which the student is placed.
- Previous federal legislation aimed at the elimination of architectural barriers to the physically handicapped will

be applied to the funding of school construction and modification.

Obviously, the 10–12% of our population who are handicapped will benefit the most from this bill of rights, but the rest of us also stand to gain, because the changes will bring schools closer to our democratic ideals.

SHARING YOUR IMPRESSIONS

1. How do you feel about being around a retarded person? Someone who is emotionally disturbed? Physically handicapped?
2. How do you feel about legislation to prevent retarded adults from having children?
3. Describe the kinds of schooling you believe should be provided for the retarded.
4. How do you suppose the life of mentally retarded children and adults is different from that of persons who are normal?
5. Make some guesses about the self-concept of school children who are retarded.
6. Explain your reasoning on the issue of whether parents with mentally retarded children ought to give up hope for normal behavior.
7. What effect does a retarded person have on the lives of other members of the family?
8. In your opinion, is it the school's function to inform parents of a realistic level of expectation for their retarded youngster? What about expectations for the normal children?

REFERENCES AND SUGGESTED READING

Abraham, Willard. "The Early Years: Prologue to Tomorrow." *Exceptional Children*, March 1976, pp. 330–335.

Apgar, Virginia. *Is My Baby All Right?* New York: Pocket Books, 1974.

Asbell, Bernard. "The Case of the Wandering IQs." In *Values and Human Development*, edited by Robert Strom. Columbus, Ohio: Charles E. Merrill, 1973. Pp. 21–35.

Bauer, David, and Yamamoto, Kaoru. "Designing Instructional Settings for Children Labeled Retarded: Some Reflections." *The Elementary School Journal*, April 1972, pp. 343–350.

Crissey, Marie Skodak. "Mental Retardation: Past, Present and Future." *American Psychologist*, August 1975, pp. 800–808.

Goodman, Leroy. "New Legislation Extends Equal Educational Opportunities to Handicapped." *Interaction*, October 1976, pp. 1–12.

Gorman, Pierre. "Handicapped by Society." *The Educational Magazine*, 31 (1974), No. 6, pp. 8–10.

Koch, Richard, and Koch, Kathryn. *Understanding the Mentally Retarded Child*. New York: Random House, 1975. Pp. 1–85.

Long, Nicholas, Morse, William, and Newman, Ruth. *Conflict in the Classroom: Education of Emotionally Disturbed Children.* Belmont, Calif.: Wadsworth, 1965.

Meyerson, Lee. "Physical Disability as a Social Psychological Problem." In *The Other Minorities*, edited by Edward Sagarin. Toronto: Ginn and Company, 1971. Pp. 205–210.

Reynolds, Maynard, and Rosen, Sylvia. "Special Education: Past, Present and Future." *The Educational Forum*, May 1976, pp. 551–562.

Trotter, Robert. "Intensive Intervention Program Prevents Retardation." *APA Monitor*, September/October 1976, pp. 4, 5, 19, 46.

Van Osdal, William, and Shane, Don. *Exceptional Children.* Dubuque, Iowa: Kendall/Hunt, 1971.

BOOKS TO SHARE WITH YOUNG CHILDREN

Fassler, Joan. *One Little Girl.* New York: Behavioral Publications, 1969. Retarded persons can lead satisfying lives. Laurie's parents are concerned about her slow intellectual development, but their doctor helps them see that Laurie can take pride in doing some things even though she is slow in others.

Fassler, Joan. *Howie Helps Himself.* Chicago: Albert Whitman, 1975. Normal children need to learn about the feelings of handicapped peers. Howie has been confined to a wheelchair, and now he makes his first attempt to take a few steps.

Klein, Gerda. *The Blue Rose.* New York: Lawrence Hill, 1974. Retarded children have feelings and want to be accepted. Jenny is likened to a "blue rose," different but beautiful in her own way.

Lasker, Joe. *He's My Brother.* Chicago: Albert Whitman, 1974. Being a brother or sister of a learning-disabled child calls for compassion. Jamie is very slow at times and always seems in trouble; yet his brother looks past these problems and is able to see the good things in Jamie.

Litchfield, Ada. *A Button in Her Ear*. Chicago: Albert Whitman, 1976. For some children, a hearing aid can make spoken words easier to understand. When Angela fails to understand the messages of family and friends, an audiologist helps by placing a special "button" in her ear.

NINETEEN

THE SURVIVAL OF IDEALS

Deciding what to live for gives a person a sense of purpose. The expression of ideals during late adolescence is therefore a sign of growing up. However, unlike other major steps in human development, such as beginning to talk or learning to read, the emergence of ideals is not always welcomed. In fact, parents who already have made career plans for their son or daughter may regard any altruistic ideals as obstacles to their child's achievement. Usually mothers and fathers identify love as the factor that motivates them to temporarily act on the younger person's behalf so that a valuable future will not be thrown away. Typically, these parents assume that a decision to leave school to join the Peace Corps or to work on a political campaign will permanently erase a youngster's chances of ever completing college.

MOTIVATION AND DROPPING OUT

It is worth examining why some idealistic young men and women decide to leave higher education; after all, many of their classmates must be people who feel as they do about the world, people with whom they can share aspirations. Perhaps those who leave realize that colleges only impose more subtle restrictions on idealism than do parents. In college, people don't object to hearing about ideals. On the contrary, we might say that higher education substitutes the clarification of ideals for their rejection. For some students, this improvement is sufficient; however, others feel that their maturity is still in jeopardy precisely because they must put ideals into practice in order to keep them. Although most college students are in the age group of high idealism, they are expected to await taking on responsibility until they are employed.

Unfortunately, this expectation fails to recognize that ideals are abandoned if they are not used. The dynamic of the disengagement process is complex, and its cost to personal development may be far greater than we comprehend. If young men and women who fervently wish to shape a better world lack confirmation that they can bring about change, it is natural for them to resign themselves to the vicarious but less constructive role of social critics. These are sufficient reasons for young people who face the alternative of staying in school or losing their ideals to decide that leaving studies is the wiser course of action. Over half of all college students who quit school before graduating do so for nonacademic reasons. In other words, they are not failing classes, but they feel that their present goals can better be achieved elsewhere. It seems ironic that we refer to such people as dropouts.

Of course, there are other ways to reconcile the demand for the prolonged education of adolescents and our accompanying regret about their lack of responsibility. If, during their college years, students were expected to perceive and respond to community needs instead of merely to read about and discuss them, chances are that they would develop a sense of civic obligation. While the importance of community service for children of the affluent seems obvious, we should also realize that some similar arrangement is essential for students from less fortunate backgrounds too.

Several years ago, I took a close look at the rationale that was then being advanced to justify the recruitment of minority students by universities. These recruitment drives had just been introduced to many universities on the premise that, without educated, indigenous leadership, every subpopulation among the poor would continue to be neglected. Supposedly the lack of leadership could be remedied by providing a college education for more minority members than the meager 5% of their subpopulations then in attendance. Numerous institutions thus established special programs. The typical approach was to grant extraordinary consideration in terms of admission criteria and to provide individual tutoring. Implicit in the notion of somehow getting the minority student through was an assumption that upon graduation he or she would return to represent the low-income community as one of its few educated leaders.

At the time, few educators foresaw the likelihood of an opposite effect—that we might be robbing the poor of their best potential spokesmen when minority students attend colleges where the curriculum invites them to succeed for themselves alone and leave the concerns of the ghetto behind. This same complaint has recently been made by foreign countries whose talented students have left home to accept fellowships from United States foundations. Here again, the humanistic purpose was to provide struggling nations with their own doctors, engineers, and scientists. But in too many cases the graduating visitors have elected to remain in the United States instead of returning to their native country. The high incidence of an effect that is exactly opposite to our intention should prompt a search for ways to ensure that foreign students are not separated from their commitments. If American minority students and foreign students both arrive at college with a sense of obligation to their nation or ethnic group, we should determine why it is that four years later the commitment no longer obtains for many of them.

To check the assumption that minority students might prefer to retain their ideals, I conducted a needs-assessment study for the Rockefeller Foundation. The 400 students interviewed were Blacks, Indians, Mexican-Americans, and Orientals enrolled at Arizona State University. Nearly half of the participants believed that community service should be included in higher education. Moreover, three-quarters of them felt a desire to be in courses that required work in the community. These figures reflect a healthy concern about using one's education on behalf of others while still in school rather than waiting until schooling is completed.

In the decade between 1960 and 1970, higher education in the U. S. doubled its enrollment from four million to eight million students. The community college came of age along with the expanding state-college and university systems. This growth was in part a reflection of our national determination to achieve equal access to higher learning for previously underrepresented groups, including racial and ethnic minorities, women, and older adults. We can be proud that more people than ever before are now able to attend college. On the other hand, when some of these students quit school to pursue their ideals in another environment, parents should realize that formal education can usually be resumed at a later date. The fact is that large numbers of adolescents enroll in higher education before they are motivated to profit from the experience. Some of them initially attend because they want to please their parents; others attend because they lack direction for their lives, and they suppose college will help them find it. Neither of these reasons approximates the motivation that is usual among returning students who are somewhat older.

What the veterans, grandmothers, and mothers whose children have reached school age seem to have in common is a sense of direction and a serious commitment to learning. Unlike their younger classmates, these people often have family responsibilities and are already accepted in the community as adults. The idea of sheltered courses for these older students seems unwise both because it prevents them from becoming a resource for younger classmates and because it reflects unwarranted assumptions about the relationship between aging and the ability to learn. As the life span is increased, colleges cannot continue to be seen as institutions for only the young.

COUNSELING AND VOCATIONAL CHOICE

Certain parents are upset when their adolescent decides to leave school early. Others are equally disappointed when sons or daughters want to study some career the parents have not chosen. The consequences of this conflict in vocational motivation are such that they ought to be considered as part of the parent-education curriculum. An illustration can be drawn from my own research on problems of academically successful students. One of these studies, involving a selected sample of 300 college sophomores, began with an attempt to identify the kinds of obstacles to achievement they had encountered during their elementary and high school years. As an aggregate, the students identified 50 obstacles that directly or indirectly related to mental health, achievement, and satisfactory completion of academic requirements. After indicating on a checklist the frequency with which they as individuals were confronted by each of the obstacles, the students were interviewed concerning their written responses.

Many of these successful students cited matters of direction as their major obstacle to achievement. A sense of direction is obviously important, since, whenever objectives are obscured, response tends to be random, energy is without focus, and doubt impedes progress. On the checklist the term "direction" subsumed a number of items relating to goals, counseling, and motivational support. When subpopulation distinctions were introduced for the purpose of comparing members of the sample, it was found that the frequency of occurrence of confusion about goals was directly related to the parents' education. That is, the more educated the parents, the less likely the student was to be confused about goals. Adolescents from homes in which parents have not completed high school show an incidence of goal confusion nearly twice as great as classmates from homes in which both parents are college graduates.

While this information would seem to argue for better-educated homes, data obtained from the student interviews discourages any such inference. It seems that one reason the offspring of well educated parents are less often confused about goals is that goals are often imposed on them, chosen early by mother, father, or other close relatives. Again and again students recounted adult intrusion into goal selection. In some cases only a professional vocation would be satisfactory. ("You can be any kind of doctor you wish.") Apparently, being less confused about goals does not necessarily favor mental health. In certain cases it may simply mean that adolescents forfeit their option—that others choose for them what they are to become. On the other hand, less educated parents—mothers and fathers who probably know less about the range of occupations—insisted only "You be what you wish to be; hopefully you'll have an easier time of it than we have had." To be sure the latter group of parents were less specific in providing direction, but, at the same time, they were more tolerant in allowing their youngsters latitude in making choices about their own futures.

Lack of counseling assistance was mentioned by students from every subpopulation. Although there is evidence that better-educated parents make available more guidance, they are also more inclined to limit the kinds of occupational information their youngsters receive and to restrict outside sources of counsel to those individuals who will reinforce their own preferences.

It is well to recognize that adolescent confusion about goals and the lack of counseling assistance are not limited to successful students. That these problems should concern everyone was first discovered a few years ago by Project Talent at the University of Pittsburgh. This project, involving 440,000 students in high schools across the nation, represented the first national census of aptitudes and abilities. The Pittsburgh researchers found that students in the ninth grade were greatly confused about goals and had very unrealistic educational and career plans but that they improved them somewhat during the high school years. About half of them made relatively radical changes during the first year after graduation from high school.

The failure of boys in particular to develop realistic career plans was well illustrated by Project Talent findings:

> Of all young men who planned to become physicians when they were nearly through high school, half abandoned the idea by the time they finished the freshman year of college.
>
> Forty-one percent of twelfth grade boys who planned a career in law obtained general academic aptitude scores below the 50th percentile.
>
> Thirty-three percent of the twelfth grade boys who planned careers as mathematicians obtained scores below the average of all boys in this grade in general academic aptitude.

This distortion of unrealistic career goals was made even more poignant by local studies. In the city of Cincinnati, 1,658 girls and boys in 35 junior high schools were asked to state their occupational choices. Results of the inquiry were summarized by Robert Hoppock as follows:

> What would Cincinnati be like if these students became the sole inhabitants of the city in the jobs of their choice, ten years from now? . . . Health services would be very high, with every 18 people supporting one doctor . . . It may be, however, that they would all be needed in a city that has no garbage disposal workers, no laundry workers, no water supply personnel, since no one chooses to do that kind of work . . . The two bus drivers will find that their customers get tired of waiting and use the services of the 67

airline pilots. It may be difficult getting to Crosley Field to
see the 40 baseball players.

Perhaps it is time to acknowledge that the unreasonable
career goals expressed by many students reflect the unrealistic
expectations held for them by their families. The 1977 National
Survey of Children illustrates that the resulting pressure for
achievement begins even earlier than high school. Some 2200
boys and girls, representing a cross section of the 7- to
11-year-old age group, were chosen to participate, along with
1700 of their parents. When asked about academic goals for their
children, Black parents revealed higher aspirations than White
parents. We know that parents' expectations are communicated
to their children from the reports by more than three-quarters
of the Black children and about two-thirds of the White children
that their mothers wanted them to be "one of the best students in
class."

The expression of lofty goals is commendable, and all children should be urged to do their best at school. However,
disappointment is inevitable when neither the parents nor the
child can accept the truth about the child's actual level of
achievement as compared to other students. Although the students in the survey represented a broad range of intelligence,
nearly 30% of them were described by their parents and themselves as "one of the best students in class." Only 5% were seen
by both parties as below the middle of the class. Finally, while
less than 4% of the students considered themselves to be near
the bottom of the class, not even 2% of the parents were willing
to acknowledge that this was a proper estimate of their child's
class standing.

A variety of research sources combine to suggest that, besides having an inflated impression of their ability, a large
number of students also lack sufficient information about the
world of work. These obstacles to career selection have serious
implications. To correct the situation, the United States Office of
Education began in 1973 to design career curricula for use at all
grade levels. The basic purpose of career education is to acquaint
children with the range of occupational choices, the nature of
available jobs, and the satisfactions they offer. The hope is that

students' exposure throughout the schooling process to the benefits and demands of various kinds of work will result in more realistic career decisions. It would be premature to evaluate the impact of career education during its still formative stage, but the enlarging scope of this kind of education is promising. As career education develops, the long-range plan is to include nonvocational objectives, those important aspects of a person's life that are not linked to employment. With this broader definition of career, encompassing parenthood training and the development of lifelong hobbies, we can anticipate that students' chances for mental health and maturity will improve.

Adolescents are often described as the idealists of our society. Yet idealism ought not be seen as a strictly adolescent condition that adults have outgrown. Because there can be no maturity without ideals, the period of idealism should extend from adolescence throughout the rest of life. Since we can now control more aspects of the future than ever before, long-range planning has become a necessity. In a sense this means that being idealistic and being practical should no longer be seen as incompatible. There is ample evidence that many students prefer to keep their ideals—to commit themselves to great causes and to become responsive to the needs of other people. Parents, career-education programs, churches, and colleges should support this desire to be responsible. If instead we withhold from adolescents the opportunity to serve society, the fiction that they are irresponsible will come true. Long ago we accepted the Biblical warning that where there is no vision the people perish. We have yet to consider that, unless the vision of youth can be acted upon, it may also vanish.

SHARING YOUR IMPRESSIONS

1. When you were a teenager, what part did your parents play in affecting your choice of a career?
2. Why do you suppose so many parents expect more from their children than they themselves achieved?
3. Parents' unrealistic expectations may get in the way of a good relationship with their children. Try to remember an unrealistic expectation your parents held for you.

4. Adolescent ideals are sometimes seen as obstacles to personal development when the ideals conflict with their parents' goals. Illustrate this circumstance with an example from your own observation.
5. Give your opinion on whether parents tend to set higher expectations for sons than for daughters.
6. How realistic are the vocational aspirations expressed by high school students?
7. How do you react to the idea that dropping out of school may sometimes be a sensible move?
8. Think of some ways in which today's adolescents might be given increased adult responsibilities.
9. How do you imagine relationships between teenagers and parents may change over the next 20 years?

REFERENCES AND SUGGESTED READING

Dubos, René. "Optimism—The Creative Attitude." *The Reader's Digest*, April 1974, pp. 61–63.

Flanagan, John C. *A National Inventory of Aptitudes and Abilities.* Pittsburgh: University of Pittsburgh, Project Talent Bulletin 4, 1965.

Gabor, Dennis. *Innovations: Scientific, Technological and Social.* New York: Oxford University Press, 1970.

Hamilton, Andrew. "Career Education Working Model." *American Education*, December 1975, pp. 22-25.

Henderson, Harold. "American Youth in Transition." *Kappa Delta Pi Record*, February 1976, pp. 67-69.

Hoppock, Robert. "The Use and Misuse of Occupational Information." Address to the Ohio Guidance Personnel Association, Columbus, June 17, 1965.

Musgrove, Frank. "The Adolescent Ghetto." In *Education for Affective Achievement*, edited by Robert Strom and E. Paul Torrance. Chicago: Rand McNally, 1973. Pp. 79-85.

National Panel on High Schools and Adolescent Education. *The Education of Adolescents, Summary, Conclusions and Recommendations.* Submitted to the U. S. Office of Education and Department of Health, Education and Welfare. Washington, D. C.: U. S. Government Printing Office, 1975.

Pine, Gerald. "Quo Vadis, School Counseling?" *Phi Delta Kappan*, April 1975, pp. 554–557.

Storr, Anthony. *The Integrity of the Personality.* Baltimore: Penguin Books, 1963.

Strom, Robert. "Recognizing Problems of the Successful." *The Urban Teacher*. Columbus, Ohio: Charles E. Merrill, 1971. Pp. 81–89.

Temple University Institute for Survey Research. *National Survey of Children: Preliminary Results*. New York: Foundation for Child Development, 1977.

Torrance, E. Paul. *Sociodrama in Career Education*. Athens: University of Georgia College of Education, 1976.

Torrance, E. Paul. *Future Careers for Gifted and Talented Students*. Athens: University of Georgia College of Education, 1976.

BOOKS TO SHARE WITH YOUNG CHILDREN

Alexander, Martha. *I'll Protect You from the Jungle Beasts*. New York: Dial Press, 1973. Children must adopt high-minded goals before they can ever pursue them. A little boy assures his teddy bear of protection; but then they get lost, and it is the teddy bear who must be depended upon.

Lexau, Joan. *Benjie*. New York: Dial Press, 1970. There are times when all of us must demonstrate our values. Benjie is afraid of the large dog and the bullies on the route home from school, but he must take the risk of traveling it to find out whether his grandmother needs help.

Ringi, Kjell, and Holl, Adelaide. *The Man Who Had No Dream*. New York: Random House, 1969. People with ideals have something to live for. Mr. Oliver had everything that money could buy and still was unhappy, because he lacked something to care about.

Velthuijs, Max. *The Little Boy and the Big Fish*. New York: Platt & Munk, 1969. Wanting someone else to be happy may require our own unhappiness. Once the little boy caught his big fish, he wanted to become its friend—but this meant giving up the bathtub idea and letting the fish return to the lake.

Watts, Mabel. *The Narrow Escapes of Solomon Smart*. New York: Parents Magazine Press, 1966. Caring enough about other people to stand up for them is an important step in growing up. Solomon's make-believe escapes help him to discover why caring adults feel obliged to protect smaller persons.

TWENTY

EDUCATING FOR LEISURE

THE PROTESTANT ETHIC

Before the Protestant Reformation, the concept of vocation and the idea of having a calling applied only to the clergy. This clerical monopoly was unacceptable to Martin Luther, because it placed the responsibility for living the gospel upon too few and because it separated religious life from secular life. Consequently, Luther urged laymen to fulfill their secular calling for Christian service through their daily labors. Thus, by relating the concept of work to the concept of calling, Luther transformed the popular definition of work from a means of providing for material needs to an expression of one's religious duty, and this view of life still shapes our values today.

We still retain the Protestant view that each person's mission is to be accomplished through his or her secular work and that, since work is morally good, unemployment is bad and being unwilling to work is sinful. The decline of religious service as a primary goal of the modern worker has changed the work ethic, which now emphasizes the belief that people must find personal satisfaction and experience meaning on the job. Yet even this modified form of the Protestant work ethic is inappropriate and must be abandoned if we are to deal successfully with some basic conflicts created by automation:

- The productive capacity of automation makes full employment unnecessary, but to be unemployed is shameful.
- Paid employment is the only way for a person to obtain dignity, but automation promises to displace many job holders.
- Workers are expected to find their sense of self-worth from a job, but automation makes jobs routine and boring.
- Automation leads to an abundance of leisure, but, since people regard nonwork activity as lacking in value, they naturally experience guilt and self-recrimination when leisure is extended.

Simply stated, our problem is how to ensure that each individual in an automated society experiences dignity and purpose while at the same time ensuring that the culture has a rationale for distributing the results of its high productivity. To accomplish these enormous but necessary tasks, we must revise our concept of work.

AUTOMATION AND THE REPLACEMENT OF WORKERS

In his testimony before the U. S. Senate Subcommittee on Employment and Manpower, John Snyder, president of U. S. Industries, suggested that it is time for popular myths about automation to give way to some unpleasant facts. The most seductive myth alleges that automation will not displace workers. A second myth contends that the need to maintain and operate automated equipment will actually create more jobs than presently exist. But in fact computers require little maintenance, and, if workers were not displaced, automation would not be economically feasible. Nevertheless, some groups still point to what they regard as equally drastic labor changes in the past, such as the introduction of knitting machines to textile manufacturing, and remind us that in time these machines increased employment. However, labor-saving devices introduced during the Industrial Revolution also led to riots, turmoil, and war. Moreover, since these changes occurred in basically rural societies, the land guaranteed food and a place to live for the unemployed. In an urban society like ours, the alternative of becoming a farmer does not exist.

A half-century ago, when the blacksmith was driven from his trade by the automobile, he alone left his job in an otherwise healthy town. But technological advancements and business failures now affect hundreds of thousands of people. When layoffs of this magnitude occur, as they increasingly do, masses of people are left in a state of volatile misery that cripples both family and community.

Many experts think that automation has only begun its replacement of people, that within the next two decades we shall see an unprecedented rise in unemployment among the skilled and middle-management groups as well as the uneducated. They predict a society in which no more than 15% of the population will be needed to provide the basic necessities and services for all. In such a society, it would be cruel and unreasonable to retain the notion that only through a job can individuals discover contentment and define who they are. One's identity, status, and sense of potency would all be expected to derive from the job, but, because the majority of people would be unneeded for employment, they would have to accept the social and psychological consequences of being regarded as worthless.

DISTINGUISHING BETWEEN A JOB AND A "WORK"

To reconcile the leisure society with an individual's need for dignity, we must stop perceiving a person's work and job as being inseparable. In a relatively jobless setting it is no longer appropriate for paid employment to be a prerequisite of dignity. If a distinction between job and work were generally accepted, the result would be in everyone's best interest. We could enlarge our inquiry of self and others from "What is your job?" to "What is your *work*?" In other words, "What is your mission as a person, the activity you pursue with a sense of duty and from which you derive self-meaning and a sense of personal worth?" It would be understood that, given the meaninglessness of some jobs, numerous people would necessarily identify their work as something apart from their employment. This would release them from the self-delusion and guilt that come from working at a job they abhor but from which they are expected to gain satisfaction.

` Industrial-sociology studies have shown that the monotonous tasks being created by automation have caused an increasing number of job holders to begin to find their major life interests outside their jobs. The idea that all people need jobs to feel good about themselves and that job holding brings satisfaction is erroneous. When people say "Thank God it's Friday," what do they mean? Do they mean that they achieve so much pleasure and extract so much significance and self-fulfillment from their jobs that the sheer ecstasy of it all cannot be sustained for more than five days at a time? Or do they mean that their jobs lack importance for them, fail to satisfy their need for potency, and force them to look to the weekend for fulfillment? Do they mean that it would be nice not to have to hold their jobs but that the need for income and social status demands it? The inner turmoil of millions of workers does not signify that they are lazy or that constructive achievement doesn't interest them. It does mean that work and job are being distinguished and that alienation from the job is becoming common. In a leisure society, the incidence of such behavior is destined to rise as industry shifts to the four-day week and people can give more attention to other interests.

"THANK GOD IT'S THURSDAY"

More than 700 U. S. companies currently have all or most of their workers on a four-day week, and at least 1000 other companies are contemplating such a shift. In 1976, the nation's largest employer, the federal government, began a three-year experiment with four-day work weeks and other flexible work schedules for nearly 3 million employees. Municipal employees in Atlanta, Long Beach, Phoenix, and other cities made the transition several years ago. A dozen companies, including Metropolitan Life Insurance, have gone even further, assigning some of their workers a three-day work week. Some political and labor leaders are suggesting that perhaps the single best way to reduce unemployment is to redistribute existing work. It is estimated that if we all move to a 35-hour work week, the resulting creation of jobs would employ six million more people.

In a leisure society, for the first time in history, most of people's time would belong to them, and they could live far away from the city of their employment. However, confidence in the leisure society seems to be declining as its arrival draws near. Previous generations believed that a relatively jobless economy would introduce greater contentment than ever before, but only 23% of the people polled in a recent national survey assume that labor-union proposals for a four-day week and three-month annual vacation will result in happier homes. Evidence from industrial sociology supports this popular doubt by indicating that a shorter work day does not necessarily increase family interaction or ensure other forms of constructive activity. Many physicians have stopped prescribing holidays and vacations for tense and anxious patients, because leisure could bring disaster rather than relief. Suicides, depressions, and other self-disabling behavior increase over weekends and holidays, when inner conflicts can no longer be repressed by the rigors of routine. In many cases leisure appears to generate domestic conflict or withdrawal. Reinforcing the danger are gerontological studies suggesting that many marriages are sustained during the career years because the people seldom see each other. Extended interpersonal contact is unpleasant unless people know how to relate well.

WORK TO LAST A LIFETIME

Slowly, our society is coming to realize that what is important is not that each of us holds a job but that each of us has work. Many people who have jobs lack work and therefore a sense of satisfaction and self-pride. The problem cannot be solved just by making jobs more meaningful, because there is a significant difference between having a work and holding a job. Nothing framed by a period shorter than a lifetime can be termed a person's work, but a given person may never have a job or may retire at age 60. The retiree who has not discovered a work may move to Florida and die sooner because he or she has lost a respected role and is unable to view his or her life as important apart from the job hierarchy. The number of people facing this prospect is growing; already over 22 million people in the U. S. are at least 65 years old. If the increased life span is to be satisfying rather than cruel, we must abandon the tradition that ties self-validation to one's job.

Recognizing that people are disenchanted with certain jobs, management has responded mainly by inventing rationalizations for investing jobs with inherent worth or greater social meaning. We all expect "What do you do?" to be the first question asked after introduction to a stranger. However, the answer becomes more difficult as a technologically advancing industry creates jobs that are new, nameless, and hard to describe. What status is there in saying "I am a relay-transmitter maintenance technician on the 609 power mag"? A substitute answer is then offered—not in terms of what one does but where one does it: "I am employed at Sears Roebuck." Despite these obstacles, the game of appealing job titles continues to expand. A person who joins a chain of department stores may immediately be given the title of executive assistant, thus temporarily meeting the beginner's need for status. In some occupations it is an accepted practice to uproot a person's family and transfer them 1000 miles from friends, relatives, and preferred location and actually lead them to feel honored because the reassignment is termed a promotion. Each of us has a need to feel significant, potent, and useful. This need will persist in an automated society, and, since the need will not be met by jobs, work is urgently required.

If more work and fewer jobs are the design for mental health in an automated society, we must soon deal with the related problems of income distribution and education. In terms of sharing our national abundance, we can choose between two inconsonant values. One value states that people gain virtue and dignity from job holding and that, therefore, no one without a job should be judged acceptable or given assistance, lest that person's chance for dignity be jeopardized. A second and more recent principle asserts that people who are unable to hold jobs or whose vocational skills are unneeded should still receive a guaranteed income so that their families are comfortably cared for. A Gallup poll taken several years ago revealed that about 70% of the U. S. population agreed with the latter principle. But it is apparent that, as automation eliminates jobs, these values will clash. The public will resist paying the unemployed, and the jobless will feel guilt and self-derogation for accepting money they haven't worked to earn. To escape from this dilemma, we must prepare tomorrow's adults for life in a leisure society.

ENLARGING EDUCATIONAL GOALS

Affluent people cannot be expected to willingly share their wealth unless they are convinced that greater importance should be attached to off-the-job work. Perhaps the schools can begin the process of changing our perceptions regarding jobs by presenting students with two basic questions throughout the school years. Unlike the present arrangement, which urges young people to decide "What is to be my job?" the goal could be enlarged to "What is to be my work?" and "What am I going to do with my life?" By raising both inquiries, we may free students from identifying who they are with the occupation they choose. We painfully recognize the mental-health outcomes when success has too narrow a definition, when the vocational side is considered the whole of our obligation. Today there are many people whose training and income qualify them as successful but whose lack of maturity and concern for others label them as failures. The fact that more people in business and industry are fired for interpersonal-relations problems than for job incompetence underscores the need for schools to help facilitate the growing-up process, the affective or emotional aspect of development.

Some futurists believe that a relatively jobless society would not need public schools, that without an occupational focus any curriculum would be meaningless. I regard this perception as inaccurate, for we are clearly undereducated in child rearing, community service, personal development, and understanding one another. Our lack of skill in the art of relating is demonstrated by our divorce rate, our treatment of the poor, and our neglect of the elderly. Supposedly these matters of relating have not been given attention because there was insufficient time in a schedule already filled with job-oriented studies. Now that more time will be available, the relevance of such curricula cannot be so easily dismissed. Of one thing we may be sure: Our schools currently devote much more effort to helping young people learn how to make a living than they do to helping students find out what their work is to be. In a relatively jobless society, the question of life purpose becomes crucial, and a new educational structure is needed to help people find the answers. With these goals in mind, the Danforth Foundation recently gave St. Louis University a multimillion-dollar grant to redesign university curricula to prepare students for life in the 21st century.

I believe that the family will survive in the coming leisure society, even though current divorce statistics reflect a high level of discontent among the married. The high divorce rate comes from the very high expectations that people now have for marriage. The recently divorced seldom complain of desertion or physical abuse; instead, the unacceptable behavior is usually a lack of understanding or communication, insufficient companionship or romance, or a failure to share goals. Many husbands and wives expect their partners to behave with greater maturity than is taught in the schools. As curricula are revised to emphasize the previously ignored arenas of human relations and continued personal development, the proportion of successful marriages will probably increase. It also seems likely that in the future fathers will be expected to play a more active role in the family. Until now, fathers of young children have justified their absence because of the job; in the leisure society they will not have that excuse.

Many adults cannot envision a future of peace and equity because they daily observe people's obsession with status, unwillingness to share, and readiness to ignore the needs of others. Yet why should we find it strange that people unschooled in personal development seldom manifest signs of maturity? Under conditions that defined success more in terms of personal growth, student motivation would necessarily be modified so that status would become a lesser need than service to others. Accomplishment would be defined in terms other than acquisition. Status is presently an accomplishment, but, if status were assumed rather than earned, accomplishment would relate instead to beneficial influence. Many older people, after a lifetime of pursuing materialistic goals, begin to ask themselves a different kind of question: "What has my life meant? How can I live the remainder in a humanistic way?" Because these questions are being asked at a younger age than ever before, and because one's self-concept rests upon the answer, there is reason to believe that maturity will arrive much earlier in the individual life span in the future. Even a casual observer is aware that the financial motive has less appeal to today's youth than it has had in the past. Mature persons see sharing, respect, and service as their chosen behavior.

WORK AND HUMAN DIGNITY

Young people are already abandoning the Protestant work ethic, the belief that personal dignity is dependent upon economic production. To the question "What are you going to be?" youngsters now say "I already *am*, and you should recognize me as a person whether I am employed or not, whether I am through with school or not." To suggest that a person without a job has no dignity is comparable to saying that a slow learner is undeserving of respect. Neither teacher nor society can dispense dignity; it is not extrinsic; it need not be earned but rather should be assumed in every act of relating. Today increasing numbers of people see themselves as less than "somebody," an underevaluation that has been thrust upon them by an archaic dictate urging each individual to determine self-worth from being classed as employed, unemployed, or unemployable.

To satisfy the human desire for happiness, a society must consider the mental health, aspiration, self-concept, and dignity of individuals. Once we thought dignity came through biology, through being well born; later we decided it occurred as a product of labor, of having a job. A proper redefinition of the status of the individual must include the assumption that dignity begins with conception. Only then will people feel comfortable in a leisure society.

SHARING YOUR IMPRESSIONS

1. What kinds of situations do you find boring?
2. Comment on the extent to which boredom affects the people you know.
3. In what ways might the school curriculum change to meet the demands of society having a four-day work week?
4. In what ways might the educational responsibility of parents change in a society with greater access to leisure time?
5. Given the emerging concept of "work," how will the role of religion need to change?
6. Suggest some ways for helping adults learn to cope with extended leisure and vacations.
7. How do you feel about parents taking a vacation without their children?
8. What advice do you have for families who cannot afford distant vacation travel?
9. Give your impressions about what constitutes a successful vacation.

REFERENCES AND SUGGESTED READING

Asher, Jules. "Flexi-time, Four Day Weeks." *American Psychological Association Monitor* 6 (1975), No. 4, p. 5.

Baier, Kurt, and Rescher, Nicholas. *Values in the Future.* New York: The Free Press, 1971.

Campbell, Felicia. "The Future of Gambling." *The Futurist*, April 1976, pp. 84–90.

Doughty, Robin. "The Three-Day American Pleasure Trip." *Natural History*, June–July 1972, pp. 22–23, 85–87.

Dunnette, Marvin. *Work and Nonwork in the Year 2001.* Monterey, Calif.: Brooks/Cole, 1973.

Epperson, Arlin, Witt, Peter, and Hitzhusen, Gerald. *Leisure Counseling: An Aspect of Leisure Education.* Springfield, Ill.: Charles C Thomas, 1977.

Field, G. Lowell. "Work, Responsibility and Service Occupations." *Phi Kappa Phi Journal*, Winter 1977, pp. 56–62.

Green, Thomas. *Work, Leisure and the American School.* New York: Random House, 1968.

LeCoutre, R. (Ed.). *Free Time and Self Fulfillment.* Brussels, Belgium: Foundation Van Clé, 1977.

Millar, Susanna. *The Psychology of Play.* Baltimore: Penguin Books, 1971.

Otto, Herbert. *The Family in Search of the Future.* New York: Appleton-Century-Crofts, 1970.

Pieper, Josef. *Leisure, the Basis of Culture.* New York: New American Library, 1963.

Pine, Gerald. "Teacher Accountability: Myths and Realities." *The Educational Forum*, November 1976, pp. 49–60.

Skinner, B. F. *Beyond Freedom and Dignity.* New York: Bantam Books, 1972.

BOOKS TO SHARE WITH YOUNG CHILDREN

Alexander, Martha. *Out! Out! Out!* New York: Dial Press, 1968. Adults who are willing to learn some things from children may adjust well to increasing leisure. When a pigeon flies into the kitchen and knocks everything around, the grown-ups try their best to get rid of it, but only the young child's idea proves successful.

Davis, Alice Vaught. *Timothy Turtle.* New York: Harcourt, Brace & World, 1940. By working together, people can solve problems that would otherwise resist solutions and leave individuals feeling impotent. When Timothy Turtle falls on his back, all of his friends try to figure out how they can get him turned over again.

Finfer, Celentha, Wasserberg, Esther, and Weinberg, Florence. *Grandmother Dear*. Chicago: Follett, 1966. The increasing leisure of grandparents means that some of them can share more of themselves with grandchildren. A little boy takes his grandmother to all the places he enjoys and finds her a willing partner who is fun to be around.

Miles, Miska. *Annie and the Old One*. Boston: Little, Brown, 1971. Personality development will be necessary for success in a leisure society. Annie's grandmother has a mature perspective about the limits of life that the young Navajo girl at first finds hard to accept.

Winn, Marie. *The Man Who Made Fine Tops*. New York: Simon & Schuster, 1970. There are benefits and dangers in becoming a technological society. This is the story of how jobs became specialized and why we will need to rely more upon one another in the future.

6

BELIEF
AND
MORAL
DEVELOPMENT

TWENTY-ONE

VALUES FOR TOMORROW

The commitment to becoming a technological society has been followed by a shift in the principal source of values. As people come to believe that knowledge is the key to success, they gradually transfer their faith from religion to education. Then, when social problems accelerate, the secular society quite naturally expects its schools to be the major corrective influence. Our society seems to be in this position now, with an increasing demand for whatever sort of curriculum is necessary to raise moral standards. Planners have already begun to design courses ranging from values clarification and simulation of social problems to gaming in the realm of interpersonal relations. In addition to these efforts, it may also be worthwhile to compare our general approach with that of the church, which for so long was the mainstay of moral instruction. In particular, let's examine some of the resemblance between the two institutions. Perhaps the schools can learn something about their important new task from a more experienced partner.

OUR FAITH IN SCHOOLING

To begin with, education and religion appear similar in the support each has given to a guilt system. According to the believer in education, Plato was right when he stated that the evil in human life is primarily due to ignorance. Thus, for the members of a technological society it is insufficient learning, more than misbehavior, that ought to generate feelings of self-recrimination. A careful observer will note that many people are more disturbed when their lack of knowledge is discovered than when their failure to help others is pointed out.

Our faith in schooling is also reflected by the stigma we attach to whomever does without it. Indeed, the most conspicuous sinners are those who decide to discontinue formal learning at an early age, the so-called dropouts. A somewhat lesser offense than being uninformed is failing to keep up with events in the technical field one has chosen to represent. Yet, given the rapid increase of knowledge, it seems unreasonable that anyone should be embarrassed at the mere mention of ideas and resources with which they are unfamiliar.

Despite our best efforts, the thesis that ignorance is a reasonable explanation for most undesirable human behavior may have to be abandoned. The assumption that learning to read will result in responsiveness to the needs one reads about lacks support. In fact, we are finding that it can be quite the other way around. With strictly academic training, people can come to regard their obligation as reading rather than responding. Thus, the educated learn to read detailed accounts of slums, war, and air pollution, to discuss them sensibly, and then to put them completely out of mind, without ever once really experiencing anything in the way they experience those things in which the whole personality is involved. After watching a riot or attempted assassination on television, the only comment some of these persons make is "Channel 3 sure has good news coverage." Similarly, their children are expected at school to talk knowingly as expert spectators about the vital issues confronting the community, nation, and world, rather than to actually try to influence affairs. This detached manner of behaving might best be described in the style of a children's textbook: "Look at the issue. See the issue. See the important issue. Talk about the issue. Talk some more about the important issue. Look at the next issue . . ." and so on.

By watching their teachers at home and in school, some youngsters learn that to be concerned about an issue means to observe it, and to be actively concerned means only to discuss or read about it more. As the schooling process continues to lengthen, we must somehow ensure that it does not compete with the equally essential need of students for responsibility— that our process of education does not make unattainable the very development at which it aims. Unless students are exposed to emotionally maturing experiences along with their academic studies, they can only become erudite adolescents. The mere passage of time makes maturity possible but never guarantees it. However extended an education may be, it fails the student if a chance to take individual responsibility is not included in it.

MORAL BEHAVIOR AND SELF-EVALUATION

A seemingly minor but noteworthy shift has begun to occur in the criteria people use for self-evaluation. When we cannot point to our responsive behavior as an indicator of success, we may compensate by seeking satisfaction in stating objectives. That is, we can at least credit ourselves with knowing precisely what *should* be done. This procedure may be acceptable for certain tasks, but we do not diminish social problems simply by clarifying our values, expressing our beliefs in a more articulate way, or engaging in marathon debates about which values deserve to be taught. Certain of the basic values we have chosen and wish to maintain are apparent to even the most casual observer. These values are implicit in the daily demands we make of those who both govern and serve us. For example, we want the police to bring about an absence of theft and assault, because such forms of behavior threaten our security. We look to our courts for equity and an end to discriminatory practices, because we believe that prejudice is wrong and that civil rights are desirable. We watch our congressmen and other political leaders for a model of cooperation and honesty, because these qualities seem indispensable to good government. It is not at all difficult to get agreement on goals like these; they are not unique to the middle class or to persons who serve in a civil capacity.

Now that some schools are trying to connect behavioral objectives with the notion of competency, there may be changes in the way some students see themselves. Unlike the religious orientation, for which self-esteem is a by-product of behaving in accord with certain established values, educators have urged all students to feel good about themselves independently of their interpersonal behavior. Granting the motivational merit of the school approach for academic work, it may be dysfunctional where interpersonal relations and moral development are concerned. If educators decide to retain the goal of a favorable self-impression for all, perhaps they should require universal student involvement in some form of responsible social service, such as peer teaching, assisting the poor, or providing companionship to the elderly. There is ample evidence that, unless young people are allowed to connect ideals with behavior and thus to enact their humanistic aspirations while still in school, these ideals may well be left behind. And the cost of this loss is considerable, because to lack ideals as an adult is to lack moral direction.

In order to hold the school accountable for moral education, our view of competency must become more comprehensive. That is, we ought not emphasize merely more precise ways of determining whether the same narrow objectives from the past are being met. In the future, competency must be seen in moral terms as well. It is not enough that students can accurately compute their assets if they have not learned to share affluence; it is not enough that they can read about the misfortune of others if they still do nothing. Education for awareness alone or for competence in skills alone is not enough, and it never has been. In a world of increased crowding, greater leisure, and greater interdependence, personal success must rest upon moral competence, on having a prior commitment to serve the welfare of others.

In contrast to moral instruction in the church, moral instruction at school faces considerable opposition. Usually the antagonists fancy themselves as defenders of personal freedom or as guardians of the scholastic standard. In either case it appears misleading to claim that learning to do some specific academic task is a matter of *competence*, while learning to use ourselves on behalf of others is a matter of *motivation*. This evasive line of reasoning makes moral competence, the type we so urgently need, a matter of option rather than of obligation. Certainly teachers recognize that some obligations are currently imposed on students. Everyone is obliged to read, to figure, and to study history, but learning how to help other people is still seen as a matter of choice. Until direct experience in moral responsibility becomes an obligation within school, we can hardly claim to be educating for maturity. On the contrary, we are making the very task of growing up optional. And it is apparent that, like Peter Pan, some people have made the choice never to grow up.

There is also a fundamental difference in how the two institutions of school and church tend to view life itself. At the
entrance to the Inferno, Dante tells us, the sign reads "Abandon
hope, all you who enter here." Persons who embrace one religion or another may not have greater evidence about the future,
but they do benefit from a different view. To hope with little
evidence while others despair is a condition favoring mental
health. In order to prepare students for the future, the school
must also foster hope rather than skepticism. Sören Kier-
kegaard said that the hopeful person has a passion for possibilities. Surely, in a technological society, there must be a view
of the humanistic possibilities if they are ever to eventuate.

The relationship between hopelessness and self-destruction
is illustrated by a recent study at the University of Pennsylvania.
Nearly 100 people who were hospitalized because of suicide
attempts were asked to declare whether certain statements
about themselves were true or false. Some statements suggested
a pessimistic view of the future; other statements were optimistic. The researchers learned that hopelessness and depression
are both positively related to suicidal risk but that hopelessness
shows a significantly higher correlation with current risk than
does depression. In other words, the lack of desire to go on living
appears to result more from a person's lack of hope for the future
than from unhappiness with the present.

TELEVISION AND VALUES

One clue concerning how to improve the success of church
and school as regards moral education can be found in a lesson
from our distant past. Long ago the Athenian Greeks received
their moral education at the theater. The Athenians realized
that, unlike other methods of teaching, a theatrical production
can hold almost everyone's attention and convey a profound
influence. Consequently, the best playwrights were commis-
sioned by the government to provide moral education, to teach
the citizens virtue through drama. All of the Greek tragedies
were based on a similar format. The principal characters were
usually persons of high social status whose departure from their
values invariably led them into desperate situations. Later, after

a renewal of commitment to his or her original values, the hero's reputation is restored and, with it, the audience's esteem. Whether the plot involved Oedipus Rex, Medea, or any of the other familiar heroes, the lesson was always the same: no one, not even the most prominent persons, can desert his or her values without experiencing in consequence a life of tragedy and remorse.

Even the Shakespearean tragedies written hundreds of years later correspond in this respect to the Greek design. Prince Hamlet, King Lear, Macbeth, and Othello are all examples of heroes who desert their values only to find that the result is great personal loss and regret. It is instructive to contrast how the Greek and Shakespearean plays differ from our modern version of tragedy. For example, in Arthur Miller's *Death of a Salesman*, the principal character, Willy Loman, is portrayed as a victim of false values. The audience is led to feel sorry and partially responsible for Willy's condition, since he has been betrayed by society. The assumption that Willy's problems are not of his own making represents a critical change, since in earlier times the tragedy never portrayed society as the villain. Neither was the failure of any individual excused on the premise that his environment was really at fault.

What does this concern for theater have to do with moral education today? Children growing up now are daily exposed to a variety of dramatic productions on television. For the most part, educators and church leaders have not learned to use television as a medium for teaching worthwhile values. As a result, neither institution has provided parents with guidance concerning how to take advantage of a major interest during childhood. It is not that anyone doubts the impact of television. On the contrary, most of the educational studies to date have been attempts to show how influential film violence is in leading children to sanction aggressive behavior. Given this persuasion, it is not surprising that parents and teachers have come to regard themselves as censors, judges who decide which programs might undermine the development of wholesome attitudes. In my opinion, this approach should be abandoned, since it overlooks the beneficial effects of television and fails to assign grown-ups the role of interpreters.

All of us can move toward a broader view by watching with children some of the programs they choose. Anyone who has ever been on a field trip with boys and girls knows that they seldom report the same experience as the adults who accompany them. One way to assess a youngster's perspective, whether on a field trip to the zoo or in the family living room watching a program like "Valley of the Dinosaurs," is by raising questions about what is taking place. Our questions can also direct a child's focus to details that would otherwise be missed. This procedure may at first be disturbing to some parents because they have always preferred silence during televiewing. However, as they begin to experience the satisfaction of listening to children share their interpretations of events, most mothers and fathers recognize the opportunity to share their own impressions. Actually, this was the original intention for rating movies "PG"—Parental Guidance Suggested.

There is much we have yet to learn about how television can help us with teaching moral development. But each of us can make an important breakthrough by expecting some new things of ourselves. In particular, parents should arrange to watch television with their children; this takes time. Next, we should be asking questions of our children during these mutual observations; this is a skill that takes practice. And, just as we want children to tell us their impressions of what they have seen, we should interpret our own experience to them; this requires self-disclosure. Finally, we should allow our sons and daughters to choose some of the programs that the family watches together; this takes acceptance of the interests held by children. Parents who subject themselves to expectations such as these soon discover that in a sense we have in television the possibility of our own Greek moral theater—except that ours requires a bit more audience participation.

SHARING YOUR IMPRESSIONS

1. Describe an experience in which you had a difference of opinion with someone who was your religious teacher.
2. What do we know about those who teach religion to our children? Those who teach them basic skills at school?

3. Make some guesses about what boys and girls learn at Sunday school and catechism.
4. How would you go about improving the religious education of children?
5. Give some reasons for the recent rise in values instruction as a part of the regular school curriculum.
6. How is education similar and dissimilar from religion in its approach to value instruction?
7. Comment about the influence of television in terms of its effect on children's values.

REFERENCES AND SUGGESTED READING

Allport, Gordon. *The Individual and His Religion.* New York: Macmillan, 1960.

Cunningham, Michael. "Television Watching and Family Tension." *Journal of Marriage and the Family* 18 (1976), 105–111.

Fiske, Edward. "New Techniques for Helping Pupils Develop Values." *Human Development in Today's World*, edited by S. White. Boston: Little, Brown, 1976. Pp. 193–196.

Fletcher, Joseph. *Situation Ethics: The New Morality.* Philadelphia: Westminster Press, 1966.

Fromm, Erich. *The Heart of Man.* New York: Harper & Row, 1964.

Goldman, Ronald. *Religious Thinking from Childhood to Adolescence.* London: Routledge and Kegan Paul, 1968.

Jeffreys, M. V. C. *Personal Values in the Modern World.* Baltimore: Penguin Books, 1968.

Kirschenbaum, H., and Simon, S. "Values and the Futures Movement in Education." In *Learning for Tomorrow*, edited by A. Toffler. New York: Random House, 1974. Pp. 257–270.

Kohlberg, Lawrence. "The Cognitive Developmental Approach to Moral Education." In *Readings in Human Development*, edited by A. Kilbride. Guilford, Conn.: Dushkin, 1976. Pp. 166–174.

May, Philip R. *Moral Education in School.* London: Methuen Educational Ltd., 1971.

Miller, Arthur. *Death of a Salesman.* New York: Bantam Books, 1955.

Singer, Dorothy, and Singer, Jerome. "Family Television Viewing Habits and the Spontaneous Play of Preschool Children." *American Journal of Orthopsychiatry*, 46 (1976), 496–502.

Strom, Robert D. "Parent As A Teacher Inventory." In *Tests and Measurements in Child Development, Handbook II*, edited by Orval Johnson. San Francisco: Jossey-Bass, 1976. Pp. 829–832.

Weissman, A., Beck, A., and Kovacs, M. "Hopelessness: An Indicator of Suicidal Risk." *Suicide and Life Threatening Behavior*, Summer 1975, pp. 98–103.

Williams, Norma, and Williams, Sheila. *The Moral Development of Children*. London: Macmillan, 1970.

BOOKS TO SHARE WITH YOUNG CHILDREN

Cole, Joan. *The Secret Box*. New York: William Morrow, 1971. Stealing is an issue that needs discussion in more homes. Ann-Marie takes a pencil from the teacher's desk and then a pencil case from her classmate before she thinks about the consequences of her behavior.

Johnston, Johanna. *Edie Changes Her Mind*. New York: Putnam's Sons, 1964. Parents can help children develop a value system by allowing them to make some decisions and experience the consequences. Edie always protested bedtime, so mother and dad let her stay up all alone and find out something about the long night, about the morning after, and about herself.

Littledale, Harold. *Alexander*. New York: Parents Magazine Press, 1964. Taking responsibility for our behavior is a sign of growing up. Chris always says the naughty things he does are caused by a pretend horse until Chris's father points out that everybody has a bad day occasionally.

Ness, Evaline. *Do You Have the Time, Lydia?* New York: Dutton, 1971. People's values are reflected by the way they spend their time. Lydia was too busy to help her younger brother, and promising to do it later wasn't good enough.

Steptoe, John. *Stevie*. New York: Harper & Row, 1969. The guilt following our mistreatment of someone can bring improved behavior. Stevie looks back with regret at how he took advantage of Robert and ignored the younger boy's needs.

TWENTY-TWO

THE POWER OF COERCION

We have become accustomed to certain disciplinary practices in school, because we suppose they lead to worthwhile results. For example, since the survival of our society requires obedience to authority, we permit coercion in the classroom. This tendency is reflected in the preoccupation of many teachers with maintaining discipline and control. In describing the kind of student they prefer, such teachers assign great value to qualities such as obedience, courteousness, and willingness to accept the judgment of authorities. At the same time, they are reluctant to accept any spirited disagreement, disruption of class routine, or guessing. Students subjected to these conditions are unlikely to fulfill their need to develop independence of judgment, courage of conviction, and curiosity. We may hope that the amount of coercion exercised in schools as well as at home will decline as more adults become aware of how it occurs and of the ways in which children are adversely affected.

One way to begin is by examining some of the common strategies that authority figures use in coercing others. Although the examples considered in this chapter are drawn from life in the classroom, the recommendations I will make apply equally well to similar circumstances involving parents.

LYING

Throughout history, people have been intimidated by others who resort to lying as a means of controlling them. Whether the untruth is a minor distortion of the facts or a complete fabrication, the purpose is similar: to undermine the victim's self-confidence and substitute a dependence on the coercing party. By arousing students' doubts about their adequacy, progress, or future well being, it is possible to eliminate any opposition they might otherwise represent in class.

Teachers usually count on the lie to bring conforming behavior from students with a reputation for trouble. This kind of lie has many forms:

"If you don't behave, you won't pass this year."

"Anyone who talks will not have recess for a week."

"Unless your math improves, you can forget about physical education."

To be sure, some of these threats will be carried out, but in most cases they are only lies to induce submission. Invariably, teachers justify the lie along these lines: "I'm doing it for the student's own good. This person needs to wake up and realize that the future is dim unless certain undesirable behaviors are discontinued." Granting the teacher's good intentions, it should be recognized that non-threatening words can serve as well as others to carry influence and convey meaning. Surely there is merit in helping students project the likely consequences of actions, discover reasons for failure, decide on alternatives for improvement, accept the need for constructive criticism, and learn to appraise themselves realistically. In these ways a teacher can replace the strategy of falsehood and fear with truth and reason.

Often the lie takes the form of a bribe. Many teachers who think they never threaten their classes bribe them instead. The bribe usually begins with the words "If you are good" or "If you get good grades . . . ." Children become familiar with this method long before they start school. Santa, for example, always asks "Have you been good?" Yet the children soon learn the irrelevance of their behavior to the number of gifts under the Christmas tree. Similarly, in the classroom children soon learn that the teacher's benevolence is not a function of their good behavior. The field trip is taken regardless of low grades in spelling; the movie is shown even if they have misbehaved the day before. They go out to play in the afternoon if the teacher feels like it; in fact, disorder may improve the possibility of going outside. Lying, in whatever form, and even when used sparingly, only serves to undermine the teacher's credibility and chance for being a good example.

CREATING A SENSE OF POWERLESSNESS

The ability to control other people's behavior is increased when they feel powerless and alone with their concerns about physiological and safety needs. Some teachers have developed a repertoire of methods for stripping students of their defenses in order to make them feel powerless. The repertoire may include constant probing and an insistence that children explain the motivation for all their behavior or an excessive concern with students' clothes, daydreaming, lack of interest in dating, or feelings of hostility—all defenses a young person may need temporarily against more threatening things.

Again, teachers can be more helpful if they reverse the powerlessness strategy and use instead techniques that enable students to take pride in themselves. Feelings of impotence diminish people and compel them to focus on merely animal concerns; a sense of self-esteem enables them to focus on human questions. Teachers who desire self-esteem for their students will respect each individual's need for defenses, realizing that these defenses may be necessary to protect the person from anxiety until more mature coping skills have been developed. For example, working with 4- and 5-year-olds requires a tolerance of the need of children at this age to sometimes depreciate the performance of others in order to feel good about themselves. In the junior high school, anxieties about pimples, obesity, or other aspects of body image are often reduced by what some grown-ups would call excessive daydreaming. Adults dealing with high school students should understand the need of adolescents to rationalize.

As teachers and parents, we should respect young people's privacy, their different manner of speech and dress, or whatever prop they may have temporarily adopted to help control inner tensions and cope with environmental demands. At the same time, a caring teacher can assist certain students to become aware of the reactions others have to their unusual behavior and its probable consequences. The self-pride strategy is implemented by being respectful of students' questions and ideas, helping individuals recognize the worth of their own thinking, encouraging the use of unique strengths, establishing group standards in which its members can take pride, keeping personal information confidential, letting students "save face," and recognizing improved performance.

EGO INFLATION

The coercive strategy of ego inflation consists of playing to people's need for esteem and then contriving a circumstance in which they lose face unless they submit. In the beginning one freely magnifies the victims' value by exaggerating their understanding and intelligence, by praising their talent, skills, sensitivity, and virtue. Often the victims have never been so charmed or felt so significant. When they are fully convinced that they are genuinely appreciated in a way they have never been before, the coercive agent threatens to withdraw the friendship, esteem, or affection unless the relationship is altered. That is, the victims must now prove themselves intellectually, emotionally, or through some behavior in compliance with the agent's wishes in order for their association to continue. Whether this strategy is employed by a father toward his low-achieving son, a young man toward his girlfriend, or teachers toward students, it comes to the same thing: taking unfair advantage of a person's need to be important to someone.

The strategy of ego inflation is understandably tempting to an inexperienced teacher, who may see it as a useful influence for working with slow learners or rejected children. It is true that such students are easy prey to this tactic, but no one wins when an individual is persuaded to accept an inflated self-impression and then challenged to justify the hoped-for image. Although this kind of lying may be intended to motivate youngsters, elevate their aspirations, and promote achievement, invariably it results in stress, frustration, and disappointment. A more sensitive teacher works toward enabling all pupils to feel important as they are, without making continued esteem contingent upon academic performance. When respect is based on achievement only, less able students receive a diminishing level of teacher esteem. By the end of the year, the youngsters who need the most support are receiving the least.

Every student has worth apart from school accomplishment. The way to reverse the ego-inflation strategy is to replace it with a respect for human dignity, a concept on which the most satisfying of human relationships are based. This is not simply a matter of choosing between telling an untruth (overestimating a child's ability for motivation's sake) and telling a supposed truth ("You're just a stupid kid who will never amount to anything, and nothing much can be done about it.") It is less a question of a truth's being damaging than it is a question of some teachers' inability to see the truth. Because they measure success in much the same way as they assess student value, some teachers are unable to accept the notion that a nonprofessional life can be satisfying and worth living and that the person who lives it can "amount to something." Such teachers end up ignoring the slow students, assigning them too difficult work, and reinforcing their negative self-concepts.

A better option than either ego inflation or telling the child our concept of success and the good life takes the form of self-questioning: "How can I help this boy (or girl) feel worthwhile as a person? How can I help him assess his weaknesses and strengths? How can he be helped to select appropriate goals and to achieve successes in the pursuit of those objectives?" Here is the test of a genuine guide, whose aspiration for all pupils is that they individually achieve whatever good in life can be theirs. Under these conditions, teachers neither ignore the unsuccessful nor assign them work that is too difficult simply to justify a low grade. Such teachers let it be known that they do care and that they are on the students' side. What is more, these teachers are able to show pride in their pupils' gains without recourse to overestimation, exaggeration, and superfluous adjectives. The future success of many students depends on increasing this kind of teacher/student relationship.

OMNIPOTENCE/OMNISCIENCE

The temptation to use the strategy of appearing all-knowing and all-powerful is constantly before educators because of their social role. Many parents who attempt to develop a child's respect for learning and school encourage perceptions of teachers that exaggerate their authority and store of knowledge. It is not surprising that, faced with the lofty expectations of students and their families, some educators succumb to the temptation of adopting an "almighty" posture. A first step is to convey to the students the suggestion that a teacher knows all about each of them and has final power over them. The teacher has aptitude, achievement, and personality test data, information from previous teachers, parents, and classmates, and confidential reports from the guidance counselor. Students commonly believe that a teacher knows things about them that they themselves do not know. It is precisely this doubt and apprehension on the part of children concerning the nature and extent of the knowledge a teacher has about them that gives the teacher the option of a bluff.

Essentially, the psychological function of bluffing is to redress the balance between one's own inadequacy and the other person's potential superiority. The insecure teacher who feels obliged to know all the answers is likely to use bluffing whenever threatened by able students. Generally, such a teacher justifies a bluff by rationalizing that its only purpose is to benefit the student—in particular, to keep troublesome students in their place and protect them from getting "swollen heads." That being put on the spot by a youngster might jeopardize the image of omniscience is given some consideration, but supposedly only for the sake of students whose learning might be adversely affected were they to lose confidence in the teacher's ability. Having thus justified the bluff as a means for "helping" threatening pupils and, indirectly, the entire class, teachers begin their act.

Bluffing may be considered unnecessary in relating to grade-oriented students. However, a few boys and girls will persist in challenging authority, questioning sources of information, and pointing to weaknesses in teachers' logic. Most members of this group can be controlled through bluff. In a private conference, the teacher might say "Larry, in many ways you are one of my better students, but the tendency to interrupt the class bothers me. In considering how to handle the matter, I talked to a number of people who know you, and I looked at your cumulative record—and, Larry, all I can say is that I am somewhat shocked by what I have learned, by what I know now." The teacher is careful not to be specific, knowing full well that his or her greatest ally is the student's own imagination.

At this point, tension begins to build within the youngster as he searches his past for a possible embarrassing issue or event. In thinking back upon the things he isn't proud of and wouldn't want to have brought into the open, the student may reason "But how could the teacher know that? How does anyone else know? Were we seen? What does the teacher really know about me?" Adding to the threat of someone knowing about the "incident" in question is the teacher's intimation that "I would hate to reveal this information to your classmates or your parents, Larry, so don't push me in class or I will be forced to play my ace. Behave, do it my way, and we will get along, everything will be alright." Because Larry fears teacher reprisal, he agrees to submit. The teacher retains control; the student has been bluffed.

A less dramatic version of omniscience is enacted daily in many classes during question periods. Since admissions of ignorance conflict with the intended image, various maneuvers are employed to convince pupils of teacher wisdom. One such maneuver is to snow the group by referring to information that is either irrelevant or outside the students' experience. Generally this performance is followed by the remark "Does everyone understand?" Because they don't want to seem stupid, students don't reply. For some boys and girls, the fact that the teacher's remarks were incomprehensible is a mark of genius. Another ploy is to avoid the questions one is unable to answer by rephrasing students' inquiries almost simultaneously, so that the new questions correspond to the answers one prepared before class. Again, some children are impressed by this kind of one-way discussion.

A third method involves penalizing the curious by regularly returning their questions with the injunction "Let's look it up." Implicit in this statement is a suggestion that all answers can be found in the library and a promise that the teacher is willing to collaborate. However, it often means that the curious youngsters stop asking questions after they learn that each inquiry involves an additional assignment. A related example of omniscience occurs when the teacher makes a mistake writing on the board. When corrected, the teacher passes it off as something done deliberately by saying "Very good, John, I wondered if anyone would catch that" or "I did that to see whether you were awake."

It would have been more instructive as well as more honest to use the incident to show that no one is perfect and that even teachers make mistakes.

Teachers who abandon omnipotence and omniscience strategies recognize that student respect can be gained without deception. They know that questions are more numerous today and that the answers are more elusive and complex. As they become guides instead of all-knowing authorities, their new intention eliminates the need for presumption and gives students the active role in learning. All youngsters need someone or something to remove the fear of the unknown; a guide serves this function. As guides, we can help students structure their world by exploring assets and liabilities, becoming aware of sources of information, viewing the feasibility of alternative courses of action, and ascertaining their own best direction. Above all, adult guides at home and in the school realize that human development is promoted not by coercive techniques but by the reversal of such strategies.

SHARING YOUR IMPRESSIONS

1. Recall some coercive techniques parents or teachers used when trying to educate you.
2. Discuss the dropout of adolescents from church attendance.
3. Discuss the place of curiosity and doubt in religious and moral education.
4. Propose a way for helping parents and teachers accept children's expression of personal opinion and thought.
5. How should parents attempt to teach religious and moral development?
6. How would you go about the selection and preparation of teachers for religious education?
7. What are some of the coercive methods peers use on each other during early childhood? Elementary school? High school?
8. Speculate about the relative amount of coercion children are subject to at home and in the school.
9. What are your feelings about corporal punishment in the home? At school?

REFERENCES AND SUGGESTED READING

Bettelheim, Bruno. "Behavior in Extreme Conditions: Coercion." In *The Informed Heart*. New York: Free Press, 1960. Pp. 106–176.

Bromberg, Walter. *The Mind of Man*. New York: Harper & Row, 1963. Pp. 43–70.

Fromm, Erich. *The Revolution of Hope*. New York: Bantam Books, 1968. Pp. 26–169.

Gordon, Ira. *The Infant Experience*. Columbus, Ohio: Charles E. Merrill, 1975.

Gray, Jeffrey. *The Psychology of Fear and Stress*. London: Weidenfeld and Nicholson, 1971. Pp. 97–180.

Milgram, Stanley. "Some Conditions of Obedience and Disobedience to Authority." *Human Relations*, 18 (1965), 5–20.

Morrison, Thomas. "Control as an Aspect of Group Leadership in Classrooms: A Review of Research." *Journal of Education*, November 1974, p. 41.

Rubin, Theodore. *The Angry Book*. New York: Macmillan, 1969.

Sargant, William. *Battle for the Mind*. London: PAN Books, 1959.

Storr, Anthony. *Human Aggression*. New York: Bantam Books, 1968.

Torrance, E. Paul. *Constructive Behavior: Stress, Personality and Mental Health*. Belmont, Calif.: Wadsworth, 1965.

Wertheimer, Michael (Ed.). *Confrontation: Psychology and the Problems of Today*. Glenview, Ill.: Scott, Foresman, 1970. Pp. 57–95.

BOOKS TO SHARE WITH YOUNG CHILDREN

Ets, Marie Hall. *Little Old Automobile*. New York: Viking, 1948. Reliance upon coercion can in time lead to disaster. The little old automobile refuses to wait for people and animals to get out of his way and delights in abusing power—until he meets a train.

Hamada, Hirosuke. *The Tears of the Dragon*. New York: Parents Magazine Press, 1967. Parents in many cultures use children's fear as one means of controlling them. A Japanese boy named Akito doesn't believe that a monstrous dragon will take you away if you are naughty, and he sets out to prove that the village elders are wrong.

Lystad, Mary. *Millicent the Monster*. New York: Harlin Quist Books, 1968. There are moments when children believe that imposing their will on parents could be the ideal way of solving family problems. Millicent is tired of the way things are run in her household; so she tries being a monster and threatening her parents.

Rosen, Winifred. *Marvin's Manhole*. New York: Dial Press, 1970. The doubts and curiosity of childhood should be viewed as desirable qualities. Mother has explained what manholes are for; but Marvin still thinks some scary thing lives down there, and he must learn more about it.

Waher, Bernard. *Lovable Lyle*. Boston: Houghton Mifflin, 1969. The anonymous threat is a familiar form of coercion. It seems everyone loves Lyle the crocodile except a secret enemy who sends him unfriendly notes but later decides that he is indeed more deserving of compliments.

TWENTY-THREE
IN DEFENSE OF PRETENDERS

Sometimes parents are embarrassed when young children announce their observations. After all, what sort of response is adequate when a boy points out that the lady at the next table is fat? We could counter his honesty with a lie by saying "Nonsense, Johnny, she's not fat at all." Another reaction is to encourage discretion: "Hush, it's not nice to call someone fat." Perhaps the least frequent answer is to agree "Yes, she is overweight." Parents in this kind of situation are later amused when they reminisce about the innocent and forthright expression of children. Yet, while the sometimes embarrassing truthfulness of little boys and girls is ultimately regarded as a favorable sign, their reliance upon fantasy is seen by some families as evidence of an opposite tendency. According to this view of moral development, a child who tells stories about events that never really took place has already begun to practice dishonesty through deception. Consequently, in homes in which pretending is interpreted as lying—as the first form of criminal behavior—fantasy is actively discouraged.

PARENTAL ATTITUDES TOWARD FANTASY

In her studies of creative play, Joan Freyberg found that the single most important factor in distinguishing between children of high and low imagination was the parents' attitude toward pretending and their quality of involvement in this sphere. Mothers and fathers who expressed positive feelings about role playing and making up stories were more apt to encourage the development of imaginative skill in their youngsters. That this kind of parental support is significant is also indicated by other research. Children who easily engage in fantasy are more able to concentrate, persist at tasks, cope with anxiety, tolerate frustration, and exercise self-control. Given these conditions, it would seem that, before parents decide to assign fantasy a low value in the home, they should acquaint themselves with its effect on some desirable moral qualities.

Children's minds are insufficiently developed to use imagination in the same way as adults; that is, their pretending does not usually produce anything that could be sold for a profit. Young children invent situations and make up stories just for the fun of it—an outcome that has little value in the estimation of some parents and teachers. Yet, if children are expected to become adults who show creativity in science, art, or technology, their inventive orientation must be preserved and developed. Fantasy must be allowed to persist in the form of dramatic play and other seemingly impractical ways until such time as children can demonstrate their originality in more sophisticated fashion, until divergent thinking is ready to impose its power on the things grown-ups accept as useful.

A second and frequently overlooked point is that children's fantasies serve a useful purpose in terms of both motivation and mental health, inasmuch as achievement usually has to be imagined before it can be actualized. Children can boast fewer achievements than they would like. Much of what they perceive as recognized accomplishment lies beyond what their minds or physical development allow. Therefore, it is only natural that they should frequent an imaginary world in which the desired goals can be reached. Parental acceptance of this need for pretending can help children believe in themselves.

It should also be expected that the product of a child's imagination will be expressed as though it represents a fact. Consider the first-grade boy who describes how, on the way home from school, he heard a cry for help. When he went to find out what was happening, he saw that a baby had fallen into a lake and was drowning; so he dived in and saved the would-be victim. Afterwards the crowd of spectators as well as the baby's parents all said they were grateful for his rescue operation. The fact that no body of water lies between the boy's school and home, that he cannot swim, and that his clothes are perfectly dry does not detract from the story. If the rescue didn't happen, it should have. His tale illustrates how he would like to act if such a situation arose; so he might as well behave as if it were true. But every so often this kind of report is treated as a moral issue, with a scolding or spanking administered because a falsehood cannot go without punishment—this response from parents who at the same time may be telling a younger brother or sister about the Easter Bunny, Santa Claus, and the Tooth Fairy. Of course, the parents might do well to encourage a desired achievement by teaching the boy to swim. But the point is that, for children, a narrow and often ignored line separates fact from wish, what is from what they would like it to be. Fantasy is able to bridge this gap, and children who first imagine themselves heroes are more likely to become heroes. These individuals have goals and can see possibilities.

Another relevant illustration of how fantasy can benefit motivation involves a father who tells about taking his 4-year-old daughter to a birthday party. The little girl was so shy and bashful that, whenever other guests approached or spoke to her, she would bury her face in her daddy's coat. All during the festivities she did not speak at all until the time came to leave. Then she remarked how very much she would like to come back again. Upon arrival at home, the girl told her mother how she had played and spoken with all the other children. Again, this so-called lie represents what the girl would like to have been doing and therefore what she imagined herself to have done. On a subsequent visit perhaps she will do what her shyness had at first prevented. However, to her way of thinking, no clear boundaries separate fantasy from fact. Indeed, the first leads to the second, and this holds true for most children in that achievements have to be imagined before they are put into effect. This principle obtains for adults as well. Anyone without the ability to fantasize lacks not only the primary source by which to sustain creative production but a great mechanism of defense that can dilute the power of stress.

FANTASY AT SCHOOL

Despite the merits of fantasy in terms of mental and moral development, its presence is sometimes unwelcomed even at school. There is a long history of research support for the claim that many children unnecessarily sacrifice imagination at about the fourth grade. At that point the previously rising creative-growth curves begin to decline. This tendency was first recognized in 1900 by E. A. Kirkpatrick, whose ink-blot study showed children in grades one through three to be more imaginative than those in grades four through six. During an investigation of written compositions, S. S. Colvin and I. F. Meyer reported a general decline in fantasy from grades three through twelve. In her song-creation experiments, Ruth Weideman found that fourth-graders submitted a smaller proportion of songs than did children in any of the lower grades. At the same time, they expressed a perfectionist trend in being the group most interested in judging work done by peers.

This same discouraging trend toward decreased imaginative production at the fourth grade is documented by Paul Torrance's studies of children's writing and by my own observations of peer teaching through fantasy play. To find out for yourself, make a comparison between the number of children in your town engaged in little-league sports and the number participating in creative dramatics.

It seems that, at about the fourth grade, male and female roles assume significance, peer standards become important, and children are expected to start behaving more like grown-ups. The emphasis of curriculum content changes to the realistic and the factual. Lessons become more formal and organized; students are invited to be critical of other people's ideas; guessing or uncommon responses are discouraged; credit is given only for what is written down; marks become an indicator of acceptability. It is commonly believed that these changes are more likely to motivate achievement than would a dreamy orientation of fantasy. Children need to learn that the world isn't all roses, that animals don't really talk, that competition is keen, and that the rewards of life go to persons who are alert, practical, and realistic.

Under these conditions, imagination is discounted. In response to the question "What are all the possible things Mother Hubbard could have done when she found no bones in the cupboard for her dog?" younger children were able to generate many alternatives, but fourth-graders found the task extremely difficult. They were so preoccupied by their judgment that she should have prevented this predicament in the first place that they could not come up with ways by which she could help herself. This story response underscores the impression that our greatest prejudice may not be a bias against certain ethnic or age groups but instead a common intolerance of fantasy. One thing is clear: Our society is presently reducing its creative talent inadvertently, by neglecting imaginative growth during middle childhood. If this were not the case, more boys and girls might grow up to be productive adults whose moral commitments would be sustained longer and whose concern for other people would be aided by the ability to come up with imaginative ways to help them.

SHARING YOUR IMPRESSIONS

1. Describe one of the "tall tales" you made up as a child and the consequences that followed.
2. Try to recall a situation in which you substituted a fictitious person as the one having a problem that was actually your own.
3. During early childhood, how normal is lying and swearing among boys? Among girls?
4. When a child makes up stories, how should the parents respond? How should teachers respond?
5. Select a grade level and illustrate the kinds of questions you recommend should be the focus of parent/teacher conferences.
6. Suggest some ways for parents to become more aware of their child's behavior at school.
7. What should parents and teachers tell a child about peers who have lied?
8. Recommend to parents and teachers some ways of reacting to children that would allow them to accept and value fantasy while still emphasizing the importance of truth.

REFERENCES AND SUGGESTED READING

Colvin, S. S., and Meyer, I. F. "Imaginative Elements in the Written Work of School Children." *Pedagogical Seminary*, 13 (1906), 84–93.

de Jouvenal, Bertrand. *The Art of Conjecture*. New York: Basic Books, 1967.

Freyberg, Joan. "Increasing Children's Fantasies: Hold High the Cardboard Sword." *Psychology Today*, February 1975, pp. 62–64.

Ghiselin, Brewster. *The Creative Process*. New York: New American Library, 1952.

Hadfield, J. A. *Childhood and Adolescence*. Baltimore: Penguin Books, 1962.

Kirkpatrick, E. A. "Individual Tests of School Children." *Psychological Review*, 5 (1900), No. 7.

Klinger, Eric. *Structure and Functions of Fantasy*. New York: Wiley, 1971.

Mead, Margaret. *Blackberry Winter: My Earlier Years*. New York: William Morrow, 1972.

Sutherland, Margaret. *Everyday Imagining and Education*. London: Routledge and Kegan Paul, 1971.

Torrance, E. Paul. "Understanding the Fourth Grade Slump in Creativity." Athens: Georgia Studies of Creative Behavior, University of Georgia, 1967.

Weideman, Ruth. "An Experiment with Grade School Children in Making Creative Song with Varied Stimuli." Masters research paper, University of Minnesota, 1961.

Winnicott, D. W. *Playing and Reality*. London: Travistock, 1971.

BOOKS TO SHARE WITH YOUNG CHILDREN

Alexander, Martha. *Maybe a Monster*. New York: Dial Press, 1968. Achievements usually have to be imagined before they actually take place. The little boy in this story decides to build a monster trap, and, even though the creature may be large and frightening, our hero insists he will not let it get away.

Black, Irma Simonton. *Doctor Proctor and Mrs. Merriwether*. Chicago: Albert Whitman, 1971. Children should be encouraged to make up stories rather than be led to feel that pretending is dishonest. Susan and Peter enact many roles during their play together and in this way demonstrate that the most honest thing children can do is report the imaginative experiences they are having.

Holl, Adelaide. *If We Could Make Wishes*. Champaign: Garrard, 1977. Children who easily engage in fantasy are more able to persist at tasks. This story reveals some of the many things children dream about and at the same time brings the difference between real and make-believe softly into focus.

Reid, Alastair. *Supposing*. Boston: Little, Brown, 1960. The attitude of parents toward pretending can influence a child's level of creative behavior. One youngster tells us what he supposes and in the process illustrates the extensive range of alternatives children can think of when they consider how their world might be improved.

Welber, Robert. *The Winter Picnic.* New York: Pantheon Books, 1970. Uncommon ideas deserve to be considered. Adam wants to have a picnic in the snow, but mother says picnics are for summer only. Then she changes her mind and also admits that she was wrong.

EPILOG

Now that educators acknowledge a close relationship between parent development and child development, they no longer oppose the idea of helping mothers and fathers become better teachers. In fact, many school systems are already trying to design worthwhile curricula for parents. In my opinion, these efforts will be more successful if they include a careful review of the expectations the school and home have for each other. Let's examine some of the prevailing assumptions about educating parents and see where changes might be warranted.

Certainly the future of parent education will be influenced by what teachers think of parent motivation. Teachers can choose to doubt whether most parents would take advantage of a curriculum for improving their influence. They can also suppose that any programs would be rejected by the families who need them most. It is not difficult to imagine the quality of instruction and level of success that would accompany this low estimate of parent aspiration. By contrast, if teachers recognize that many people wish to become better parents, then schools are more likely to take the task of parent development seriously. Obviously, once parents agree to participate, their further motivation will be determined by the program itself.

The content of parent curriculum may have to be revised to go beyond school problems. Many parents whose children have reached the upper elementary grades can no longer be helpful with assignments. Some teachers ignore this fact and continue to regard homework assistance as a proper expectation of all par-

275

ents. Apart from the decline in children's respect for parents that this procedure causes, it also suggests that the only things worth learning take place in school. Perhaps we need a separate curriculum of learnings to be offered by the home, one that supports the family relationship and takes into account the need for important nonacademic learning not offered at school.

In this connection, it would be misleading to use programs serving families with preschoolers as a model for educating parents with older children. The tendency to rely on these programs is tempting, because they are the most common, and they have been carefully planned. However, certain premises about the parental role remain appropriate for only a short period of time. To illustrate, the stage during which boys and girls spend most days at home with parents as the only teachers is limited to early childhood. Accordingly, the nature of parent education then consists mostly of content intended for the child. Once a youngster enters school, the curriculum for mothers and fathers should shift to emphasize their enlarging guidance function rather than readiness or remedial teaching on behalf of the school.

Another beneficial change we can anticipate before long is the provision of continuity. Since parents are a child's only continuous guides, they must acquire a broad understanding of human development, encompassing at least the period between birth and adolescence. Parents have a role unlike that of a third-grade teacher who works exclusively with 8-year-olds or, for that matter, any teacher at school whose students are always in the same age group and taught for only a year. Parents are expected to educate children who keep getting older. Yet, although access to learning about preschoolers is widely available, it is rare to find a curriculum for parents who have elementary or adolescent youngsters. Some parents may infer from this lack of continuing education for them that their child-rearing responsibility is complete once the youngster enters grade school; someone else called the teacher is then to be held accountable. Other parents of adolescents live with the false impression that the family problems they experience are uncommon and qualify them for clinical treatment. I believe such parents would not suffer the levels of anxiety and guilt they now do nor seek the services of psychologists and psychiatrists in as large numbers if they had access to parent education on a long-term basis. For one thing, their feeling of aloneness would decline when, through sharing, they discovered that other mothers and fathers face similar situations. Moreover, their feeling of helplessness could be reduced as they learn possible solutions to common problems of parenting.

Finally, there is the question of who should be expected to develop and present parent curriculum. At the moment, many profit-making organizations advertise brief courses in parent effectiveness, techniques that supposedly are successful with boys and girls of any age. This expensive source of help was indirectly encouraged by the government's policy of restricting participation in publicly funded programs to poverty families only. An opposite extreme would require voters to approve a new labor market of parent experts attached to the public schools.

I believe our best choice lies in raising the current low level of collaboration among educators. School systems can form consortiums whereby each assumes responsibility for developing separate aspects of parent curriculum. Federal agencies and private foundations could earmark some financial support for projects that try to fill the void in curriculum for later stages of parenting. University researchers should begin to link the parent curricula they have separately designed. Teachers enrolled in graduate work could receive supervision and credit for projects dealing with parent curriculum.

At the same time as educators attempt to collaborate with one another more, they should reserve a place for the indigenous leadership of parents. Many individuals who now devote their volunteer efforts to other institutions could provide capable direction in parent education. All of these changes call for a greater willingness to work together, a higher degree of mutual respect, and a better relationship among those who expect to help children grow.

NAME INDEX

SUBJECT INDEX

Work *(continued)*
distinction from job, 234–235
Protestant ethic, 232, 239
reduced work week, 235–236
source of identity, 236–237, 240

Work *(continued)*
volunteerism, 17–18, 190

YMCA, 175–176